Corporate Nature

Critical Green Engagements

Investigating the Green Economy and Its Alternatives

Jim Igoe, Melissa Checker, Molly Doane, Tracey Heatherington,
José Martínez-Reyes, and Mary Mostafanezhad
SERIES EDITORS

Corporate Nature

An Insider's Ethnography of Global Conservation

Sarah Milne

THE UNIVERSITY OF ARIZONA PRESS
TUCSON

The University of Arizona Press
www.uapress.arizona.edu

We respectfully acknowledge the University of Arizona is on the land and territories of Indigenous peoples. Today, Arizona is home to twenty-two federally recognized tribes, with Tucson being home to the O'odham and the Yaqui. Committed to diversity and inclusion, the University strives to build sustainable relationships with sovereign Native Nations and Indigenous communities through education offerings, partnerships, and community service.

© 2022 by The Arizona Board of Regents
All rights reserved. Published 2022

ISBN-13: 978-0-8165-4700-5 (hardcover)
ISBN-13: 978-0-8165-4701-2 (ebook)

Cover design by Leigh McDonald
Cover photo: Community members and conservation staff inspect forest clearing, Chumnoab, Cardamom Mountains, Cambodia. Photo by Sarah Milne, 2007.
Typeset by Sara Thaxton in 10/14 Warnock Pro with Trade Gothic Next LT Pro

Publication of this book is made possible in part by support from Australian National University.

Library of Congress Cataloging-in-Publication Data
Names: Milne, Sarah, 1975– author.
Title: Corporate nature : an insider's ethnography of global conservation / Sarah Milne.
Other titles: Critical green engagements.
Description: Tucson : University of Arizona Press, 2022. | Series: Critical green engagements: investigating the green economy and its alternatives | Includes bibliographical references and index.
Identifiers: LCCN 2022007196 (print) | LCCN 2022007197 (ebook) | ISBN 9780816547005 (hardcover) | ISBN 9780816547012 (ebook)
Subjects: LCSH: Nature conservation—Cambodia. | Conservation of natural resources—Moral and ethical aspects—Cambodia. | Non-governmental organizations—Moral and ethical aspects—Cambodia. | Business ethics. | Environmental ethics.
Classification: LCC QH77.C16 M55 2022 (print) | LCC QH77.C16 (ebook) | DDC 508—dc23/eng/20220331
LC record available at https://lccn.loc.gov/2022007196
LC ebook record available at https://lccn.loc.gov/2022007197

Printed in the United States of America
♾ This paper meets the requirements of ANSI/NISO Z39.48-1992 (Permanence of Paper).

The conquest of the earth, which mostly means the taking it away from those who have a different complexion or slightly flatter noses than ourselves, is not a pretty thing when you look into it too much. What redeems it is the idea only. An idea at the back of it; not a sentimental pretence but an idea; and an unselfish belief in the idea—something you can set up, and bow down before, and offer a sacrifice to.

—Joseph Conrad, *Heart of Darkness*, 1899

Contents

	Acknowledgments	*ix*
	Abbreviations	*xiii*
	Introduction	5
1.	Corporate Subject, Corporate Object	30
2.	The Policy Idea as Corporate Product	55
3.	Situating the Field in Cambodia	87
4.	Brokering and Transforming the Idea	119
5.	The Idea in Village Life	149
6.	Encountering the Violence of Corporate Conservation	182
	Conclusion	213
	References	*229*
	Index	*249*

Acknowledgments

What is the point of writing a book that is critical of nature conservation in the midst of a global ecological crisis? This question has plagued me at my desk, especially as the forests of my Australian home burned in the Black Summer of 2019–2020 and as the landscapes of the Cardamom Mountains in Cambodia—the setting and inspiration for much this book—now face unprecedented threats due to new dams and land enclosures. It is not possible to write away these man-made crises, but writing with purpose *can* help to navigate troubled times. The point of this book, therefore, is to explore how actions that intend to conserve nature can go wrong: they often fail to achieve their stated goals or, worse, they can undermine the conditions required for social and ecological justice. Although there is no time to squander in a crisis, it is also futile to rush and reproduce old logics that no longer serve. Crises demand that we take time to reflect. For this reason, I write in the hope that my reflections will contribute to new ways of nurturing life on our imperiled planet.

If there is one message to convey, then it is that we need to rework the old cliché of environmentalism: think globally, act locally. Global thinking about the environment often fails in practice, especially when insufficient attention is paid to local perspectives and Indigenous knowledges. We know, for example, that global concepts like "biodiversity protection" and "ecosystem services" do not translate well on the ground. Delving further, as I do this book, these global concepts can even have insidious side effects when they are implemented in places like Cambodia, where violence and authoritarian power prevail. I therefore propose that mainstream environmental initiatives learn to *think locally*—a notion that should not be just another cliché but a substantive proposition with epistemological, practical, and ethical implications. Only through conservation practice that is locally engaged, and situated in every sense, will it be possible to foster life-inspiring relationships between all beings on Earth.

In this spirit, I acknowledge that most of this book was written on the unceded lands of the Ngunnawal and Ngambri peoples, where the Australian National University (ANU) is now located. I acknowledge the Ngunnawal and Ngambri elders, past, present, and emerging; and I thank them for their role in sustaining Country, the foundation for all life. I acknowledge, too, that Australia's potent decolonial movement and sensibilities have influenced how I perceived the struggles of Cambodia's Indigenous people—especially the Chong people of the Cardamom Mountains, whose lives have now become entangled in an unfortunate combination of state developmentalism and global conservation. Having seen this entanglement unfold from 2002 onward, I have tried in my writing to bear witness and therefore to contest the processes of Indigenous dispossession under way in Cambodia today.

From the outset of my work in Cambodia, the people of the Cardamom Mountains in Thmar Bang, Tatai Leu, Chumnoab, Areng, and Prolay responded patiently to my questions and ideas. In Tatai Leu, I thank Chan Saron—one of the few female Indigenous leaders in the area—who took me under her wing in 2003. In Chumnoab, I acknowledge Ven Vorn, who tirelessly sought to protect his homeland, especially as a leader of the campaign against the proposed Stung Areng dam. Cambodian authorities jailed Ven Vorn in 2015, leaving his young wife and children to fend for themselves. He has now been released, but threats and violence against environmental activists is an ongoing specter to contend with in Cambodia.

Importantly, my access to the field in the Cardamom Mountains relied on incredible Cambodian colleagues and friends. First and foremost, I thank Thap Savy, who patiently showed me the workings of the field and the village while also translating Khmer language for me over the years, as I gradually learned to speak and listen for myself. Other Cambodian colleagues and critical thinkers to whom I am indebted for support and inspiration include: the late Chut Wutty, Hot Chanthy, Keo Piseth, Ouk Lykhim, Prak Chanthy, Ken Rotha, Keo Omaliss, Meas Nee, and Chea Sokha. All of my Cambodian informants in this book have been anonymized for security reasons, and

Acknowledgments   xi

some cannot be named here. While most of my field research was conducted in Khmer, I have always relied on my Cambodian interlocutors to check meanings—and I am grateful for all our conversations. In my writing, I bring some of this to life by using key Khmer terms, which I have transliterated in accordance with common practice. Any errors in translation or interpretation are my own.

Also in the Cambodian realm, I found incredible non-Cambodian allies, friends, and scholars who variously offered me ideas, solidarity, companionship, and critical feedback—not to mention spare bedrooms and sustenance. Here, I am indebted to Robin Biddulph and Casper Bruun Jenson for reading and commenting on early drafts of this book. For inspiration and collaboration, my sincere thanks also go to Jeremy Ironside, Marcus Hardtke, Alejandro Gonzalez-Davidson, David Boyle, Ron Jones, Jean-Christophe Diepart, Daniel Adler, Mathieu Pellerin, Hanneke Nooren, Gordon Claridge, Natalie Bugalski, David Pred, Veronique Audibert, Colas Chervier, Jonathan Padwe, Frederic Bourdier, Wayne McCallum, Moeko Saito-Jensen, and Megan McInnes. Indomitable Australian women in Phnom Penh also kept me afloat: Bronwyn Blue, Kathryn Bennett, and Sharee Bauld.

In global conservation, I retain enormous respect for colleagues with whom I worked over the years. Thank you to Eduard Niesten and Jake Brunner for teaching me so much, for maintaining a sense of humor, and for giving me opportunities. Alongside these two are so many more outstanding colleagues to whom I am indebted but shall not name for the sake of confidentiality. I am grateful to all of my conservation colleagues for sharing insights with me: while you may disagree with some of the critical sentiments in this book, please know that I write in full respect for those who choose to defend our natural world, with justice and integrity. There is so much important work to be done, and my intention is to support this.

On the academic front, the research and writing for this book was completed across various stages and locales. Initially, I completed large portions of the research as a doctoral student at the University of Cambridge, under the supervision of Bill Adams. It was Bill who introduced me to terms like "institutional ethnography," so I have him to thank for the early intellectual framing of my work, along with other advisors, Bhaskar Vira and Tim Bayliss-Smith. Chapters 2, 4, and 5 draw from my 2009 doctoral thesis, which includes full documentation of my early ethnographic sources. Also in Cambridge, I found a remarkable cohort of scholars and friends who guided my thinking, including Rob Small, Catherine Corson, Richard Paley, Deepta Chopra, Eszter Kovacs, Chris Sandbrook, and Justin Welbergen, among others. Later, as the critical literature on global and neoliberal conservation gained momentum, I was fortunate to meet other incredible researchers at the vanguard who encouraged me to publish my work. Thank you especially to Paige West, whose generosity I will not forget. Thank you also to Jim Igoe, Ken MacDonald, Peter Brosius, Raymond Bryant, Dan Brockington, Bram Büscher, and Wolfram Dressler.

Years lapsed in the writing of this book. Major events also unfolded in my life and in Cambodia, too, which changed the story—not least distressing struggles over illegal logging in the Cardamom Mountains, which led to the murder of Chut Wutty in 2012, which I explain in the book. In these circumstances, the generous support of the Wenner Gren Foundation in the form of a Hunt Postdoctoral Fellowship in 2014 was vital for my completion of this book. So too was ongoing moral support from the General Sir John Monash Foundation in Australia, especially from Peter Binks. The Foundation deserves special thanks for having funded my PhD scholarship in 2005, which is how this story began.

In Canberra, I found my institutional home at the ANU, where I was fortunate to meet a stellar group of colleagues in the Resources, Environment and Development group at the Crawford School of Public Policy, College of Asia and the Pacific. Here, I am so grateful to Sango Mahanty for her endless support, especially for sustaining and extending my work in Cambodia over the years. Also at the ANU, I sincerely thank Siobhan McDonnell, Colin Filer, Carina Wyborn, Rosie Cooney, Lia Kent, Rebecca Monson, Sophie Dowling, Anna Hutchens, Andrew Walker, Nisha Phillips, and Judith Pabian for keeping the faith in various ways. Sandy Potter and Karina Pelling at the ANU cartography-GIS unit also provided essential assistance with map making.

Finally, everyone knows that it takes a village to write a book. In this regard, I have been surrounded by magical people who helped me on all fronts over the years with advice, proofreading, moral support, babysitting, and more. Heartfelt gratitude to Ginger Gorman, Jodi Neale and family, Olivia Boyd, Paul Wyrwoll, Arnaud Gallois, Tara Darlington, Lizanne Van Scheppingen, Dede Da Cruz, and my own amazing family, especially Jenny Milne and Mario Navarro. Most of all, I thank my little daughter Elena, for bearing with me: may the world that you inherit be teeming with life and hope!

Abbreviations

BINGO   Big international NGO

CBNRM   Community-based natural resource management

CCPF   Central Cardamoms Protected Forest

CI   Conservation International

CNRMCs   Commune Natural Resource Management Committees

CPP   Cambodian People's Party

CSP   Conservation Stewards Program

FA   Cambodian Forestry Administration

FFI   Flora and Fauna International

ICDPs   Integrated Conservation and Development Projects

IUCN   International Union for the Conservation of Nature

MAFF   Cambodian Ministry of Agriculture, Forestry and Fisheries

MoE   Cambodian Ministry of Environment

NGO   Nongovernmental organization

PES   Payments for environmental services

PLUP   Participatory land use planning

REDD+   Reducing Emissions from Deforestation and Forest Degradation

TNC   The Nature Conservancy

WWF   World Wildlife Fund

Corporate Nature

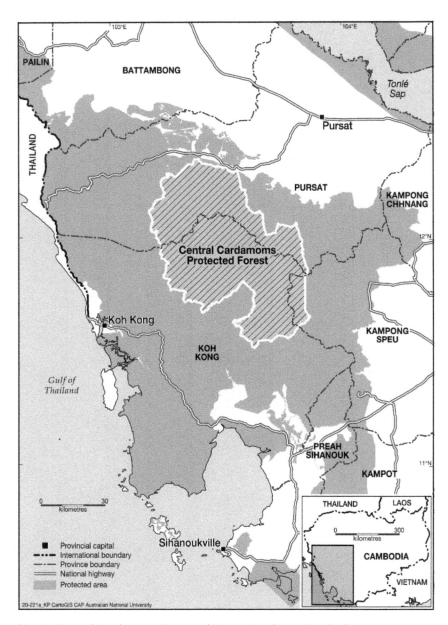

Map 1 Central Cardamoms Protected Forest, Southwest Cambodia.

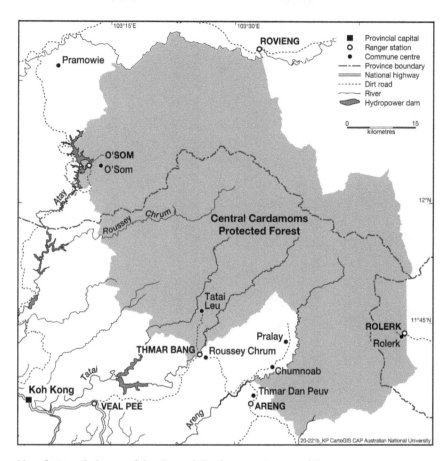

Map 2 Detailed map of the Central Cardamoms Protected Forest.

Introduction

April 26, 2012, Cardamom Mountains, Southwest Cambodia:
The forest pulses slowly, as if weighed down by the stifling pre-monsoon heat. Beside a remote dirt track lies an illegal logging compound, from which agitated voices emerge. Tensions rise, then shots ring out. Nature heaves. Chut Wutty, Cambodia's most prominent environmental activist, slumps at the wheel of his beaten-up red Toyota . . . bleeding, murdered, just as he was trying to drive away from the scene. The screams of two female journalists reverberate as they flee into the forest, their investigative trip with Wutty gone horribly wrong. More gunfire, and now Wutty's assassin lies dead: a young military policeman, sprawled in the dust, killed by one of his uniformed superiors. Any hope for justice evaporates in that moment, as the perpetrator of Wutty's murder has also been murdered. The forest, voiceless, has witnessed everything.

This book begins with the murder of Chut Wutty, my former colleague, because his violent death exposes deep flaws and contradictions in contemporary environmental governance. The fact that Wutty's murder occurred within a major biodiversity conservation landscape—one orchestrated by international donors and nongovernmental organizations (NGOs) in partnership with the Cambodian government—is unsettling. One might ask: What has become of the apparently noble cause of saving nature? Such questions prompt us to look inside the black box of global conservation, to see how it operates across scales and on the ground in the world's biodiversity hotspots.[1]

---

1. Hotspots are globally significant areas of biodiversity under high threat (Myers et al. 2000).

The core aim of this book is therefore to explore the politics and practice of global conservation, so that we may appreciate how it works as a system and as a human endeavor replete with injustices, passions, and deep contradictions. By studying how global conservation thinks and acts, we may observe how it is generative of various potential "socio-natures" (Haraway 1997; Latour 2010), each with its own biophysical, ethical, and philosophical contours— what Lorimer calls "the multi-natural" (2015). For example, we know of "colonial nature" (Adams and Mulligan 2003), "imperial nature" (Goldman 2005), "neoliberal nature" (Castree 2008), and "ecological-modernist nature" (Christoff 1996), among others (see Escobar 1999). But my focus is on what I call *corporate nature*—that which emerges from the technocratic, bureaucratic, and power-laden practices of mainstream global conservation organizations. Here, I use the notion of "mainstream" to refer to the "particular historical and institutional strain of Western conservation" that "dominates the field of conservation in terms of ideology, practice and resources" (Brockington, Duffy, and Igoe 2008, 9). This is a form of conservation that aligns with the contours of global power, capital, and coloniality.

When Chut Wutty was murdered, he was on yet another investigative mission through the backroads of the Cardamom Mountains, arguably one of the wildest and most remote pockets of rainforest remaining in mainland Southeast Asia. Since 2002, he had doggedly recorded and exposed the illegal exploitation of forests throughout Cambodia. Yet Wutty's work in the Cardamom Mountains had commenced earlier in 2000, when he left the Royal Cambodian Armed Forces to join Conservation International (CI), a major player in the global conservation movement, with a strong presence in Cambodia. After two years with CI, Wutty moved on to form his own local NGO, which was notably activist and anti-government in stance. Wutty then became a thorn in the side of Cambodia's ruling elite, who, backed by Prime Minister Hun Sen, were intent on ravaging the country's public forests for private gain (Cock 2016; Milne 2015). At the time of Wutty's murder, Cambodia's deforestation problem had reached crisis point, with the country clocking the world's third highest national deforestation rate from 2000 to 2012 (Hansen et al. 2013); the exploitation of protected forests has not slowed since (Amnesty International 2022).

Talk of deforestation rates, however, obscures the specific dynamics of what has happened in the Cardamom Mountains. While the area appears to retain most of its forest cover today, it is hard to overstate the logging

Introduction

scandal that occurred there from 2009 to 2012, which involved extensive extraction of high-value timber. With most of the landscape legally protected, the Cambodian government took advantage of its territorial monopoly over the forest. It fostered major illegal logging operations, which relied on the manipulation of timber removal permits for the clearing of hydropower dam reservoirs before flooding: in practice, however, timber was removed from throughout the surrounding conservation areas (Milne 2015). Most of this timber was a locally occurring species of rosewood (*Dalbergia siamensis*), highly valued for luxury furniture in China. Two companies, run by tycoons with familial ties to Hun Sen, operated the logging, together collecting roughly US$440 million over a three-year period (Milne 2015). Their operations were backed by the military police and the Royal Cambodian Armed Forces, who also profited from the logging. Everybody's rice bowl was filled by rosewood—local villagers, park rangers, government officials—and for some players, it was extremely lucrative. From somewhere inside this extractive complex, the command to murder Chut Wutty was issued. A proper investigation was never conducted.

News of Wutty's murder, and the circumstances around it, prompted international outcry. Articles adorned the front pages of all major world news outlets, and human rights groups called for action, decrying the impunity in Cambodia. But the hyped-up press was short-lived, and ultimately too narrow. Missing from the discussion was the puzzle that I grapple with in this book: that Wutty was murdered within one of Southeast Asia's most iconic and well-funded conservation landscapes, a poster child for global conservation. Specifically, he was murdered in what was then the Central Cardamoms Protected Forest (CCPF), an area managed jointly by CI and the Cambodian Forestry Administration.[2] So, we must ask: Why was an underfunded local environmental activist trying to expose illegal logging in this protected area? Why weren't international conservation NGOs trying to stop the logging, which was destroying Indigenous homelands and the very biodiversity and ecosystem services that they were there to protect? To answer these questions, we must observe the global conservation NGOs' responses to Wutty's assassination.

---

2. After jurisdictional reforms in 2016, this is now the Central Cardamom Mountains National Park (CCMNP), under the Ministry of the Environment. CI remains engaged in managing the area with the Cambodian government.

May 2012, Phnom Penh, capital of Cambodia:

The convention room in one of Phnom Penh's most luxurious hotels is thickly curtained and air-conditioned, as if hermetically sealed from the outside world. A gathering of well-dressed government officials, journalists, and conservation professionals is present—the latter a predictable mix of Western expatriate advisors and their Khmer counterparts. All are here for the launch of The Cardamom Conundrum, *a new book about conservation and development in the Cardamom Mountains, published by a reputable academic press. Guests are treated to a spectacle in which the jungle is celebrated through images projected onto a screen. Attached to these images is the idea of a green economy, replete with win-win opportunities that are achievable through the marketization of nature's services, especially watershed services in aid of large-scale hydropower development, currently under way in the Cardamom Mountains. The area is to become an icon of green development. Or, in Hun Sen's words, "the battery of Cambodia."*

But these PowerPoint dreams are interrupted by newspaper journalists pushing for answers about Wutty's murder just three weeks prior. Eventually, the journalists conduct an interview with the book's author, Timothy Killeen, a besuited employee of CI, who offers a set of responses about Wutty and illegal logging in the Cardamom Mountains. These were reported in the *Phnom Penh Post*, a key English-language newspaper in Cambodia at the time, as follows: "I am not one to comment on the political will of the Cambodian government . . . I am an optimistic person by nature . . . [Wutty's death] is a tragic incident that grew out of the altercation of two individuals who were not engaged in the types of dialogues that can avoid conflict and identify positive opportunities for the nation" (*Phnom Penh Post* 2012). While this voice is strategic, I argue that it is a voice of corporate avoidance. It is technical, pragmatic, and couched in apolitical optimism. I also argue that this voice signifies a key dilemma in mainstream conservation today. In CI's statements to the press, we witness one of the world's biggest and most influential conservation NGOs denying the existence of a multimillion-dollar illegal logging racket in its project area and downplaying a politically motivated murder that occurred just a short drive from one of its ranger stations. This is an archetypal and unusually visible moment of dissonance, which enables us to glimpse the potential for darkness at the heart of global conservation—a potential now evident in recent observations of conservation NGOs' complicity in "atmospheres of violence" against environmental defenders around the world (Menton and Gilbert 2021).

This book explores conservation's dark corners and institutional character through project ethnography. My subject is CI and its conservation project in the Cardamom Mountains of Cambodia: an exemplary case of mainstream global conservation practice crafted around influential neoliberal policy ideas. As a former project insider, once employed by CI, I had privileged access to this project over the course of a decade (2002–2012). During this time, I observed the intricacies of transnational conservation in practice. And, inspired by emerging ethnographic approaches to conservation (Anderson and Berglund 2003; Brosius 1999a; Larsen and Brockington 2018; West 2006), I adopted a hybrid stance as a former-insider-cum-ethnographer to develop this book. The result is an attempt to reveal some of global conservation's deepest contradictions and ethical pitfalls, including its capacity to inflict various forms of direct and indirect violence (see Menton, Navas, and Le Billon 2021).[3] As for my motivations, I am conducting this critique in a time of ecological crisis because it is a necessary first step toward reimagining socio-natures for the future: socio-natures that are grounded in care, diversity, conviviality, and decolonial solidarity (e.g., Büscher and Fletcher 2020; Haraway 2016; Kashwan et al. 2021).

The remainder of this introduction frames my endeavor: first, I outline what is wrong with the global conservation industry; second, I show how perspectives from anthropology can help to make sense of the complexities and failings of mainstream environmental intervention; third, I describe my empirical approach and outline the chapters that comprise this book.

Problematizing the Global Conservation Industry

Efforts to conserve wild nature and natural resources around the world have expanded dramatically in recent decades, and they have never been more urgent. This has produced a global conservation movement that is powerful, compelling, and able to leverage significant financial and scientific resources.

---

3. Menton, Navas, and Le Billon (2021) provide a thorough review of how indirect violence has been conceptualized, drawing from foundational notions of "structural violence" (Galtung 1969) and "symbolic violence" (Bourdieu 1977) while extending this to the contemporary context of environmental defenders.

The scale and ambition of global conservation is reflected in initiatives like the Millennium Ecosystem Assessment (MEA), which engaged over one thousand scientists to assess the status of the world's ecosystems in the early 2000s (see MEA 2005), or, most recently, the Intergovernmental Science-Policy Platform on Biodiversity and Ecosystem Services (IPBES), which in 2019 released another global assessment of biodiversity and ecosystems. Unfortunately, the prognosis is dire, with stark warnings issued about nature's "unprecedented" and "dangerous decline" (IPBES 2019).

These disturbing findings have prompted fresh calls for urgent action and new resources to achieve a massive upscaling of conservation action. For example, early targets set through the international Convention on Biological Diversity call for "maintenance of 17% terrestrial and 10% marine protected areas" on Earth, at an estimated cost of US$76.1 billion annually (McCarthy et al. 2012). These figures suggest that current conservation spending must increase at least tenfold, as though the problem of nature's decline could be solved merely by increasing the level of effort. Even more ambitious is the influential Nature Needs Half movement, which calls for greater increases in protected areas, as though this too were a plausible fix.[4] Amid these calls for more money and more protection, however, I argue that we must evaluate the dominant organizational form of global conservation. Before scaling up, we must ask: How does conservation operate, and with what effects? How do conservation actors make decisions and strategies, and to whom are they accountable?

Studying the magnitude and distribution of current conservation funding provides some initial answers. Estimates of global spending on conservation suggest that US$21.5 billion was spent between 2001 and 2008 (Waldron et al. 2013), or over US$3 billion per year. A large portion of this is government and multilateral spending, but big international nongovernment organizations (BINGOs) play a significant role in moving investments around the world. There are about six BINGOs of note in this niche industry, with the top three often referred to as the "big three" (Chapin 2004). They are Conservation International (CI), The Nature Conservancy (TNC), and the World Wildlife Fund (WWF). Notable others include the International Union for the Conservation of Nature (IUCN), the African Wildlife Foundation, and the Wildlife Conservation Society. In 2017, the top three BINGOs together spent US$1.23 billion on biodiversity conservation, or over 40 percent of global

---

4. See "Nature Needs Half" campaign, accessed June 2, 2020, https://natureneedshalf.org/.

Introduction

conservation spending.[5] This signals the vital importance of understanding how BINGOs function, if we are to engage critically with the nature-society trajectories that they produce. In the remainder of this section, I describe some of the notable characteristics of BINGOs, namely their corporate and capitalist tendencies, and what this means for organizational culture.

CORPORATE TENDENCIES

A key aspect of mainstream conservation BINGOs is their corporate form. Fundamentally, this refers their formal institutional structure, which enables a group of people to act as a single entity (Bakan 2012). The corporate form allows conservation organizations to achieve impressive global reach and operational scale while maintaining organizational coherence and branding. For example, the top three BINGOs have headquarters in the Washington, DC, area, which oversee field programs in most of the world's biodiversity hotspots. CI, the organization responsible for spawning the idea of hotspots, now has offices in thirty countries worldwide and has supported interventions in seventy-seven countries.[6] Concepts like the hotspots, and other similarly conceived prioritization tools like WWF's eco-regions and IUCN's Red List, work discursively and conceptually to give BINGOs a scientifically justified global mandate (Brosius and Russell 2003; Campbell 2012). These concepts in turn generate corporate identity and purpose. Tellingly, CI has registered "hotspots" as a legal trademark.[7] Through such devices, BINGOs exert strong influence over conservation priorities and spending in developing countries (Marchese 2015; Rodríguez et al. 2007). Unfortunately, a corresponding "accountability regime" (Jepson 2005) for these NGOs has not emerged.

A key challenge for accountability in global conservation is that organizational success does not depend upon transparency. For private sector corporations, accountability is typically driven by profit-seeking shareholders

---

5. Aggregate spending figures come from Charity Navigator in 2019. US$1.23 billion is the sum of declared BINGO spending on "functional expenses." US$1.23 billion is 40 percent of global spending on conservation, estimated to be US$3 billion/annum (Waldron et al. 2013).

6. See CI's website, accessed February 16, 2022, https://www.conservation.org/about/global-offices.

7. Ownership specifications on Hotspots Revisited outlined here, accessed September 1, 2021, https://databasin.org/datasets/23fb5da1586141109fa6f8d45de0a260/.

(Bakan 2012). Yet the not-for-profit sector works differently. Conservation BINGOs are instead assessed by their achievement of organizational goals, like halting biodiversity loss and safeguarding ecosystems. For example, CI's mission statement reads: "Building upon a strong foundation of science, partnership and field demonstration, CI empowers societies to responsibly and sustainably care for nature, our global biodiversity, for the well-being of humanity."[8] In a mission of this kind, BINGOs are accountable not to share-holders but to their donors, partners, various publics, and in some cases their members. Organizational success is therefore closely tied to a BINGO's ability to persuade these stakeholders that it implements efficient and effective con-servation action. This has produced an industry in which ideas, branding, and appearances play a major role. Igoe calls this the "spectacle" of global conser-vation (2010), in which the *illusion* of saving nature is fetishized just as much as any material product or action. Representations of success are therefore a foundational element of conservation's corporate form, akin to "virtualism" in environmental governance (Carrier and West 2009) and "organizational hypocrisy" in global development (Weaver 2008): both concepts point to how nonprofit agencies must compensate for ongoing gaps between vision and execution.

Another contributing factor to the corporate style of global conservation has been its courting of powerful interests, often in exchange for funding. For example, a significant source of conservation funding now derives from Amer-ican philanthropists and their foundations, such as the Gordon and Betty Moore Foundation, which provided one of the largest one-off conservation grants ever: US$261 million to CI in 2001 (MacDonald 2008). Other similar philanthropic sources for conservation include the Walton Family Trust and the MacArthur Foundation. Yet donations from self-made billionaire philan-thropists can be complicated because celebrity donors often want to specify how their funds are spent (Holmes 2012; McGoey 2015). This can lead to personalized and opaque relationships between conservation NGOs and their patrons, which again raise questions about accountability in global conserva-tion (Ramutsindela, Spierenburg, and Wels 2013). Similarly, heavy reliance on bilateral donors like USAID can produce perverse effects within NGOs, like top-heavy organizational processes (Sachedina 2010). Ultimately, the prob-

---

8. Mission statement on CI's website, accessed June 2020, https://www.conservation.org /about.

Introduction

lem is that environmental funding tends to serve donor interests, which are "congenial to industrial capital" (Ramutsindela, Spierenburg, and Wels 2013) and often emulate dominant logics of neoliberal governance (Corson 2016).

CAPITALIST TENDENCIES

Questions about global conservation's accountability are most pointed when one considers the significant role of private-sector partnerships and corporate donations. Most major conservation organizations now maintain relationships with and receive funding from mining, fossil fuel, and agribusiness conglomerates (Adams 2017; MacDonald 2010). The fact that these private partners emerge from resource-extractive sectors is no coincidence: these industries rely on nature's bounty, they operate in remote locales that are often the target of conservation projects, and they need to maintain their social license to operate (Adams 2017; MacDonald 2010). Critics therefore accuse big conservation organizations of greenwashing for environmentally destructive companies, or selling out on their original altruistic motivations (Chapin 2004; MacDonald 2008). For this reason, mainstream or corporate-friendly environmental NGOs are considered to be exemplary of a wider "corporatization of activism" in civil society (Dauvergne and LeBaron 2014).

More fundamentally, NGO entanglements with the private sector point to conservation's intimate relationship to capitalism. A large literature illustrates how the practices and ideas associated with "neoliberal conservation" (Büscher et al. 2012) exhibit and enable many of capitalism's key processes at resource frontiers, including primitive accumulation, appropriation, dispossession, privatization, and commodification (Brockington, Duffy, and Igoe 2008; Igoe and Brockington 2007; Kelly 2013; Nevins and Peluso 2008). In short, neoliberal conservation involves the reregulation of nature-society for the purposes of market expansion (Castree 2008), especially through conservation's embrace of market mechanisms to solve environmental problems or "selling nature to save it" (McAfee 1999). This approach has spawned a suite of new economic instruments, aimed at facilitating market-like transactions for "ecosystem services" and "carbon credits": mechanisms that form the cornerstone of neoliberal conservation (Büscher et al. 2012). A key thread in this book is the genesis and fate of one such policy idea, that of payments for environmental services (PES) implemented by CI, as I explain below.

Alongside the adoption of market-based policies and tools, mainstream conservation practice has also become more businesslike. This is partly due to intense competition for funding, which forces NGOs to market their wares to prospective donors, corporate partners, and members. To use a business analogy, NGOs offer virtual and intellectual products to their clients, which are often couched in spectacular imagery (Igoe 2010) or laden with value-adding, performative, or marketing practices (Carrier and West 2009; Milne and Mahanty 2019). These NGO products typically include scientific prowess, new policy models, promises of win-win solutions, and the proclamation of "results-oriented" or "evidence-based" strategies (Adams and Hutton 2007; Büscher 2008). Indeed, global conservation offers us an array of toolkits or fixes, which seem to provide an easy way out of the profound structural and existential contradictions that society faces, namely our dependence on capitalist growth at nature's expense (Büscher and Fletcher 2020). Furthermore, as global conservation continues to embrace capitalist logics and modalities, its institutions have begun to exhibit their own forms of corporate behavior.

ORGANIZATIONAL PRACTICES

The rise of corporate organizational practices and culture in environmental BINGOs is now recognized as a key aspect of neoliberal conservation (Adams and Hutton 2007; Büscher et al. 2012). In part, this is due to a concentration of power at the top of conservation organizations, which brings a degree of opacity to decision-making (Brockington 2009; Sachedina 2010). Scholars of global conservation also note how the movement's leadership is dominated by a small and well-connected transnational elite (Holmes 2011). This "elite network" includes the senior staff of conservation BINGOs, renowned scientists, high-level government officials, celebrities, corporate sector leaders, and media actors: herein, personal connections are the primary mode through which "money, influence and ideas are mobilized" (Holmes 2011, 2). Obviously, this is not a democratic or transparent form of governance.

To explore the businesslike form of global conservation, this book focuses on NGO practices and knowledge making. For example, "business models" are now prevalent in NGO articulations of strategy and fundraising, and these often involve the embrace of generic policy models that can be "rolled out" or "scaled up" across the globe (Adams and Hutton 2007; Rodriguez et al. 2007). Global NGO practice therefore implies a preference for cookie-cutter tools, which are co-produced with centralized or top-down programming. But trouble arises here: when NGOs approach conservation in this way, highly problematic knowledge-making processes emerge (Brosius 1999a). This is because NGO actors need to make the field "legible" (Scott 1998) for their projects and policies, through simplified forms of knowledge that un-see complexity and silence local voices (Brosius and Hitchner 2010). Furthermore, information that is inconvenient for the business model or policy tool at hand must be filtered out, leading to the production of NGO-friendly forms of knowledge or "non-knowledge"—the latter a product of efforts either to suppress uncomfortable things or to "kindle endless new forms of ambiguity and ignorance" in service of powerful interests (McGoey 2012, 3). NGO-produced non-knowledge can therefore conceal or even extend various forms of violence in the field (Milne and Mahanty 2019; Sachedina 2010).

Furthermore, with global conservation being highly reputation-based and image-driven, honest communication about field challenges is often precluded. This means that conservation practitioners can sometimes find themselves in a realm of empty rhetoric where "consensus is assumed," and critique of an organization's impacts or methods is not tolerated (Büscher 2008). This points to another aspect of global conservation's corporate culture, which is a strong need for loyalty and obedience among staff. Correspondingly, some conservation practitioners and researchers have been known to self-censor after witnessing the suppression of dissenting views by BINGO leadership (Büscher et al. 2012; Igoe and Sullivan 2009). I provide an ethnographic account of this kind of suppression, which I experienced at the end of my relationship with CI in 2011. My findings suggest that what is at stake in such conflicts is knowledge, or the interpretation of conservation action and its impacts in the field.

To summarize, corporate culture in conservation may be distinguished by efforts to control knowledge. As I have explained, these efforts involve the production of spectacular imagery and representations of success, as seen in the fundraising materials and websites of conservation BINGOs (Igoe 2010). Yet this success is often political, because it involves the erasure of dissonant perspectives from the field (Brosius and Hitchner 2010; Igoe and Sullivan 2009). My ethnographic task, therefore, is to explore the persistent gaps between global ideas and local realities in mainstream conservation practice:

Making Sense of Green Intervention

To study global conservation, I approach it first as a form of intervention. This enables me to explore whose ideas and perspectives prevail in conservation practice, and how power relations shape this. To do this, it is also necessary to attend to disconnections between stated goals and actual outcomes, including how contestations are dealt with. Scholars of international development have much to offer in these analytical tasks. The anthropology of development especially provides a point of departure, as I now explain.

THE IMPORTANCE OF IDEAS

To begin, it is helpful to explore the notion that "saving nature" is a form of intervention, shaped by the ideas and intentions of those involved. In general, interventions entail a set of *externally driven* activities, which are guided by an overall rationale to ameliorate or govern the relationships between people and things (Li 2007).[9] Conservation's political nature therefore emerges from the theories, assumptions, and approaches of those who devise and implement its interventions. Core here are ideas about the global and intrinsic value of biodiversity, and our duty to protect it through strategies such as the creation of protected areas (Adams and Hutton 2007). The parallels between conservation's virtuous mandate and other well-intended global interventions such as colonial improvement, missionary projects, and contemporary poverty alleviation are obvious. If we have learned anything from the past, it is that the formulation and implementation of good intentions is not apolitical, and that it can have perverse side effects in practice (Crush 1995; Easterly 2006; Hobart 1993).

Of course, the ideas that motivate intervention are discursive: they reflect the co-evolution of knowledge and power (Foucault 1980) or a distinct politics of knowledge (Jasanoff 2004). In the context of conservation, we have learned how discourses frame problems, produce so-called facts, and simplify

---

9. Here I refer to "government" in the Foucauldian sense (see Li 2007, 9).

Introduction   17

complexity in ways that silence or privilege certain voices (Brosius 1999a). Similarly in international development, Tania Li (2007) describes the power-laden yet depoliticizing processes of problem definition as "rendering technical." This is a fundamental dynamic in development interventions, which Ferguson (1994) famously called the "anti-politics development machine." A recurring theme here is how the rural world is discursively constructed by NGOs and development agencies as a set of problems to be solved, often in ways that disguise underlying resource struggles and marginalized voices (Bryant and Bailey 1997; Leach and Mearns 1996; Peet and Watts 2004). In particular, the practices of mapping, calculation, and regulation make unruly places "legible" for government through the erasure of local context (Scott 1998). These insights provide a starting point for understanding the politics of conservation: we must recognize how its discourses enact and disguise power.

Of vital importance, then, is the role of policy and policy making in conservation practice. As Shore and Wright deftly explain, in the development context "policy is the ghost in the machine—the force which breathes life and purpose into the machinery of government" (1997, 5). In other words, policy ideas fundamentally guide organizational practices, by shaping problem-solving *and* knowledge making: in short, policy is a source and form of power. For this reason, Michel Foucault (1991) spoke of policy as a "political technology" or a "means by which power conceals its own operation" through the deployment of language that is apparently objective, neutral, rational, and technical (cited in Shore and Wright 1997, 8). Ethnographies of policy in action, therefore, provide a way to read the politics of intervention.

Here, I draw on two key insights about policy to study conservation practice. First is the apparent intellectual coherence of policy. As Dryzek notes, adherents of a given policy discourse all use a "particular kind of language when talking about events, which in turn rests upon common definitions, judgments, assumptions and contentions" (1997, 3). This uniformity of knowledge is also identified by Mosse (2005) in the context of rural development, where he observes that project designs, policy models, and institutional approaches are all connected by common underlying assumptions and causal theories. Environment and development organizations therefore appear to produce or require a degree of uniformity of thought among their staff, including ideological frames and intervention logics that all can adhere to.

The second insight is that policy formation often relies on constituent storylines or narratives. Policy narratives—or stories that have a beginning, a middle, and an end—have become a powerful analytical tool in political ecology (Keeley and Scoones 2014; Roe 1991). Relatedly, Hajer's storylines (1995) describe "connected sets of ideas" that occur and recur within policy discourses. By identifying policy storylines or narratives, we may observe how policy makers cope with uncertainty and complexity. In other words, we can see how narratives are used to frame problems and prescribe solutions (Li 2007; Roe 1991). These acts are political because evidence is not required to demonstrate the truth-value of a narrative. Political ecologists famously demonstrated this by exposing recurrent flaws in "expert understandings" of environmental problems, such as in relation to the causes of African land degradation (Blaikie 1995; Fairhead and Leach 1995). Policy narratives persist in the face of contravening evidence because they have inherent appeal: they provide simple and unified interpretations of circumstances so that policy makers, project staff, and donors can intervene (Roe 1991).

By implication, changes in dominant policy narratives can signal ideological shifts or struggles within organizations. Policy struggles are often articulated in terms of dominant narratives and counternarratives: one giving way to the other, and vice versa (Roe 1991). This is evident in conservation, which has seen a range of policy ideas come and go over time. For example, until the 1990s, conservation was dominated by the creation of protected areas in the style of "fortress conservation" (Brockington 2002). A major policy shift then occurred toward "community conservation," with new narratives that supported integrated conservation and development projects (ICDPs) or community-based natural resource management (CBNRM), in response to outcry over the negative human consequences of protected areas (Adams and Hulme 2001). Questions over the effectiveness and efficiency of so-called integrated or community-based approaches then prompted a return to protectionist thinking within conservation organizations, alongside the embrace of new market-based or neoliberal approaches (Brockington, Duffy, and Igoe 2008; Hutton, Adams, and Murombedzi 2005). Yet, to understand *how* new paradigms take hold in conservation, we must attend to the organizational processes and human drama of policy making.

THE SOCIAL LIFE OF PROJECTS

While policy ideas and discourses are important for understanding conservation practice, so too are the everyday social and political interactions

Introduction   **19**

among practitioners and their "subjects" in the field (Fairhead and Leach 2003; Kiik 2019; Mosse 2005). Importantly, the social life of projects or interventions can play a strong role in influencing outcomes on the ground, whether intended or not. To explore this, we must observe the interactions between people within conservation projects, including the interactions between NGO practitioners and those they are trying to help or influence, such as villagers or government officials. This also means studying the distinct subjectivities and perceptions of each person involved.

Early inquiry into this interactive realm emerged from rural sociology in the 1990s. Here, a focus on individuals or actors within development projects highlighted "the central role played by human action and consciousness" in determining the processes and effects of external intervention (Long 2001, 13). Encounters between individuals of different "lifeworlds" were studied in the development context: between bureaucrat and peasant, or NGO worker and villager (Hilhorst 2003; Long and Long 1992). This analysis revealed the productive nature of such encounters, wherein meanings would be negotiated and actors' agendas pursued. Much focus was directed toward the typically messy "interface" between those doing the intervening and their subjects or targets (Long 2001).

In parallel, science and technology scholars began to focus on project actors involved in crafting and executing other kinds of complex interventions, including consultants, engineers, economists, and politicians. Combining discourse analysis and ethnography, these scholars interrogated the power-laden practices involved in making scientific knowledge and technology, often revealing internally contested and contingent processes (Latour 1996) or interactive effects in which project processes *co-produced* the social context in which they were acting (Callon 1986; Jasanoff 2004). These perspectives have helped to interpret project dynamics across sectors like transport engineering, irrigation, and biodiversity conservation: projects are now seen as complex networks or systems of social production, involving various power and knowledge struggles (see Latour 1996; Mosse 2005; West 2006). In this book, I adopt a similar view of conservation projects as dynamic networks of individuals engaged in ongoing processes of negotiation over ideas and knowledge about the field.

For global conservation, the cross-scalar or transnational dimensions of projects require special attention. Observing the often awkward or loaded encounters between so-called global and local actors provides a way forward here. These encounters are sometimes said to occur through an "interface" (Long 2001), in which the global and the local are "mutually produced" through social, cultural, and economic exchanges across space and time (Appadurai 1996). The productive nature of these interactions has been described as "friction" (Tsing 2005), a set of processes that generates new dreams, expectations, worldviews, and realities. In conservation projects, Paige West articulates "the transnational" (2006) as a productive realm that emerges when global concerns about biodiversity meet the unique worldviews and interests of local communities and Indigenous people. Or, as Brosius observes regarding rainforest conservation in Malaysia, "it is no longer clear what is local and what is not: the origins of representations are obscured in the processes of translation and distribution" (1999b, 281). Thus, scale appears to collapse, and friction generates new possibilities, even new socio-natures.

To study the significance and effects of global conservation, therefore, it is necessary to look beyond the formal boundaries of a given NGO project. This is especially true as conservation projects shift into hybrid organizational forms, such as those that blend NGO action with state institutions, private partnerships, and market logics. The case of CI's work in Cambodia is exemplary of this blending of ideas and intentions: it involved a partnership with the Cambodian government *and* the implementation of PES with local communities. Projects like this must be seen as productive spaces that generate new knowledge, rework local realities, and make new subjectivities among staff, project partners, and villagers. For this reason, I focus my ethnography on *project effects*, whether planned, unplanned, deliberate, or unconscious.

INTERPRETING PROJECT EFFECTS

To study the significance of conservation action, it is necessary to recognize that a neat causal relationship between a project's objectives and its actual effects is unlikely. Development scholars have long observed a measure of unpredictability or nonlinearity in the relationship between project intentions and outcomes (e.g., Hobart 1993). Problems begin when the *anticipated* results of a project, which typically derive from theoretical policy models, contrast with actual project effects that emerge in the local context (Lewis et al. 2003; Mosse 2004; van Ufford and Giri 2003). As Mosse (2005, 19) argues, the effects of aid projects have more to do with their "infusion into regional and historical processes of change" than actual policy design. Or, for those working in an actor-oriented approach, it is project life itself that reworks the goals of intervention, since project actors must continually negotiate and mediate between the competing demands of policy and reality (Long 2001). For Norman Long, this leads to "the reinterpretation or transformation of policy during the implementation process" (2001, 25). The outcome of this, however, is not just a product of random social processes: some argue that the most significant aspects of an intervention may well emerge from its side effects or unintended consequences (see Ferguson 1994).

Indeed, the prevalence of unintended consequences in conservation and development may be viewed as systematic and political in nature. One argument here is that projects in practice can possess a logic or intelligibility of their own. Ferguson (1994) famously showed this in his analysis of the "side effects" of World Bank intervention in Lesotho: here, specific policy intentions became irrelevant, as foreign development interventions instead facilitated the expansion of bureaucratic and state power.[10] In other words, unintended project effects can end up having political uses, because they "accomplish important strategic tasks behind the backs of the most sincere participants" (Ferguson 1994, 256). This does not mean that a conspiratorial or hegemonic "development machine" is always present (Harrison 2003). Rather, the insight is important because it shows how interventionist environmental projects can inadvertently expand or enhance local governmental processes, which often entail dynamics of exploitation and marginalization (Anderson and Berglund 2003).

The problem of perverse local transformations is a key theme in this book, particularly with regard to how CI's project enhanced government power in Cambodia. Global conservation appears to be particularly adept at producing such effects, as scholars inspired by Foucault's notion of governmentality readily show. For example, Li (2002) describes how community-based natural resource management projects unwittingly enabled state control in the remote uplands of Indonesia; while Bryant (2002) argues that conservation NGOs in the Philippines, regardless of their explicit agendas, essentially "prepare" Indigenous people to be governed. These studies also resonate

---

10. Ferguson describes this phenomenon in terms of Foucault's (1977, 255–56) "instrument effects."

with the notion of "environmentality" (Agrawal 2005), in which environmental subjects are made and governed through the processes of environmental intervention. My observations of CI's project in Cambodia confirm but also problematize these interpretations. I argue that the key issue with Foucauldian optics is that they can attribute too much power and control to global conservation, without attending to the ways that local actors and processes can subvert and manipulate NGO intentions. Indeed, my findings indicate a distinct lack of NGO control over what happens in the field, which leads to dissonance between intentions and outcomes.

INTERVENTION IN THE FACE OF DISSONANCE

If the field effects of conservation and development projects are typically unpredictable, or even unknowable, then we must ask why policy models are still so important. Here, I return to the role played by ideas in the course of intervention. As I explained above, global conservation is underpinned by policy ideas: they are built into its business models and project designs; they provide templates for action in the face of complexity (see Mosse 2005). This attachment to ideas is especially evident in the way that BINGOs seek to generalize their approaches by producing models or solutions for replication across multiple sites. Reflecting a positivist epistemology, this approach sees policy models as tools to be neatly transferred from one context to another. Mainstream conservation's ongoing commitments to "evidence-based conservation" (Sutherland et al. 2004) and the use of quasi-experimental methods to measure policy "effectiveness" (Ferraro and Pattanayak 2006) illustrate this mode of thinking. Such approaches all fit into global conservation's technical obsession with "what works" or "getting the model right" (see Burivalova et al. 2019)—key constructs for bolstering the apparent authority of one's intervention, giving the appearance of control (Scoones and Stirling 2020).

A key problem with conservation's policy-centered view is that it allows policy models to acquire a unique power of their own. Here, the model becomes the treatment, as though it possesses a magical power to act upon the field. Tess Lea explains this in the context of government intervention in Indigenous Australia: "policy artefacts are . . . not simply statements of logical intent. They are also fetish objects or magical relics that travel through time and space . . . that are attributed great expressive power and controlling capacities" (2008, 20). Thus, policy models enable intervention by giving it form and purpose. They persist not because they work but because they animate NGO life. In the context of international development, Mosse (2005, 2003) observes similar dynamics, pointing to the organizational function of policy ideas. For him, policy models and their counterpart "project designs" provide an overarching metaphor to guide action. They provide a lens or template through which to interpret field complexities into "authorized categories" (Mosse 2005) for the purposes of intervention.

Policy ideas also serve to mobilize resources and maintain political support for projects. Latour (1996) refers to this as "political mobilization around ideas," an inherent aspect of project life. In Mosse's interpretation, "policy ideas are important less for what they say than for *who* they bring together" (2005, 15). The success of a project therefore depends on the ongoing "enrolment" (Latour 1996) of actors and institutions into a policy idea or project model, which happens through activities like staff field visits, planning meetings, and report writing. In this way, projects socially produce their own success through representations that derive from actors' interpretations of events, using the policy metaphor at hand (Latour 1996; Mosse 2005). It follows that project failure results from a breakdown in coherence or "fragmentation of meaning" shared between actors within a project (Lewis et al. 2003). These insights are relevant to global conservation, because they help to explain how and why project actors proceed with interventions, even when field realities diverge sharply from policy assumptions. The magic of "good" policy ideas is that they enable NGO staff to factor out what is uncomfortable, by making it either irrelevant or invisible.

These insights also point to the role of ignorance and hypocrisy in global conservation projects, which I explore in this book. Linsey McGoey's (2012) work on "strategic ignorance," or the ability to unknow things that conflict with a dominant paradigm or organizational need, is prescient. So too are observations about the behavior of international bureaucracies like the World Bank, where "organized hypocrisy" is seen as a necessary condition for organizational survival (Weaver 2008). This is because "talk" can become systematically separated from "action" when organizations must respond to ongoing, and often conflicting demands from external stakeholders on the one hand and organizational leaders on the other. My research shows how this occurs in conservation practice, too, with NGOs often stuck in cycles of managing dissonance between policy ideas and field realities.

Overview of the Book

This book is an ethnographic journey through the politics and practice of global biodiversity conservation, which I approach as a form of transnational intervention. My focus is on the organizational processes of mainstream conservation NGOs and the "socio-nature" (Haraway 1997) that they produce, which I call *corporate nature*. As indicated, corporate nature emerges from the practices of a handful of big international NGOs, all of whom pursue technical and market-friendly "solutions" to conservation problems; the appearance of coherent knowledge and action; and ultimately organizational success in the newfound "business" of saving nature. My ethnographic gaze is focused on this neoliberal-corporate phenomenon, which in practice is like an "assemblage" of actors and institutions (Anderson and McFarlane 2011) that intervene in nature-society through the deployment of powerful policy ideas and knowledge-making practices. Herein, I observe how ethical compromises and various forms of violence can emerge in practice, because corporate nature involves a reliance on strategic ignorance (McGoey 2012), including the glossing over of deep complexities and dissonance in project field sites, where endemic violence often prevails and can be amplified by conservation interventions (Menton and Gilbert 2021; Milne and Mahanty 2019). This maintenance of ignorance can also involve "institutional violence" (Ahmed 2021, 179) against those who complain or dissent. A core contribution, therefore, is to show how corporate organizational practices and neoliberal ideas in global conservation give rise to undesirable socio-natures.

My findings derive from a decade-long project ethnography, focused on the case of CI and its work in Cambodia. I therefore address a dearth of ethnographic writing on the inner workings of global conservation. The internal logics, everyday practices, staff subjectivities, and organizational cultures of big conservation organizations remain understudied, especially from the perspective of insiders or those who have had insider access (Corson et al. 2019; Kiik 2019; Larsen and Brockington 2018). A key reason for this is difficulty gaining access to the inner workings of BINGOs as an ethnographer, often due to their limited appetite for criticism (Igoe and Sullivan 2009). In my case, rather unintentionally and serendipitously, I was able to use my former employment with CI in Cambodia as a way to conduct project ethnography in a multisited and multipositioned way—as other rare ethnogra-

Introduction

25

phies of conservation have done (see Corson 2016; Hussain 2019; Sachedina 2010). This approach inevitably entailed an array of epistemological, ethical, and personal challenges, which I explore throughout the book.

STUDYING CORPORATE NATURE

This book presents the case of one exemplary conservation project—that of CI in Cambodia—across scales and over time, from 2002 to 2012. This was not a neat study, planned from the outset: rather, my practitioner-researcher journey unfolded in surprising ways. It was only in retrospect that I was able to name and define corporate nature as something produced by big conservation organizations that fetishize the appearance of technical expertise and effectiveness at the expense of diverse knowledges and ethical conduct.

To focus my analysis, I trace the institutional life and effects of a prominent global policy idea: that of payments for environmental services, or PES,[11] which was deployed over time at CI. From 2005 onward, I observed the emergence of CI's PES program in Washington, DC, alongside its implementation in the Cardamom Mountains of Cambodia. By following the policy idea in this way, I open a window into global conservation practice more generally. My analysis observes the social and political dynamics around CI's mobilization of PES, tracing its whole life cycle from policy model to global program, from project metaphor to mechanism through which nature-society is remade on the ground. In short, I illustrate how conservation policy is crafted and then translated into practice by project actors across scales, including how knowledge is controlled and produced in the process.

Although my approach could be replicated for any policy idea, it is important to note the significance of PES. With its defining feature being contractual and market-like transactions for environmental services, PES is an archetypal element of neoliberal conservation: it emerges from aspirational thinking that "the market" can be harnessed, almost magically, to achieve conservation outcomes (Büscher et al. 2012). Testament to the power and appeal of PES, it has now spawned a veritable subindustry in global conservation. This includes billions invested in REDD+, a PES-like mechanism for

---

11. PES was originally defined as a willing buyer-seller transaction for well-defined ecosystem services (Wunder 2005). An earlier version of this was "direct payments" for conservation (Ferraro and Kiss 2002).

reducing carbon emissions from deforestation and forest degradation (Milne et al. 2019), as well as other global efforts to mainstream and financialize the idea of ecosystem services (MacDonald and Corson 2012). These remarkable policy developments are reshaping socio-nature, in ways that involve the commodification of elements of nature and the formation of natural capital (Castree and Henderson 2014; Corson et al. 2019)—a phenomenon often referred to as "Nature Inc." (Büscher, Dressler, and Fletcher 2014).

With these philosophical implications of environmental markets in mind, my focus here is on PES in practice. This story began when CI was inspired by early notions of PES known as direct payments (Ferraro and Kiss 2002), which led CI to develop a community-based version of the idea, called conservation agreements (Milne and Niesten 2009). This new policy became a global program at CI, known as the Conservation Stewards Program (CSP). From 2005, CSP grew in prominence: it now operates in twenty countries, with over 3,000 agreements, supported by over US\$17 million in grants and leveraged funds (CI 2020). By tracing the development and implementation of this global program, from Washington, DC, to Cambodia, this book observes the discursive and organizational practices, human contingencies, and power dynamics that define corporate nature.

OUTLINE

My account of CI's work in Cambodia unfolds in six substantive chapters. First, in chapter 1, I introduce the conservation project that is my ethnographic focus. Here, I portray the project as a transnational network of actors through whom ideas flow and implementation occurs. I also introduce the cast of characters who feature in this book, using pseudonyms. Having introduced the project, this chapter then addresses my experiences of doing ethnography within it, as an insider. Many dilemmas arose here, as my relationship with CI changed over time. Initially, I was a staff member in Cambodia from 2002 to 2005. Later, my engagement with CI involved a multisited mixture of research, collaboration, consultancy, and employment until 2012. As a result, my access to CI as a researcher was privileged but complicated, due to my changing role and perspective over the decade— something that I capture with the notion of multipositionality. I also discuss how some of the material in this book derives from unplanned and contentious events that happened to me: events that I feel ethically compelled

Introduction 27

to describe, even though they fall beyond the boundaries of conventional research (see Scheper-Hughes 1995).

With the introductions complete, I turn to CI's implementation of PES. The story begins at its source, which is CI's headquarters in Washington, DC—the subject of chapter 2. Here, I examine how the idea of PES was adopted by CI in 2005, and how it was made into a policy model for deployment in over ten countries. I focus on how the policy model was articulated, contested, justified, and promoted within CI's global head office. I also explore how the model was formulated for "scaling up"—an operational approach that reflects positivist logics, whereby policy tools are tested and replicated around the world, regardless of the context in which they are implemented. Ultimately, this chapter shows how neoliberal thinking took hold at CI through the PES model: the process was top-down and power-laden, but it was not seamless, nor was it uncontested among staff.

Having described the global realm, I turn my attention to the local realm in chapter 3. Here I illustrate the social and political context of CI's conservation project in the Cardamom Mountains, Southwest Cambodia. After outlining the complex post-conflict history of the area, I show how contemporary global conservation took hold from the year 2000 onward, to build a protected forest landscape of over one million hectares (see map 1). Here, a key issue has been how the Cambodian government maneuvered itself over time to territorialize forested land, with little consideration for local Indigenous people. In this light, I describe CI's partnership with the Cambodian Forestry Administration, which was marked by conflicts between conservation interests, government officials, Indigenous people, and other villagers living in the Cardamom Mountains. Amid this complexity, CI implemented its first PES-like conservation agreements with local communities in 2005: six agreements in six communes that persisted for over a decade.[12]

With implementation of the conservation agreements under way, chapter 4 examines the translation of CI's policy idea into practice. In this account of transnational policy implementation, I show how the policy model travels from CI's global headquarters to the NGO's country office in Phnom Penh, and then on to target villages and communes in the Cardamom Mountains.

---

12. Communes are an administrative unit in Cambodia, which in the Cardamom Mountains contained 50 to 250 families each. They became a de facto category for "community" in conservation practice.

The key point of this chapter is to show how the policy idea is transformed by processes of transnational implementation, to the extent that it becomes something else in practice: a PES-like policy in name only. I argue that this transformation occurred through the workings of local context, which in the Cambodian case involved two key dynamics: government manipulation of project processes and cross-cultural communication blockages between Khmer and foreign staff. At this point, the powerlessness and clumsiness of transnational NGO action become apparent, calling into question the assumed power of global conservation.

In chapter 5, I examine the untold or private life of CI's policy idea in the field. Through careful analysis of local villagers' perceptions and experiences, vivid gaps between the policy model's intentions and local realities are exposed. In particular, the side effects of CI's market-inspired yet government-partnered project practices are revealed in an unfortunate scenario whereby villagers are rendered into governable subjects or ecosystem service providers through apparently voluntary conservation agreements. Here, we witness how authoritarian state power can be elaborated through NGO action, which in this case occurred under the guise of CI's neoliberal rhetoric of "community choice," which framed communities as willing participants in the PES transaction. While CI might have believed in the effectiveness of its policy model, what happened in Cambodia shows how global conservation actually has relatively little capacity to control, or even to detect, what happens locally alongside its interventions.

Finally, chapter 6 shows how global conservation interests protect themselves in the face of dissonance. This chapter describes how CI's conservation project unwittingly became host to a major government-backed illicit logging racket from 2009 onward. CI's relationship with the highly corrupt and patronage-dominated Cambodian Forestry Administration at this point became a liability. Yet CI denied any aberrations within the project area and maintained a public narrative of project success. This occurred even as some CI staff, along with villagers and activists, dissented and tried to tackle the illegal logging themselves. I was involved in this struggle, eventually becoming a reluctant whistleblower on CI's role in the logging. Tellingly, those involved in exposing the logging were all variously defamed, dismissed, or forced to resign, while Chut Wutty paid the ultimate price with his life in 2012. In describing what happened, this chapter lays bare the violent processes through which corporate nature emerges, which include the production of ignorance about uncomfortable or unethical project side effects, like illegal logging or dangers faced by local activists. Ultimately, this chapter points to how policy ideas can persist in the face of dissonance: CI's PES scheme lives on as a chimera, composed of narratives, performance, and changing faces, all guided by corporate behavior.

Together, these chapters present a multifaceted portrait of mainstream global conservation, which shows how powerful policy ideas emerge and operate across scales and over time, as well as how they are upheld by corporate organizational practices. Furthermore, by maintaining ethnographic focus on CI's implementation of PES, I trace the discursive practices, human contingencies, and sociopolitical effects that unfold around policy ideas and their implementation. A key finding here is how policy ideas transform in practice, leading to gaps between intentions and outcomes. The ways in which global conservation then absorbs, deflects, and ignores this dissonance is a defining characteristic of corporate nature. My motive in offering this ethnography is not to dismantle global conservation but to prompt reflection in the hope of generating a more reflexive, ethical, and critical practice. Without this, we cannot begin to enact the new and radically different approaches to saving nature that we urgently need (see Büscher and Fletcher 2020; Collard, Dempsey, and Sundberg 2015)—approaches that acknowledge complexity and uncertainty; that are decolonial and caring of people and nature; and that ultimately nurture a thriving diversity of human and nonhuman life on our damaged planet.

Chapter 1

Corporate Subject, Corporate Object

October 2002, Cardamom Mountains:
It's my first trip into the forest, and I am a fresh Aussie volunteer—the kind
that is full of hope, and even ambition, about what I might achieve in the year
ahead. My job description is unusual, but somehow it chimes with my self-
made can-do style. Handed down the day before, in a single word, "WHAM."
The directive came from my enigmatic Australian boss, a Vietnam War vet-
eran, and country director for Conservation International (CI) in Cambo-
dia. Not understanding, I looked at him questioningly. "Winning hearts and
minds," he answered, as he handed me a pair of jungle-standard army boots.
"We've been good at holding the line, keeping the forest intact, but not so good
at working with the locals . . . that's your job, the communities bit."

With this in mind, I am now being ushered around the field site by my new
Cambodian colleagues. Their language is so foreign, I grimace; the surround-
ing forest is so green that it's unnatural, even sickly. Meanwhile, my head is
full of ideas from Australia—Indigenous rights and self-determination—the
language of my central Australian NGO job and desert home of just one week
prior. But there are no outback horizons here. The rainforest on either side of
the muddy track we're following seems impenetrable, somehow claustropho-
bic. I'm also uncomfortable because, in this stage-managed tour of the field,
I am being made into the quintessential foreigner. They call me barang*—the*
Khmer word for Frenchman or white person, deriving from colonial times. It's
the only word I understand in the unfamiliar chatter. At least I know when
they're talking about me.

Blindly riding this wave of NGO teamwork, I find myself en route to a pre-arranged village event, which will involve us—CI—handing out large sacks of rice and parcels of salt to the local Indigenous people. "This is because they are hungry," I'm told by my translator, "because the conservation project prevents them from doing slash-and-burn farming." As we arrive at the local temple grounds, I'm horrified to discover a large crowd of villagers waiting for us. Squatting in the hot sun, they stare as we get off our motorbikes and organize our things—cameras, water bottles, sunglasses ... too much stuff, in front of people who have nothing. This is the first time representatives from CI or any NGO have formally visited this village. Thus, there's a sense of anticipation and expectation, plus awe at the sight of a foreign woman who is dressed rather like a man. I now feel doubly self-conscious, unbearably hot, and somehow oversized in my Australian outback field gear.

Even though this is the first official public engagement between villagers and the conservation project, it seems that the proceedings are scripted. Dignitaries like the village chief and the local Forestry Administration boss are greeted and thanked, monks arrive to bless the bags of rice piled high at our feet, and villagers applaud on cue. Then, to my alarm, I'm told that I must give a speech. Totally unprepared, I hesitate, but saying no is not an option. Cringing privately, I begin in English, with my translator standing ready beside me: "Hello, everyone, my name is Sarah, I'm here to help you." As the conservation project's new communities officer, I have now entered the story. I'm on stage, in what will become an intoxicating role play, one replete with its own offstage dynamics of fear, manipulation, and passion that I cannot yet imagine.

I share this account of my arrival in the Cardamom Mountains because it marks the beginning of this story: the beginning of my decade-long engagement with CI and its work in Cambodia, from 2002 to 2012. My account is intended to convey something of my own subjectivity as an NGO insider. As any foreign NGO worker will tell you, expat life or working in the field is often exciting, but it is not always comfortable at an intellectual or personal level. In my case, I was painfully aware of being "matter out of place" (Trembath 2018), an experience that I compensated for, or perhaps even overcompensated for, through my learning of the Khmer language and attempts to bond with Khmer staff and villagers over the years. For others, the expat experience can morph into something that is all too natural, in which expat becomes expert and an intoxicating relationship with power forms. Notably, these two personal experiences of NGO work are not mutually exclusive. Rather, I see them as intertwined in a constantly shifting emotional and identity-making experience, unified by one common denominator: that being an expat, by definition, entails a relationship to global power. How each of us deals with this expat status—the ethnographer, her subjects, her colleagues—is a key factor in insider ethnographies such as this one. It is also a central consideration in this chapter, where I explain my efforts to achieve an empathetic and reflexive account of global conservation, as perceived from the inside.

The purpose of this chapter, therefore, is to explore the methodological and ethical contours of my ethnographic voice. I write as former insider, now academic, and *always* an advocate for forests, including the human and nonhuman beings who sustain and inhabit forested worlds. From this standpoint, I study global conservation. As Laura Nader explains in her treatise on "studying up," it is frequently this kind of "normative impulse" that "leads one to ask important questions about a phenomenon that would not be asked otherwise" (1969, 285). The phenomenon in question here is mainstream conservation, which is global in scale and corporate by nature. It is a phenomenon that demands ethnographic attention because it entails a concentration of power, held by a small group of people, who purport to influence the trajectories of society and nature around the world. The first part of this chapter therefore explains the methods I have used for studying up, which draw principally from the approach of "institutional ethnography" (Billo and Mountz 2016).

The second part of this chapter introduces my ethnographic subject, Conservation International (CI), and my unique and changing relationship with it. Here, I give an overview of CI's history and makeup, attempting to characterize the key elements of its corporate identity and culture. I then map the transnational project that is the focus of this book, including its cast of characters, who appear throughout the empirical chapters. Finally, I describe how I got to know CI as a staff member, and how my relationship to the organization changed over the course of a decade, along with changes to my personal perspective and identity. For this reason, I consider my work to be a *multipositioned ethnography*, to echo Marcus's multisited ethnography (1983).

This chapter's title—corporate subject, corporate object—intends to convey the multipositioned experience of insider ethnography. It's like wearing two hats at once, or various hats in sequence. The title is also intentionally circular because I want to convey how subject and object collapse in the context of studying up as an insider. By this, I mean that the ethnographer is simultaneously object and subject of the organization being studied, given its potential power and influence. This is true even when the ethnographic subject—an NGO, a policy, a project—comes into being post hoc, through an "ethnographic exit" from professional practice (Mosse 2015), as was the case for part of this ethnography. Thus, I describe the various stages of my relationship with CI so as to disclose the shifting methodological and ethical dilemmas of being an *observing participant* within a conservation project.

Studying Up for Global Conservation

As I have indicated, "studying up" (Nader 1969) involves turning our gaze toward people and organizations in positions of power, to observe how they operate and what makes them powerful. The notion of studying up has traveled far and has produced new lines of inquiry, such as "elite studies," which can involve ethnographic research into organizations and individuals in businesses, government, churches, or the military (Gusterson 1997; Marcus 1983). Similarly, the new field of science and technology studies involves ethnographic attention directed toward scientists, engineers, and other experts involved in the production of knowledge and authority (Jasanoff 2004; Latour 1996; Rottenburg 2009). Anthropological methods, therefore, provide unique ways to observe powerful institutions and their effects.

A key method for studying up is "institutional ethnography," which involves observing how individuals are embedded within and affected by institutions (Billo and Mountz 2016). Nominally, the main motivation for doing institutional ethnography is to understand how "ruling relations" or dynamics of subordination arise, as explained by Dorothy Smith (1987), who first proposed the method in the context of collaborative feminist studies. These days, institutional ethnography can examine how formal organizations such as government agencies or NGOs function, and in particular how they act upon their staff and subjects. Critical scholars have produced rich ethnographies of interventions and their politics, as I described in the introduction, but relatively few studies actually derive from participant observation of projects and professional practices (Billo and Mountz 2016). This approach, which may also be referred to as "project ethnography" (Latour 1996; West 2006), is what I pursue here.

Ethnographic studies of conservation and development projects are gradually emerging. Some leading examples from development studies broke new ground, including Mosse's (2005) remarkable ethnography of aid policy and practice in the case of the UK's Department for International Development interventions in India; Rottenburg's (2009) ethnography of Development Bank activities in a fictive African country; and Hilhorst's (2003) account of "the real world of NGOs" in the Philippines. All involved the researcher being embedded within the development organization in question. This is now becoming more common with the practice of "engaged research," which blurs the boundaries between ethnography and normative practice (Kirsch 2018; Lashaw 2013; Mosse 2015). In relation to conservation, calls for ethnographies of environmental intervention led to innovative work, such as team-based "collaborative event ethnography" at global meetings like the World Conservation Congress (Campbell et al. 2014). Ethnographies of conservation in various field settings have also begun to emerge (see Büscher 2013; Hussain 2019; McElwee 2016; Thaler 2021; West 2006). Two scholars in particular draw from an insider's perspective: Catherine Corson on USAID's biodiversity conservation work (2016) and Hassanali Sachedina on the African Wildlife Foundation's work in Tanzania (2010). Both write ethnographically about conservation initiatives in which they were formerly employed.

A key methodological challenge to conducting such work is putting boundaries around what exactly is being researched. This is especially true as conservation governance is increasingly seen as an assemblage or porous network (Corson et al. 2019). For this book, West's (2006) ethnography of conservation in Papua New Guinea is instructive, as her study is bounded around the notion of "the project," even though the project involved diffuse and transnational processes of social production. Similarly, I focus on a transnational conservation project, but I bound my study by focusing on the *policy idea* being implemented across scales. This approach considers the field to be a multisited phenomenon, spanning various locations and social spaces (Marcus 1995).[1] This book is therefore a multisited project ethnogra-

---

1. Alternatively, Markowitz (2001) talks of "multi-local" research, especially for understanding NGOs, as it provides a way to study the transnational connections or "interconnecting systems" within NGOs.

phy, but with the unusual extra dimension of multipositionality, due to my changing role over time.

The principal research method for project ethnography is participant observation. Applied to projects, the key advantage of this method is that it provides an "inside" view, which gives a much richer analysis than is afforded by observations from "the outside" (Markowitz 2001). However, participant observation is a research technique that "does not travel well up the social structure" (Gusterson 1997, 115), meaning that gaining access to organizations for research purposes can be hard. This means that researchers often work as staff members or consultants within the organization or project they wish to study—or at the very least, they become involved in some way (Mosse 2015). Achieving this requires building and maintaining relationships—a potentially complicated process that involves personal effort and emotional labor, harking back to the open and collaborative origins of institutional ethnography (Smith 1987). As Billo and Mountz explain of Dorothy Smith's work: "The approach is considered an ongoing, evolving practice, rather than a clearly demarcated or completed project; the practice grows through networking, relationships, and group meetings among feminist scholars" (2016, 204). Thus, project ethnography conducted *on the inside* is necessarily contingent upon an array of unpredictable, interpersonal factors.

Being embedded in a project is a legitimate research strategy, but it poses unique ethical issues in relation to the researcher's relationships with the organization and staff being studied (Mosse 2015; Gusterson 1997). Particularly tricky is informed consent, because researcher-practitioners often find themselves privy to sensitive information when they are conducting engaged work as consultants, advocates, and advisors (Kirsch 2018; Lashaw 2013; Mosse 2015). Furthermore, unexpected things can happen in the course of research, leaving all participants in unnegotiated territory. In such cases, tensions can emerge when one's colleagues resist being treated as research subjects, especially if they disagree with the researcher's "ethnographic rendering" of past shared experiences (Mosse 2015). Given this potential awkwardness, I endeavor to take an empathetic stance in this book, often turning the critical lens upon myself. I therefore interweave elements of "auto-ethnography" (Ellis, Adams, and Bochner 2011) into the text, where I analyze my own experiences and perceptions. This offers a way to explore my own subjectivity in relation to CI.

Conservation International:
Corporate Subject and Exemplar

When I first started working for CI in 2002, I had no idea that I would end up studying my employer. At the time I was excited about working for an international organization. It felt like the realization of a childhood dream—especially when I first visited CI's headquarters in 2004 in downtown Washington, DC. That was the year that CI's biodiversity hotspots coffee-table book was launched by a stellar lineup of authors, with corporate sponsorship.[2] At the time, the hotspots concept was conveyed compellingly throughout the head office on glossy color posters that displayed photos of exotic primates, birds, and painted-up Indigenous people. Something like a naïve sense of possibility and purpose stirred inside me when I first saw these images.

As I explained in the introduction, CI is an exemplar of the global conservation industry. It has pioneered innovative but controversial partnerships with the private sector, including with major fossil fuel companies; it has spearheaded new marketing strategies with celebrities like Harrison Ford; and it is known for its embrace of science and market-based approaches (see MacDonald 2008). Over the years, I found that most of the senior technical staff at CI were biologists or economists: importantly, this meant that they subscribed to a common powerful language, underpinned by positivist and often reductionist views of the world. Initially, I fitted into this space, given my undergraduate training in science and engineering. I thought that I could easily belong, and for a while I shared the language and worldview of those on the inside.

One of the appealing things about CI is that it seems to possess a unique entrepreneurial spirit, as conveyed through the organization's own mythology. Key here is the figure of Peter Seligman, CI's founding chief executive officer and charismatic leader for three decades, now chairman of the board. Tales of heroic risks and unassailable principles emerge from accounts of CI's origins: Seligman, with a small breakaway group of loyal colleagues from the international division of The Nature Conservancy, formed CI late one evening in a humble hotel room in 1987. Fresh and inspired, this group of innovators vowed to save biodiversity around the world, in a way that was free from the colonial and bureaucratic baggage of the past. With this trailblazing spirit, the organization grew around its leadership and core team,

---

2. See *Hotspots Revisited* by Mittermeier et al. (2004), part of the CEMEX books on nature series.

Corporate Subject, Corporate Object

giving rise to a uniquely coherent organizational identity, and eventually its own signature, top-down corporate culture.

Given CI's appeal and momentum, it is not surprising that the organization now operates globally and is recognized as one of the biggest, most influential conservation NGOs in the world. CI operates in over thirty countries, with 2,000 partners from business, government, and civil society.[3] It has roughly 400 staff working at its head office, and hundreds more based at field offices. Annual spending in recent years averages around US$160 million, 40 percent of which goes to country and field programs. Telling of mainstream conservation's territorial gaze, CI articulates its global impact in terms of the area of Earth that it helps to protect, which in 2018 was cited as "4.6 million square kilometers of land and sea" (CI 2018). This reflects the dominant underlying paradigm of global conservation, which is that of protection—even as protected areas are now asked to meet human needs and deliver ecosystem services too (Corson et al. 2019).

In spite of the overall emphasis on protection, CI has tried hard in recent years to refocus on the connections between people and nature. This was most obvious in 2010, when CI changed its logo and mission statement to reflect Seligman's new "key message" which was that "people need nature to thrive."[4] The shift was not entirely welcomed by CI's staff, especially the more traditional conservation biologists. For example, staff at the head office joked about the new logo: "It looks like a toilet seat" and "It looks like Korean writing" were mutterings I heard in the corridors. Indeed, these comments corresponded with a sense of unease, as staff realized that to deliver on CI's new mission, a massive re-skilling and re-staffing would be required. Some long-term staff sighed, as they were now used to Seligman's never-ending "startup" genius, which apparently drove him perpetually to reinvent the organization that he had created.

DERIVING POWER FROM SCIENCE

Despite recent organizational shifts, CI's mainstay of "science, partnership and field demonstration" has prevailed since the 2000s. These key elements

---

3. From CI's "impact statement" drawing from the 2018 Annual Report (CI 2018).

4. See "CI Unveils New Organizational Identity," Conservation International, accessed May 2019, https://www.conservation.org/NewsRoom/pressreleases/Pages/New_Logo.aspx.

of organizational identity were forged through the hotspots idea, which was published in the prestigious journal *Nature* (Myers et al. 2000). From then on, CI's largesse only grew, especially when it received the largest ever philanthropic grant for biodiversity conservation in 2001, from the Moore Foundation, valued at US$261 million. This grant enabled CI to build an in-house scientific task force dedicated to monitoring the status of biodiversity hotspots and conservation outcomes around the world.[5] Apart from producing peer-reviewed journal articles, CI's science team focused on what they call "metrics," as its website explains: "At CI, we've given a lot of thought to the way we measure our success. Our science team has landed on a unique, human-focused set of criteria that will help us determine where to place our efforts, track progress toward our goals and communicate the results of our work" (CI 2015a). This language conveys global expertise, rationality, and oversight. In short, CI's embrace of science is intimately related to its organizational identity.

CI's discourses of scientific application and success also constitute the organization's discursive power. The quote about the "science team" and its "unique criteria . . . to track progress" is indicative of CI's techno-corporate voice, which conveys a sense of control over project activities in the field. Somehow, CI's metrics convert the unruliness of postcolonial socio-natures into something that can be quantitatively measured and tracked, like the blood pressure of a sick patient. CI even uses medical analogies in its program design and marketing, as seen in the "vital signs" program for measuring "ecosystem health" in sub-Saharan Africa (CI 2015a). These discourses work to abstract and simplify complex phenomena, by "rendering technical" the politics of intervention (Li 2007), and by generating the possibility of an unproblematic and objective form of global governance (Merry 2011). Yet, as this book shows, CI's generic indicators of conservation success quickly become nonsensical in the face of messy field realities. Nevertheless, they persist because they support intervention, and create a sense of accountability and control that appeals to donors and the public.

---

5. See "Conservation International unveils solution to prevent global species extinctions," Gordon and Betty Moore Foundation, accessed April 2019, https://www.moore.org/article-detail?newsUrlName=conservation-international-unveils-solution-to-prevent-global-species-extinctions.

EMBRACING NEOLIBERALISM

Alongside science, CI's corporate identity may also be characterized by its seemingly easy embrace of capitalism, elite networks, and market-based approaches—all signature elements of neoliberal conservation (Büscher et al. 2012). This is evident in the composition of CI's board, which includes household names and brands like the Hollywood actor Harrison Ford; Rob Walton, retired chairman of the board of Wal-Mart Stores Inc.; and Robert Fisher, the chairman of the board of Gap Inc. (CI 2019). The leadership also demonstrates close ties to the US government, particularly in relation to security and defense. For example, CI's former president (for the short period of 2014–2015) was Gary Edson, a deputy national security advisor under George W. Bush, now lobbyist and philanthropic advisor (CI 2015b). Furthermore, CI's chairman of the executive committee is Wes Bush, an aerospace engineer who is close to the Pentagon and was formerly chairman of Northrop Grumman Corporation—the world's fourth largest arms trader in 2017.[6] This remarkable lineup is, of course, assembled to leverage funding and political influence—not insights from ground-level experience with conservation and development. This is an executive leadership that can advance a late-capitalist vision of nature conservation, in which corporate power, consumerism, accumulation, state violence, and extraction can exist apparently naturally alongside the mission to save nature.

For this reason, Guy Debord's *Society of the Spectacle* has been used to illuminate and critique neoliberal conservation (see Igoe 2010). Spectacle refers to the role of images and illusions in capitalist transactions: here, we consume ideas and virtual products, just as much as any material commodity. In conservation, this can involve the consumption of promotional imagery made by NGOs, depicting idealized human–environment relations or rarefied images of wild nature and what is being done to save it (Igoe 2010). For critical scholars, this is a form of hyperfetishization, which propagates illusory fictions about capitalism's synergy with mainstream conservation practice (Brockington et al. 2012; Igoe 2017). CI's "Nature Is Speaking" cam-

---

6. Details on Northrop Grumman from Wikipedia (https://en.wikipedia.org/wiki/Northrop _Grumman) and see CI's board website, accessed May 2019, https://www.conservation.org /about/Pages/board-of-directors.aspx.

paign is exemplary of this spectacular form of production and consumption. Operating as an interactive website, this campaign involves celebrities like Robert Redford and Julia Roberts speaking *as* nature and its elements, using voiceovers of dramatic videos of wilderness and its destruction.[7] Viewers experience a sense of distress at the prospect of losing the natural world, which is personified through celebrities. They also feel a sense of relief that something is being done, not least by CI.

What CI produces, therefore, is not just measurable scientific results for donors but also emotive images and powerful ideas. The focus of this ethnography, as I explained in the introduction, is on one of these virtual products: the idea that market mechanisms can be used to conserve nature. This idea is fundamental to the production of neoliberal nature (Castree 2008; McAfee 1999), and CI has played a leading role in promoting it as a new "solution" or strategy for global conservation. Again, Seligman's entrepreneurialism and commitment to translating blue sky policy ideas into practice was critical here. He ensured that CI was able to hire a small team of economists to develop new market-like tools such as conservation agreements, conservation concessions, direct payments, and payments for environmental services (see Milne and Niesten 2009). Seligman's philanthropic networks also secured a major grant for CI to implement its conservation agreements model around the world, under CI's flagship Conservation Stewards Program, as I show in chapter 2.

In attempting to summarize CI's relationship with capitalism, elite power, and neoliberal ideas, it is important to acknowledge that this has not gone unnoticed or uncriticized. Many observers now accuse CI of greenwashing due to its relationships with multibillion-dollar corporations, especially those involved in extractive and agricultural industries like Rio Tinto, Cargill, Monsanto, Starbucks, and ExxonMobil (e.g., Adams 2017; Lang 2018; MacDonald 2008). CI's apparent lack of principles has also been targeted. For example, in 2011, CI's willingness to "sell out" was exposed in a spoof in which undercover comedians posed as representatives from Lockheed Martin, the arms manufacturer, seeking a relationship with CI for image improvement—a proposition that CI's staff welcomed at the time. Needless to say, the resulting exposé went viral (see Zeller 2011). Others have observed

---

7. See CI's Nature Is Speaking website, accessed March 3, 2020, https://www.conservation.org/nature-is-speaking/Pages/default.aspx.

the organization's incompetence and arrogance in some field settings, for example in cases where CI spent donor funds on conspicuous luxury items for executives, instead of on project needs (Balboa 2014; Chapin 2004). The critique is easy and potentially endless. What is of interest, therefore, is that CI seems to be impervious to most criticism. In general, it appears that CI either maintains silence or responds with careful public statements of deflection or denial. I explore this dynamic in chapter 6, because it was a key aspect of my own experience with CI, and I argue that it reveals how corporate organizational processes can shape the behavior of ostensibly virtuous not-for-profit groups, generating new forms of violence in the process.

The Project System

Rather than attempting to conduct an exhaustive study of CI as a whole—a formidable task, given the organization's sheer scale and dynamism—this book focuses on one project over time. As explained in the introduction, I trace the genesis and implementation of CI's PES-like conservation agreements, from Washington, DC, to rural Cambodia from 2005 to 2012; and my aim in doing so is to reveal the inner workings of global conservation across scales. To approach this study, I therefore took my realm of inquiry to be the "project system," which is basically a "set of relationships" that connect project actors in a loose and porous network (Mosse 2001, 2005), like an "assemblage" (Anderson and McFarlane 2011).

The project system does not represent formal organizational structures or boundaries; rather, it conveys dynamic, transnational processes of social production in which global and local realms simultaneously "produce" the other (Appadurai 1996; West 2006). Ideas, information, and money flow through the system, along with influence and power. The fluid connections between actors are also spaces of negotiation in which political pressure and personal agendas are advanced (Mosse 2001), along with efforts to find common meanings at project interfaces (Long 2001). Here, the most influential actors may be called "brokers," or those who do the work of "translation" across scales and interfaces (Lewis and Mosse 2006, after Latour 1996). I draw from these concepts in subsequent chapters, to show how processes of brokering and translation played out in CI's project work, especially in relation to the PES-like conservation agreements.

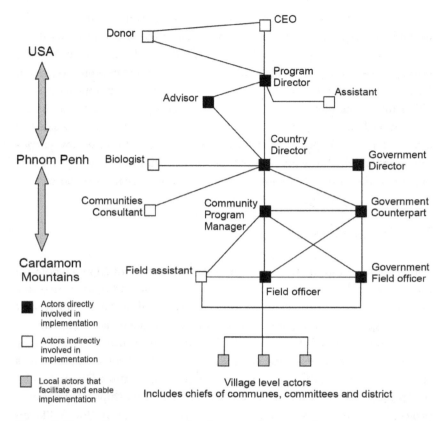

Figure 1 The project as a transnational system of connected actors.

For now, my aim is to introduce the key players and to map out the project. As shown in figure 1, the project system includes all people who had some involvement, direct or indirect, with implementing the conservation agreements in Cambodia. Part of this system exists in Washington, DC, where the policy model and funding opportunities originated; another part exists in CI's country office for Cambodia, in Phnom Penh, where much of the brokering and translation work occurred; and the final part of the system is on the ground in the Cardamom Mountains, where field staff enacted the project through engagements with local villagers and government officials. My project diagram is indicative only, being a snapshot view from 2009. It does not represent all the complex interactions between actors over time, nor does it show their constant movement between offices and the field. Alongside figure 1, I also introduce the project brokers in personal terms, as the cast of characters that feature in this ethnography (see table 1). From this point forward, I will refer to them by their pseudonyms and/or their position title. A decade on, none of these actors now works on CI's project in the Cardamom Mountains.

A final point about the project system is that it exhibited overall system dynamics. That is, even though the project was made up of a cast of characters, these individuals were all influenced by separate personal and institutional demands—coming either from the Forestry Administration in Cambodia or from the various departments of CI's head office, each with their own lines of accountability. A key dynamic here was the interplay between the head office and the field, in which the Cambodian agreements served CI's global purpose of testing and "scaling up" its ideas and solutions. As the DC-based director explained, these agreements are "setting a precedent . . . they're tremendously important." Correspondingly, field stories from Cambodia were used in promotional presentations to the CI board, to donors, and at the World Conservation Congress in 2008.[8] CI's project in Cambodia therefore functioned as a web of relations and knowledge production, becoming an exemplar of global conservation, replete with internal tensions and contradictions, as this book shall describe.

My Relationship with CI

As I have explained, this ethnography derives from ten years of personal involvement with CI and its work in Cambodia. My role changed over time, from insider to outsider, twice, as follows: I was employed by CI Cambodia from 2002 to 2005 to work on its Cardamom Mountains project, as the community engagement advisor; as a doctoral student, I returned to the field to conduct project ethnography from 2006 to 2007, during which time I also acted as a short-term consultant for CI to gather household survey data; I rejoined CI in 2010 as a part-time director hired by the head office to advise on the social aspects of the conservation agreements globally; by January 2012 I had resigned from CI, after the organization's refusal to acknowledge allegations of illegal logging at its field site in Cambodia.

---

8. As conveyed by key staff, and as I witnessed at the World Conservation Congress.

Table 1 The cast of characters, 2007 to 2009

Pseudonym	Role in the project
Maria	**Program director**, based in Washington, DC. Has authority over design and financing of all conservation agreements globally. Young, charismatic Latin American woman, with field experience. Resource economist, with postgraduate degree from a top US university. First went to Cambodia in 2006 to initiate the conservation agreements.
Jan	**Technical director**, based near Washington, DC. Provides expert advice to CSP globally. Significant intellectual influence over CI's conservation agreements policy. Experienced, multilingual European man with a PhD in resource economics from a top US university. Made several visits to Cambodia from 2004 to 2009.
Kiry	**Country director** of CI Cambodia, based in Phnom Penh. Charismatic and competent Khmer man; many years' experience with international projects; postgraduate degree from Australia. Heavily involved in implementing the conservation agreements in the Cardamom Mountains. Began at CI as the community program manager, promoted to country director in 2007.
Chung	**Government director** for CI Cambodia project, based in Phnom Penh. Forestry Administration employee, co-managing the Cardamom Mountains site with Kiry. Young man, experienced with international NGOs; earned a postgraduate degree in forestry from Japan. Began with CI in 2006.
Sok	**Community program manager** for CI, based in Phnom Penh. A Khmer man with many years of NGO experience, responsible for reporting aspects of the conservation agreements, but with limited field involvement. Recruited in late 2006, resigned from CI in 2009.

Aung	**Government counterpart**, based in the field and in Phnom Penh. Works for the Forestry Administration, involved in everyday running of the conservation agreements in the field, especially administration. Young and ambitious, with a background in forestry. Empowered by Kiry in this role from 2006 onward.
Nhet	**Field officer**, based in the Cardamom Mountains. Employee of CI, whose community relationships and liaison skills underpinned the conservation agreements. Educated Khmer man in his early fifties, who survived the Khmer Rouge and fought armed resistance against Vietnamese forces in Cambodia for twenty years. He left the army to join CI in the Cardamom Mountains in 2001.
Kim	**Government field officer**, Cardamom Mountains. Employee of provincial FA, responsible for community liaison along with Nhet. Middle-aged Khmer man; member of the original Community Engagement team from 2002. Clever, charismatic, educated, but not ambitious like Aung.
Luke	**Conservation biologist**, Phnom Penh–based expatriate who provided technical advice. Became CI's regional director in 2007. Passionate about wildlife and biodiversity, he first came to the Cardamom Mountains in 2003. Not involved in implementing the conservation agreements directly, but from 2007 had an oversight role.

As a result of this relationship with CI, I had privileged access to my subject. I participated in and observed from the inside the daily behaviors, actions, and logics of the organization's staff, as well as its donors and partners. I also witnessed ongoing project interactions with local villagers in the Cardamom Mountains and with Cambodian government officials. As a result, the social and political processes of policy making and project implementation were laid bare to me, and I was often an actor involved in shaping these processes.

Furthermore, although my normative stance in support of social and environmental justice changed little over time, I did change as a person. My scholarly knowledge, Khmer language skills, confidence, and experience all increased, contributing to an evolving personal identity. Initially, I suffered from my own delusions, as a starry-eyed and well-intended NGO worker in her late twenties. Later, I would recoil from the power-laden and highly flawed NGO encounters with villagers that I witnessed, feeling as though I had become a more seasoned observer. Yet my desire to do research only, as a fly on the wall, also entailed its own delusions of detachment or non-involvement. I therefore offer an ethnographic rendering of my journey *through* global conservation practice, being as true to my observations as possible, while accounting for my changing role as professional, scholar, and activist, outlined below.

BECOMING A CONSERVATION PROFESSIONAL

My first three years with CI Cambodia were marked by a personal determination to grow what was then the Community Engagement Program, a core aspect of CI's project in the Cardamom Mountains. My concerns were strictly applied, in the sense of wanting to achieve practical goals that were ambitious but, in my mind, achievable and meaningful. Those goals included protecting forests and strengthening local livelihoods, in line with CI's strategy and Cambodian government policy. I was a team player, working with a group of Khmer staff called the "community team."

I remember feeling excited about working for CI and what might be achieved. This sentiment related largely to timing: in 2002, there was a distinct sense of hope and possibility in Cambodia. The heavily forested frontier was just opening up to NGOs—especially big international conservation organizations—after more than thirty years of civil war that had made access impossible. Furthermore, the first ever commune council elections were to be held in late 2002, in what appeared to the beginnings of democracy in Cambodia.

My sense of hope in those early days was surely a product of naïveté too. I knew little of Cambodian history, political culture, or local context. This is a condition that I now see as endemic in global conservation practice, and in some ways facilitative of interventions. That is, a certain level of ignorance is *required* in order for policy models to make sense to those responsible for implementing them. In addition to my lack of local knowledge, I was also not particularly aware of the scholarly critiques of development and conservation at the time. Thus, I was not inclined to deconstruct what "we" were doing. Rather, my inclination was to try to improve "our" project strategy. And I did this in the most professional and ethical way that I could: gathering data on local conditions, questioning assumptions from the head office, seeking input from local communities. In these things I *had* been trained, and my instinct was to attend to the local social and political conditions influencing the conservation project. Perhaps because of this, I often found myself at odds with the attitudes that prevailed within CI, especially when it came to community engagement.

Spurred on by a desire to be useful, I threw myself into this work for three years. I became one of the NGO workers whom I would later observe: obsessed with the project, with little work-life balance, and a personal identity that became fused with the mission to save the Cardamom Mountains and its people. In this all-consuming condition, life and work can meld into an amplified sense of purpose. I felt like my team and I were really making a difference! I also had a great affinity with my Khmer counterpart, Nhet, with whom I shared ideas and made decisions. He and Chut Wutty were the first Khmer people I worked with in 2002, as they were the only ones who spoke English at the ranger station. Nhet was an ex-guerrilla fighter from the US-aligned Khmer People's National Liberation Front, who had remarkably survived the Khmer Rouge period as an educated youth. He was practical and strategic; we shared values, jokes, and observational instincts; and he became the charismatic Khmer face of CI's early community engagement. The outcomes of our work are hard to judge, but on our last joint visit to the field in 2015, after years of absence, we were still warmly received.

I recount these experiences because I wish to demonstrate that I have lived the NGO worker's personal sense of purpose and significance, which can even become addictive. I relate to the sentiments, aspirations, and pressures of being a conservation practitioner with empathy. It is meaningful work, often laced with a sense of power to change the world in a virtuous way.

BECOMING A SCHOLAR

As I became more aware of the nuances and complexities of conservation, I drafted a proposal for doctoral research. Initially my research questions were about the "effectiveness" of direct payments schemes, which were the most compelling policy idea in conservation at the time (Ferraro and Kiss 2002). However, under new intellectual influences at Cambridge University, I soon discovered the critical literature that enabled me to pursue other questions about conservation politics and practice. What began as a policy-relevant doctoral proposal in 2005 soon became a critical ethnographic study. I emphasize this transformation in intention because it relates to the ethics of my research. That is, I never set out to do an ethnography of CI, but it happened as my perspective and disposition changed over time.

At the outset of my doctoral research, I established a practical working relationship with CI, of mutual benefit. CI saw me as someone who could help to collect socioeconomic data on the impacts of its new PES scheme—something that CI contracted me to do. Furthermore, the CI Cambodia staff knew me well and trusted me as their former colleague, which meant that I could still play an informal advisory role. Thus, I was granted full access to the project, benefiting from CI's assistance in the field. This way, I continued to work with the community engagement team, as a doctoral researcher.

I was very grateful to have this level of access, and in many ways, I felt at home. Yet my high comfort level also led to a conflicted identity on my part. That is, I still wanted to fix and improve things, especially as I saw changes in the project style that I did not agree with—even though I was meant to be on the sidelines. Most notably, this related to a fading emphasis within CI on community rights and empowerment, which had been my priority. My first trip back to the field as a researcher, only six months after I had left the role of community program manager, was characterized by this conflicted sense of purpose. I vividly recall the moment when I realized that I had to let go of my prior involvements. Sitting on the bank of the Areng River, during a field trip, I finally saw that it was no longer my place to advise on how things were done. With time I got used to my new positionality of detachment, but I still retained an "applied hat." For example, I remained in dialogue with various CI staff at the US headquarters and in Phnom Penh, informing them of what was happening in the field and suggesting how things might be improved.

This pragmatic relationship continued for a while. I offered information and insights to CI, and key staff in Cambodia and DC allowed me to have access to the project. The arrangement worked well for the conduct of household surveys and interviews with villagers, but as my research interests expanded into project ethnography, it became more complicated. I tried to explain to the CI staff who were giving me access to the project that I was also observing them; that I was interested in how they did things, and how project life happened. But in retrospect, I doubt that they really understood what project ethnography was or why anyone would bother with it.

The key issue in trying to explain my research to CI was epistemological. That is, the senior staff who facilitated my access were typically natural scientists, whose training made it hard for me to communicate the qualitative nature of my investigation. For example, shortly after commencing my PhD I visited CI DC and met with the global head of field programs at the time. He was interested in my research, and he asked me: "So, what are your dependent variables?" All I could say was that my study was not quantitative. Similarly, CI supported me as a graduate student to present my work on direct payments at a Society of Conservation Biology meeting. My sponsor, who was then the "human dimensions" expert in CI's science team, asked me beforehand, in bewilderment: "Why are you presenting in the environmental anthropology panel?" But after hearing my talk, he said, "Well, you pitched it beautifully for that audience." Thus, most CI staff still saw me as a member of their team but I was beginning to belong elsewhere too. My production of anthropological knowledge about conservation might therefore have seemed quaint, but not threatening.

For me, too, this transformation in identity and positionality was gradual, and to some extent I remained in a state of duality. I started my PhD as a conservation professional, but by the end I was a hybrid anthropologist, having unraveled most of the knowledge constructs that were once the basis of my working life. I still identified as a conservationist and as a practitioner, but it was getting complicated. This hybridity deeply affected my research praxis. By 2006, I had begun to see my colleagues as subjects to be observed: I had become fascinated with their ideas, their language, and their assumptions, and almost constantly took notes "about them" while we interacted. However, I was also a participant and collaborator in project life. I attended team meetings and global workshops, sharing my best insights on how to solve difficult field problems. This dual stance of insider-outsider remained with me throughout the research: the only antidote was to cultivate an awareness of my switching subjectivity, between technical advisor and ethnographer.

Inevitably my dual role and positionality produced ethical and analytical issues. I had privileged access to the project because of the long-term relationships that I had established with staff over the years, and I did not want to abuse their trust. Furthermore, it was important to me to maintain the relationships that I had with people at CI and to conduct my research in a way that reflected my sincere intention to contribute to conservation practice that was effective and socially just.

This desire to maintain relationships, and a foot in both worlds, meant that I tried extremely hard not to offend my colleagues in the write-up of my findings. I anonymized CI and the staff that I wrote about, even though this was not really practicable. Mainly, I wanted to show that I was not out to attack them but that my findings could be about *any* large conservation NGO. My critique was also empathetic, as I could personally identify with the challenges faced by practitioners. Eventually, I ensured that CI had an opportunity to respond to my thesis before it became available in the university library. Rather nervously, I sent hard copies to my key contacts at CI, wondering what response I would receive. But no formal response ever came. Months later, Jan said that he had read it, commenting only briefly, "Well, you didn't pull any punches!"

All these efforts to tread lightly were observed by my thesis examiner in 2009. He challenged me: "You are being disciplined by them . . . you could have gone much further with your critique!" He was right. Apart from wanting to keep the trust I had been given by certain colleagues, I was afraid of potential backlash. Would my colleagues think I was being overly critical or even unethical? Would I be able to work in conservation again? My concerns were partly pragmatic, as I explained to my examiner: "I am too young to burn bridges . . . I don't even have a job." In this sense, my thesis was the product of a cautious researcher writing about a powerful subject. The notion that I had been disciplined by my subject stayed with me though. It became an intellectual challenge to delve into more deeply.

BACK INTO THE FOLD

Postdoctoral life was fraught with insecurities and change. After completing my PhD, I moved back to Australia to live for the first time in nearly a decade. With only insecure and part-time academic work available, my internal deliberations continued over whether to pursue a scholarly path or to follow my desire to be a conservationist. It was at this moment that CI's head office advertised the position of social development director with the Conservation Stewards Program, and Jan contacted me to suggest that I apply. It seemed that he saw the value in my critique, and CI wanted to hire someone who could track the social impacts of its new conservation agreements. I decided to apply.

The possibility of becoming an insider again provoked mixed feelings. On the one hand, it seemed like a ridiculous idea, given the intellectual ground that I had covered in deconstructing and critiquing big conservation. On the other hand, it seemed like a chance for me to do something with the insights that I had gained from my PhD. I did not make the decision lightly, as I was also concerned that I would lose my ability to publish from my hard-won doctorate. Furthermore, some colleagues who knew me and CI well tried to persuade me not to take the job: "Don't go back, working for them will change you," one friend and ex-CI staffer said. He was referring to the risk of me being disciplined again by CI, through the pressures of transnational, professional employment. He was alluding to that whirlwind sense of busyness and purpose that can preclude deep and humble engagements with the field. I was conscious of these things but took the job anyway.

What followed was eighteen months of employment with CI, working at 60 percent of a full-time load. My base was in Canberra, where I maintained a part-time postdoctoral role. Life was punctuated by late-night Skype calls as I attempted to advise on the social dimensions of ten CSP projects in ten countries, across Latin America, Africa, and Asia. One of the countries was Cambodia, and it was in my new capacity as CI's social development director that I was able to return to the Cardamom Mountains and to reengage with the very project that I had studied and helped to create. It was tantalizing to return to Cambodia in late 2010, after a three-year absence. I was warmly received by old colleagues, who were now more senior. Kiry, who I had recruited to run the Community Engagement Program in 2005, was now country director. Furthermore, the field biologist Luke was now

CI's technical director, the most senior expatriate in the region. Upon my return to the office, he said to me: "I read the abstract for your thesis, and I thought, 'Wow, this woman really knows what she's talking about.'... It will be great to have you involved again." I was chuffed, even if it was only the abstract that he had read.

The project had indeed matured over my three-year absence, and as I reengaged, I discovered the ways in which it had changed. Unfortunately, the changes resembled an extreme version of what I had anticipated in my thesis write-up in 2009: rising government control, weakened community voices. Naïvely, I thought that the flaws could be remedied. I began to advocate for improved local participation in project activities; greater attention to the *quality* of project processes; and more honest reporting about emerging challenges in the field, which included dealing with rumors about illegal logging in the project area. However, when I raised these matters there was pushback from the project leadership in Cambodia, and after months of tension our relationships unraveled.

I describe this unraveling in chapter 6 as a series of events that eventually forced me to become a whistleblower, exposing CI's role in illegal logging in the Cardamom Mountains. It was an exhausting and traumatic experience, which I did not foresee. Because of this, my ethnographic voice is now that of a former insider—a scholar-practitioner who could no longer remain on the inside of the NGO machinery. This ruptured or tainted positionality reveals the consequences of knowing too much, or of possessing the kind of knowledge that insiders either should not have or are expected to conceal. Ultimately, my relationship with CI ended because of my own conviction: I found it unethical to hide knowledge about illicit logging and corruption in CI's project area, which had been disclosed to me by field staff and villagers, along with their pleas for help. It was a case of having to speak out.

Final Reflections on Insider Ethnography

The production of ethnographic knowledge involves being in relationship to people and place. Long-term engagements and dialogue are required, and this must entail a sense of reciprocity and respect toward one's subjects, both human and nonhuman (Kiik 2019; Lather 1986). Questions for the researcher arise here about what to do when one bears witness to injus-

Corporate Subject, Corporate Object

tices, even violence, in the field (Scheper-Hughes 1995). Under such circumstances, ethnographers can describe and expose what is happening in powerful ways—as Mosse indicates (2015), the power of ethnography is not to be underestimated.

In my case, I found it impossible to remain silent about what I was hearing and witnessing in Cambodia in 2010–2011, even though CI's in-country management deflected my concerns and suggested that I attend to the "bigger picture."[9] I felt that my main commitment was to those who had asked for help, including villagers who said, "Please tell CI in Washington about the logging." I was in a position to speak up, and I felt an obligation to do so: not just because of my role at CI but also because of my history in the Cardamom Mountains. Thus, my intention was only ever to strive for social and ecological justice—a stance that unfortunately brought me into conflict with CI.

My ability to write about these events now involves an appeal to the "primacy of the ethical" (Scheper-Hughes 1995). Although I was not officially conducting research when I returned to the Cardamom Mountains with CI in 2010, my approach and commitment to the field was still ethnographic and normatively engaged. I could not erase my old relationships to place and people in the project area, and the reciprocal ties that this brings. Thus, I have used an "ethnographic rendering" or "auto-ethnography" (Mosse 2015) to analyze how CI treated the illegal logging problem, and how this acted upon me.

Ultimately, I hope that my approach will reveal why we need insider ethnographies of conservation, but also why they are so hard to achieve. This is an ethnographic form that emerges over time, often serendipitously: very rarely can it be neatly planned from the outset. Furthermore, researchers must tackle complex, multipositional identities, along with the problems of gaining and maintaining access to organizations. Few social scientists have been allowed inside conservation organizations with the explicit purpose of studying their internal processes. After all, why would a self-preserving nonprofit organization willingly open itself to the scrutiny of an ethnographer who is curious about power dynamics and justice? Furthermore, can the dominant epistemology in conservation science ever accommodate or tolerate qualitative inquiry into its own practices? The prospects of achiev-

---

9. See chapter 6. It was Kiry who asked me to focus on the bigger picture, rather than pushing for the illegal logging to be dealt with.

ing a fully consenting or collaborative insider ethnography for conservation are slim.

There is also a history of malaise between social scientists and conservationists to contend with here. This includes incidents of intimidation of conservation's critics (Igoe and Sullivan 2009), along with NGO-backed attempts to discredit the knowledge that qualitative social scientists produce.[10] A key battleground is how different actors—conservationists, biologists, ethnographers—relate to and interpret data from the field. These differences may never be settled epistemologically, but how they are contested can at least be examined. Too often, researchers fear the consequences of being critical, and this has a disciplining effect upon knowledge production. In this sense, I propose that corporate nature depends on, or indeed emerges from, hegemonic control over interpretations of what happens inside projects; a proposition that propels my research into the inner workings of global conservation.

---

10. For example, in 2013 WWF allegedly petitioned the journal *Global Environmental Change* to remove a peer-reviewed journal article that was critical of one of its African projects.

Chapter 2

The Policy Idea as Corporate Product

In this chapter, I describe how the idea of payments for environmental services or PES became one of Conservation International's key global policy instruments, akin to a corporate knowledge product. By focusing on the social and organizational processes involved in making this product, which became known as the conservation agreements model, I illustrate the discursive and intellectual workings of global conservation at the head office. By understanding *how* and *why* some policy ideas gain precedence over others, and *who* is involved in these processes, key insights into the power of corporate nature emerge. Importantly, this chapter shows how neoliberal thinking caught on at Conservation International, including how it was contested, settled, and ultimately operationalized into global policy and programs.

This chapter is organized around two key policy processes. First, I examine the *adoption* of the idea of PES, which became a key new way for CI to work with communities from 2004 onward. Here, I attend to the discursive material that circulated through CI's head office at the time, which was used to justify the policy shift to payments-based approaches. Second, I explore the *deployment* of the PES idea, which was achieved through CI's formulation and dissemination of the new conservation agreements policy model. This part of the chapter reveals the policy-making practices of global conservation, which were socially dynamic and contingent on the one hand, yet deeply bound by corporate organizational structures and logics on the other. Ultimately, a powerful policy product emerged, which CI staff referred to proudly as "the model." I explore how their model could apparently transcend complexities in the field, through the discursive magic of simplification, problem formatting, and the prescription of solutions. My analysis draws from interviews with CI staff and CI policy documents from 2004 to 2008.[1]

Crafting a Silver Bullet

CI's adoption of conservation agreements was not underpinned by an obvious policy decision or coherent theory. Rather, it was a messy and contested process, in which multiple ideas were deployed to justify the organization's policy shift. Understanding this shift requires that we analyze the discursive makeup of policy, which can be examined through its storylines (Hajer 1995) or narratives (Roe 1991). Here, I explore the multiple narratives that came into play during CI's adoption and formulation of its conservation agreements policy. This approach shows how CI staff used a specific collection of arguments, from published literature and authoritative sources like the World Bank, to produce and promote their policy product. In effect their product was a complex assemblage of ideas, like a discursive *bricolage* drawn from the "policy environment" (Blaikie 2006), mobilized to build the case for conservation agreements. The product was yet another silver bullet: a new policy idea to solve protracted conservation problems and to remedy past failures.

Five key policy narratives underpinned CI's explanation of the merits of conservation agreements. I define and explain each of these in the remainder of this section, drawing from interviews and policy texts. I also demonstrate how these often contradictory narratives were deployed intellectually and persuasively by CI staff. Overall, my analysis reveals how powerful theoretical arguments, mainly from the discipline of economics, were used to justify the embrace of payments-based policy. There was no evidence to support the policy change, only hypothetical scenarios derived from neoliberal logics. This finding resonates with wider observations on the absence of evidence in environmental policy decisions (see Leach and Mearns 1996; Roe 1991).

---

1. I drew materials from forty-six project documents to develop this chapter. A full list is in my PhD thesis, which attributes each quote to an individual document (Milne 2009, 313–14). For ease of reading here, I simply attribute quotes to "CI policy documents."

NARRATIVE 1: "CONSERVATION INVESTMENTS SHOULD BE TIED TO RESULTS"

A foundational argument used to promote payments-based instruments, both within CI and beyond, was that they were apparently more effective in achieving conservation results than other methods. Here, CI staff especially promoted conservation agreements as a way to overcome the "failure" of so-called "indirect approaches" like integrated conservation and development projects (ICDPs). They referred to empirical studies of ICDPs, mainly commissioned by the World Bank yet coauthored by CI staff, showing that ICDPs were often expensive and unable to produce desired outcomes (see Brandon and Wells 1992). Project staff in turn explained to me that ICDPs fell short because they relied on flawed, even romantic, assumptions about the "natural connections" between conservation and development. The problem with ICDPs, they said, is that they do not link conservation investments directly to conservation results. This argument about "directness" can be attributed to the original article on "direct payments" in the journal *Science* by Ferraro and Kiss (2002), which had been circulated among CI staff at the time.

CI's narratives therefore created a dichotomy between payments-based approaches and ICDPs. This emerged through policy memos, explanatory emails, and public presentations. For example, one senior staff member wrote in an early memo: "direct payments differ from classic ICDPs by making the link between conservation and development explicit." He went on to call for a move away from vague and unaccountable "indirect" approaches toward more effective "direct" approaches. By the time of the 2008 World Conservation Congress, CI was publicly promoting the conservation agreements as a way to "avoid ICDP logic," so as to deliver more effective and efficient conservation outcomes. This new narrative became so pronounced within CI that integrated or indirect approaches to conservation and development—like sustainable use, agroforestry, and ecotourism—became considered as quaint or passé among some staff. As one CI policy document put it at the time: "Promoting conservation and development via sustainable resource use is potentially limited by unreliable markets for green products from a remote location; difficulty in ensuring that development benefits are broadly distributed; and no clear need to protect biodiversity to earn income."

CI's avoidance of the integrated conservation and development paradigm also fit with its renewed and persistent emphasis on "the need to protect biodiversity" over other objectives—reflecting a neoprotectionist turn in global conservation at the time (Hutton et al. 2005). Indeed, staff often referred to literature calling to refocus conservation *back* onto its original objectives, so that the work of saving nature would not be diluted by development concerns (see Terborgh 1999). This narrative began in 2002, when a CI economist published a piece in *Scientific American* saying: "For all the money we spend on making conservation pay for itself, we may as well just pay for conservation" (Hardner and Rice 2002, 70). This statement, part of a sales pitch for direct payments, refutes attempts to harmonize conservation and development goals through integrated strategies. Its rallying cry was for conservation to refocus on achieving biodiversity protection above all else.

This focus on linking investments to results also implied making a shift away from so-called "project-based" approaches to "market-based" approaches. As argued by one of the early champions for direct payments at the World Bank, the problem with projects is that they "focus on activities rather than results" (Kiss 2004, 102). In other words, projects involve paying a group of people to carry out specific tasks in the hope that these tasks will deliver conservation outcomes, but with no guarantee. This notion was readily adopted by CI's economists to make the case for payments-based approaches, one of whom explained to me in an interview in 2006: "Conservation agreements take an economic point of view . . . [so it's up to] the community to find the solution. This is attractive because it lowers transaction costs . . . so there's not much that we have to do."

Such remarks signal CI's discursive move toward paying for conservation services, in line with emerging PES narratives at the time.[2] The neoliberal logic is that conservation investors like CI should no longer be responsible for running projects. Rather, their chief concern should be to get what they paid for. Thus, notions of "performance-based payments" and "conditionality" began to emerge, in line with early definitions of the PES mechanism (see Wunder 2005). Correspondingly, CI embraced an explicit quid pro quo element in its conservation agreements model, which prescribed "regularly scheduled compensation [to communities] in return for conservation per-

---

2. Other big NGOs promoted their adoption of direct payments in this way, too; for example, the title of the Wildlife Conservation Society's review of direct payments was "Paying for Results" (Svadlenak-Gomez et al. 2007).

The Policy Idea as Corporate Product   **59**

formance based on measurable indicators." Thus, conservation investments were to be tied to results through conditionality mechanisms.

NARRATIVE 2: "PAYMENTS RESOLVE CONFLICTS BETWEEN CONSERVATION AND DEVELOPMENT"

Through the rejection of integrated approaches aimed at harmonizing conservation and development, another aspect of pro-payments logic emerges: that conflicts between humans and nature are inevitable, and can be fixed through economic transactions. Some prominent voices in global conservation echoed this view at the time, and it became a basic premise in CI's adoption and formulation of the conservation agreements.[3] Direct payments could therefore be pitched as a *mechanism* to resolve conflicts between conservation and development, as seen in CI's explanation of its conservation agreement model in 2007: "The model requires making direct links between conservation and the benefit provided: it requires identification of the conflict to be solved."

With the notion that payments could fix conservation conflicts, CI's economists became the new gurus for resolving nature–society dilemmas. Power-Point presentations and workshops for staff in 2007 then began introducing the language of "trade-offs" and "opportunity costs" to conceptualize the conflicts between conservation and development. This thinking underpinned the design of the conservation agreements, which was pitched in policy documents as an "approach [that] acknowledges that conservation strategies often incur a significant opportunity cost for local communities." It then followed that payments, or "benefit packages," could be used to compensate local communities for the costs of conservation. For those in the head office, as one economist explained, the explicit purpose of the conservation agreements was "to make sure that conservation doesn't come at a cost to local people." The agreements therefore became a compensation mechanism of sorts, with the power to resolve conservation's most difficult trade-offs.

The apparent simplicity of the fix became a key selling point of CI's conservation agreements. No one questioned the assumptions embodied in the fix, which were that the costs of conservation could be measured and quan-

---

3. For example, see WWF's work on tradeoffs and WCS's intellectual work on conservation and development conflicts (Redford and Sanderson 2000).

tified financially, and that they could be neutralized through monetary payments or benefits. Rather, the ability of conservation agreements to establish solutions *rapidly* simply became another aspect of CI's pitch. As one senior advisor put it, "Conservation agreements are good because they can be implemented in a short period of time . . . one to two years . . . [which is] the window of opportunity for project staff to be present and to implement . . . so it's an appropriate policy tool for developing countries." These claims of simplicity, speed, and effectiveness somehow dissolved past difficulties with integrated conservation and development practice. They were a deft discursive maneuver, appealing to donors and other constituents in search of quick and easy solutions.

CI's framing of the conservation agreements as a neat new tool for "developing countries" was also highly innovative at the time. This represented a key adaptation of the original theory of PES, which posited that payments were best applied to privately held resources, where property rights were clear (Wunder 2005). By applying PES thinking to the contested realms of the hotspots, CI also appealed to parallel policy developments in conservation at the time, about poverty and protected areas. For example, a 2003 letter to *The Economist* was circulated widely among CI staff for consideration in policy design, the key phrase being: "Costs borne by the very poor, as a direct result of Western desires for conservation, often go uncompensated, leading to conflict between people and parks. Mechanisms must be found to match these local costs with a global willingness to pay" (Hockley 2003).

Thus, the stage was set for CI to adapt new payments-based models to the old problems of conservation and development. Ten years on, this innovation would be the subject of a burgeoning literature on PES and PES-like adaptations in developing countries, alongside a swathe of policy and project experiments like REDD+ (reducing emissions from deforestation and forest degradation), backed by billions of dollars in donor funding (see Milne et al. 2019; Tacconi 2015). Few saw this coming back in 2005.

NARRATIVE 3: "BIODIVERSITY IS A GLOBAL PUBLIC GOOD THAT REQUIRES EXTERNAL FINANCING"

Another element in CI's case for direct payments was the notion that biodiversity is a global public good. This idea had begun to appear in the conservation literature, often associated with authors from the World Bank.

For example, an article in the *World Bank Research Observer* argued that local economic benefits derived from biodiversity were insufficient to drive conservation action, meaning that external financing for the "global value" of conservation was required (Chomitz and Kumari 1998). Senior economists at CI often used this idea to support their proposition that conservation agreements or conservation concessions could function as mechanisms to capture the "global willingness to pay" for biodiversity (Hardner and Rice 2002; Niesten and Rice 2004). As one economist explained to me: "Conservation should be like a running a museum . . . we pay for its contents to be maintained and looked after . . . Biodiversity should be treated in the same way." This statement reveals how economic theory and protectionist thinking went hand in hand at CI. The reasoning was that public goods like biodiversity would not be secured by "profit-oriented private suppliers," and so a market correction or policy fix was required (see Balmford and Whitten 2003). Furthermore, the museum analogy implied that nature was best locked up by benevolent outsiders for the greater good.

With this thinking in play, a logical mechanism to secure global biodiversity became the use of ongoing payments, or conservation agreements. These were to be secured in perpetuity through "sustainable financing" or "endowment funds." As one internal CI policy document stated, "we need to set the critical precedent of endowing conservation incentive agreements to make them sustainable." This reasoning, from 2004, has now fed into the prominent field of "conservation finance" (see Corson et al. 2013). Indeed, by the time of the 2014 World Parks Congress in Sydney, CI was prominently positioned as a leader and innovator in the field—especially through its promotion of "conservation trust funds," its latest policy product.[4] CI continues to argue that conservation trust funds can ensure sustainable financing for conservation agreements—indeed, this remains a core part of its strategy in Cambodia.

NARRATIVE 4: "MARKET MECHANISMS ARE THE MOST EFFICIENT WAY TO DO CONSERVATION"

A corollary to the view that biodiversity is a global public good is that "market failure" has caused the undersupply of conservation services. Here, econ-

---

4. I observed this firsthand when I attended CI's sessions at the 2014 World Parks Congress.

omists argue that markets and incentive structures at the local level do not favor conservation (e.g., Kremen et al. 2000). Therefore, they suggest that local markets should be adjusted through external funding, so that conservation becomes desirable for local actors as a "viable and competitive land use" (Kiss 2004). CI adopted these notions to argue that markets can be corrected and harnessed through the application of direct payments. As CI policy statements argued at the time: "decisions to convert forest to other land uses often respond to market incentives that do not incorporate the value of ecosystem services. . . . In order to correct for this market failure, policy instruments or incentives are required to change undesirable behaviors." Conservation policy therefore became a game of adjusting local incentives or engineering markets to achieve desired changes in human behavior. Of course, this idea is not unique to conservation: it corresponds with the spread of neoliberal ideology into all aspects of public and private life (Harvey, Slater, and Farrington 2005).

Another part of neoliberal reasoning, akin to the idea of correcting markets, is to *create* markets for ecosystem services. This too was a resounding message in the conservation literature at the time, with proponents calling for ecosystem services to be properly valued and marketed (see Balmford et al. 2002; Kremen et al. 2000). This thinking was then reflected in CI's policy documents, which argued: "Indirect approaches to biodiversity conservation . . . fail to address the root cause of biodiversity loss, namely the missing market for biodiversity values. Conservation incentive agreements seek to address this missing market by providing direct compensation in return for biodiversity conservation services."

Thus, whether creating or correcting markets, direct payments were framed as a way to incentivize potential providers of conservation services. The neoliberal premise for this was that people are economically rational "creatures of the marketplace" (Brohman 1995). For CI's economists, this meant that, if provided with the right incentives, local actors would conserve biodiversity as a rational choice. This became what CI called the "guiding premise" of its conservation agreements, phrased as follows: "People will conserve if the benefits outweigh the costs of doing conservation and if they have the option to do so." This thinking recast conservation for CI and its partners into a deceptively simple matter of reconfiguring local economic conditions to facilitate rational choices in favor of biodiversity. This made intervention a mere technical matter (see Li 2007).

The Policy Idea as Corporate Product

Another aspect of CI's market embrace was the suggestion that governments and NGOs could not offer effective solutions to biodiversity loss and should be bypassed. This corresponds with neoliberal notions like "rolling back the state" to enable market forces to function freely (Castree 2008). Notably, CI used this very argument to justify the use of direct payments in Cambodia in 2005. This took the form of a memo, circulated by one senior director, stating that the Cambodian government had "proved itself to be generally corrupt and ineffective" and that it was more efficient to engage local communities in conservation directly through "private agreements." Other written statements from the head office also suggested this approach. One stated: "Based on the knowledge that much biodiversity is currently in private hands, and to make progress on its conservation we need to work with local people." Bypassing governments to engage local people directly therefore became the new approach. Implicit here were assumptions that private property rights existed, or could be easily established, and that local people could be empowered to self-govern on this basis, without state interference (see McCarthy 2006)—conspicuously neoliberal assumptions that do not hold in places like Cambodia, as this book reveals.

NARRATIVE 5: "PAYMENTS CAN ALLEVIATE POVERTY"

The final narrative employed by CI was that direct payments could help to alleviate poverty and achieve development outcomes. Although in tension with earlier arguments about needing to avoid "integrated approaches" (see narrative 1), this narrative harnessed the appeal of win-win solutions in conservation and development, which are persistent and compelling (Muradian et al. 2013). As one academic observer explained to me, conservationists will always seek "the holy grail" of achieving poverty alleviation with biodiversity conservation.[5] This was openly acknowledged by the director of the conservation agreements program, who also stressed the need to address poverty alleviation for pragmatic reasons: "We want to . . . demonstrate that the incentives can be used as a welfare tool, [so] we can tap into development donor money," she said in 2006. Thus, CI's internal and public program documents were laden with rhetoric about how the incentives agreements could

---

5. Interview with economist and direct payments proponent at the 2006 Society of Conservation Biology meeting, June, San Jose, California.

reduce poverty, as though the original theoretical basis for direct payments had been temporarily forgotten. For example, one document ambitiously stated: "Agreements are a tool to: (i) efficiently support community interests in both conservation and development; (ii) bundle carbon, water and biodiversity provision, while improving the quality of life of local communities; (iii) allow communities to maximize their utility, and thus offset the opportunity cost of doing conservation."

Another aspect of CI's pro-development narrative was that payments were more empowering for communities than alternative project-based approaches, which were framed drably as "supply-driven." In contrast, payments were appealing because they were "demand-driven": that is, they supposedly enabled communities to make *voluntary* commitments to conservation on their own terms. This was articulated as the "core idea" of CI's conservation agreements: "To conserve biodiversity as a community choice, by building agreements that provide communities with benefits and capacity building in exchange for delivering effective conservation." The agreements were therefore framed as opportunities for communities to choose what they wanted. CI's conservation agreements policy, however, still allowed for the buyer of conservation services to get involved in the community development process. For example, CI's policy guidance stated: "For more complex agreements, it may be valuable to support the steward in creating short- and long-term development visions which will guide their use of benefits in future." Thus, for all the rhetoric of community empowerment and direct incentives, CI's implementation still held the potential for old-school development approaches in the field, as eventually occurred in Cambodia.

Despite this, head-office staff continued to claim that they were implementing a new and entrepreneurial form of development. In line with neoliberal narratives, they took pains to explain that they were not in the business of giving "welfare" or "handouts," as these would create "local dependency," One head-office manager even gave cautionary advice to the Cambodia program via email about the field situation it had created prior to the introduction of the conservation agreements: "Villages are in a position of waiting for [CI's] delivery of expected development benefits . . . this must be reversed, or they will forever be awaiting welfare donations with no commitment to conservation or collective development."

The advice went on to highlight how conservation agreements instead "require accountability from communities," which would lead to "sustainability." Of great influence here were neoliberal discourses from the development sector, on "social entrepreneurship" and "smart development" (Oxfam 2008), in which "active citizens" should foster growth through their own efforts (Edwards 2008). This new businesslike thinking was readily adopted by the CI staff who were driving the conservation agreements: as innovative young economists in the DC scene, this was the policy groove. It was also the core interest of one of CI's donors, a private foundation that eventually bankrolled the conservation agreements globally through a single major grant in 2005.

Organizational Processes and the Neoliberal Turn

Like changing the course of a ship, a range of organizational processes came into play to enact CI's embrace of payments-based approaches to conservation. I witnessed these diverse processes from the inside, over five years (2002–2007). In my account below, I show how neoliberal thinking became established at CI in a variety of ways. These included incremental, persuasive, and entrepreneurial behavior on the one hand, and authoritative, even "symbolically violent" behavior on the other (Bourdieu 1977). Examining these organizational processes helps to explain how neoliberal thinking came to influence global conservation as a whole, becoming assumed, as though it were common sense.

ENACTING AND FINANCING THE POLICY SHIFT

When it comes to community engagement in conservation, CI has not had a coherent approach. In 2002, various programs existed for ecotourism, agroforestry, sustainable livelihoods, population and environment, and Indigenous rights. These programs operated separately, each funded by a different donor and crafted by its individual manager. This enabled a variety of agendas and ideologies in relation to community-based conservation to coexist at CI. It was from within this context that the conservation agreements rose to dominate CI's thinking about field-level community engagement. The idea began to gain traction in 2003, and it eventually became a global policy model in 2006.

The first conservation agreements caught on in an ad hoc fashion. They emerged where country programs had the right combination of ideas and resources to experiment, in dialogue with the head office. Three country programs led the way, using their own funding, before the global program was established: Cambodia, Ecuador, and Madagascar. Each of these cases involved expatriate individuals in the field who were receptive to the new policy ideas coming from the head office. For example, in Cambodia, the concept of direct payments was introduced to field staff in 2004, through the Indo-Burma regional director, who had heard about it from CI's head-office economists.

In parallel with these early field experiments, major changes were under way to CI's main community engagement program at the head office, then known as the Healthy Communities Initiative (HCI). This global program ran from 1998 to 2003 with generous support from a private philanthropic foundation—the same foundation that would go on to fund the conservation agreements. The original HCI approach espoused ideas of community participation, local empowerment, and sustainable livelihoods. Popular in the 1990s, these ideas were falling out of favor at CI, given the new policy environment of the 2000s. This eventually meant that HCI lost support from key figures in CI's leadership, and after some contestation, it came to an abrupt end in 2003. Its two directors were dismissed without warning and escorted from their offices in what was described by some as an "investment-banking-style" sacking.

The timing of this event was auspicious. HCI's old grant was ending, and negotiations were under way with its donor foundation for a new grant. CI's leadership was in charge of this process, as CEO Peter Seligman had personal connections with the foundation. Under his auspices, a new multimillion-dollar grant for conservation and communities was negotiated. But this time it was ideologically different. The new focus was on conservation incentives and performance-based agreements. Thus, a period of transition began.

From 2003 to 2005, negotiations over the new grant continued. During this time, an American woman with significant grassroots community development experience was tasked with conceptualizing the new program in consultation with the donor. However, she was not an economist, and she was resistant to some of the arguments being used by the pro-payments clique within CI. Another problem was that she had originally been recruited by the now-fired former HCI directors, which marked her with the stigma of their old ideas. For example, pro-payments staff commented that she was "out of touch" and in "ICDP land." Eventually this prompted the foundation, which was openly keen to pioneer incentives-based approaches, to request a change in personnel at CI. The new grant was made conditional upon the appointment of a different director: an entrepreneurial young economist from Latin America who was a strong advocate of payments-based conservation. In late 2005, a multimillion-dollar grant was issued to CI to initiate what became the Conservation Stewards Program.

With this major grant in place, CI could consolidate and formalize its new policy ideas. As the funding only came from one source, this process was inevitably influenced by the donor—a New York–based foundation created in 1968 by a single benefactor, the son of wealthy bankers who had fled Nazi Germany. The foundation is notably discreet, but it *is* known for its entrepreneurial approach to effecting change in developing countries. The foundation's manager, a medical doctor and friend of the original benefactor, was largely responsible for this policy emphasis. From the outset he played a role in the design and implementation of CI's new program, drawing from his medical training. As one head-office staff member explained: "He is very involved. . . . He has pushed the idea of *the model* so that incentives agreements can be scaled up . . . so that they can be replicated and repeated."

Thus, the foundation's view of policy models, and how they could be deployed at scale, significantly influenced CI's approach. This shows how CI's policy change was contingent on personal connections and ideological alignments between a small group of people. The unique circumstances of a generous and engaged donor, combined with strong organizational leadership, enabled the conservation agreements experiment to begin.

THE ROLE OF POLICY ENTREPRENEURS

CI's adoption of direct payments can also be associated with a small group of individuals based at the head office. Within this group, four people from CI's Conservation Economics team stood out as "policy entrepreneurs": tenacious and ambitious people, who are skilled and authoritative (Kingdon 1984). All had postgraduate qualifications in resource economics, and they enjoyed strong connections with CI's leadership. These connections, combined with the persuasive quality of the team's ideas and language, enabled them to influence policy at CI. They were instrumental in achieving the paradigm shift from old project-based or integrated approaches to newer payments-based approaches.

A key function of the team was to craft and promote its new silver bullet—the conservation agreements—whose discursive dimensions I illustrated at the outset of this chapter. The team published articles with academics, wrote reports with consultants, and presented their ideas at conferences. They had a clear strategy to set the agenda and build the case for conservation agreements within CI and beyond. One team member described his work as "spreading the gospel" as he traveled from the remote Pacific to West Africa, raising awareness about conservation agreements and scoping out opportunities for new projects. He also spoke of the need "to educate donors" to convince them that "incentives agreements are the way to do conservation." The Conservation Economics team also initiated bold field projects to demonstrate their ideas. The most notable of these was the world's first conservation concession in Guyana in 2003, which generated great excitement among staff and in the media (Ellison 2003).

Having sparked people's interest, the policy entrepreneurs then embarked on a steady process of "enrolment" (Latour 1996) of staff at CI into the idea of direct payments. With backing from CI's leadership, this process unfolded from 2004 through the sharing of emails, memos, and articles among staff. One proponent also described how they "lobbied" CI's management and board members to ensure that their ideas gained currency. For example, once the CSP was launched in 2006, its director met regularly with senior managers to ensure that they were "on board with using the conservation agreements model." She also sought to integrate CI's other community-based conservation activities, such as ecotourism, into the CSP program and its overarching framework. This was achieved partly through CSP-led global workshops, attend by experts, partners, head-office managers, and field staff.[6] These events meant that the conservation agreements, referred to by CSP staff as "the idea," could be mainstreamed into CI's wider activities.

Ultimately, the policy entrepreneurs' persuasive work was grounded in a *belief* that their new policy model would work. There was no evidence base, but they were convinced by a set of theoretical justifications. By mid-2006, the presumed effectiveness of conservation incentives had become what one senior manager called "conventional wisdom at CI . . . even though we don't have data to prove that they work." There was not even anecdotal evidence about direct payments in practice. Yet this did not stop some staff

---

6. I attended two of these workshops: one in China in 2007, the other in South Africa in 2010.

The Policy Idea as Corporate Product   **69**

from claiming that the policy had a "proven track record," especially when promoting the idea to external partners.[7]

DISCURSIVE STRUGGLES, AND THEIR CONTAINMENT

Despite the policy entrepreneurs' deft work, CI's adoption of payments-based approaches was not uncontested. Specifically, there was internal resistance from other global programs that worked with communities at CI, which relied on alternative concepts of local empowerment and well-being, such as the old HCI program. As the new CSP director and her assistant explained at the time:

> **Director:** The response to direct payments depends upon the people . . . business-oriented people are those who have been on the ground . . . field staff get it . . . but the community development people are more resistant.
>
> **Assistant:** There are two sides: the soft people, development workers with social objectives; and the hard economic rationalists who say, "We just want a deal for conservation." When people consider conservation to be a moral truth, then incentives become problematic . . . incentives take the morality out of the equation.

The notion that those who adhered to the "old ways" were too emotional or overly moral was one that I frequently heard from the pro-payments economists. Most fundamentally, this appears to reflect personal and ideological responses to markets and the commodification of nature. As one advisor to the Conservation Economics team observed: "Environmentalists have big ideas [including] moral claims that you shouldn't pay for nature. They see that direct payments have taken a noble idea and commodified it . . . therefore they're emotional." Accordingly, the resisters were depicted as people who held romantic ideals about communities living in harmony with nature. As the CSP director said: "These are people who infantilize communities . . . They believe that you can't pay for change, and this denies local people an economic opportunity they wouldn't otherwise get . . . it's threatening to them that they spent the last twenty years doing something that was a waste of time."

---

7. I heard this claim being made by the then Indo-Burma regional director in his efforts to promote conservation agreements to other NGOs in Cambodia.

Tensions between the two sides manifested in a series of conflicts at CI from 2004 to 2009, as the new policy terrain was forged. For example, those critical of payments-based approaches expressed concerns about their sustainability and the potential for negative social impacts. As one former CI DC staffer said in 2006: "Incentives are really controversial . . . [The CSP director] has created quite a stir because her values are different. . . . I'm concerned about sustainability, how are payments to be maintained? Peter [Seligman] is pushing incentives, but he has little awareness of local impacts."

Other critics perceived ethical and reputational risks associated with the use of direct payments. For example, conflicts arose with CI's population and environment program around the use of incentives to change people's behavior. This program, funded by USAID, was specifically concerned with links between reproductive health, family planning, and the environment. Given the program's remit, USAID had sent an email to CI warning against the use of incentives to encourage birth control, which was legally prohibited by Congress. The population-environment director remarked: "There's going to be another Mac Chapin article on incentives if we're not careful."[8] Because of the sensitivity, the conservation agreements in Cambodia were told to keep a "healthy breathing space" from all population-environment activities, which were being implemented at the same field site. Community engagement in Cambodia therefore ran two parallel and contradictory tracks: one that promoted nonincentivized health services and family planning for conservation, and the other that promoted conservation agreements. This bizarre situation was only tenable because the two programs had mutually exclusive funding and reporting mechanisms, through distinct networks at CI's head office.

Ultimately, the accommodation of parallel, even contradictory, policy ideas in the field seemed to be tolerated by CI so long as the money flowed. For this reason, CI proposed the notion of "mixed models" for landscape planning at the 2008 World Conservation Congress. This approach evidently provided a way to engage "the agroforestry and ecotourism people" *and* the "incentives people" in one place—all being valuable to CI for their discrete funding streams.[9] In this way, CI managed to contain potential ideological conflicts arising around the idea of direct payments. The neoliberal turn

---

8. She was referring to the earlier Mac Chapin article, "A Challenge to Conservationists," which was highly critical of big international conservation NGOs. See Chapin (2004).

9. As discussed with CI's lead on "mixed models" for landscapes at the 2008 WCC in Barcelona.

was therefore never uniformly or completely implemented. Instead, I observed a mix of old and new ideas working in concert, during the policy transition—just as Sally Jeanrenaud (2002) observed when WWF moved away from protectionist approaches to embrace community-based conservation in the 1990s.

That said, it is often the very presence of vagueness and contradiction that enables new policy ideas to take hold, eventually to become stable models or implementable tools, as Jeanrenaud (2002) suggests. In the case of CI, the pro-payments staff learned to be more careful about the language that they used, to make their ideas more palatable. As one of the policy entrepreneurs explained: "It's when you say 'payments' that people don't like it." Another told me, "I don't use the word 'market'—it creates too many problems." Furthermore, after the polemic over the word "incentives," caused by USAID's email to the head office, that word too was removed from CI's language. This careful filtering was how the more neutral-sounding conservation agreement policy model was born.

Operationalizing the Policy Idea

Having illustrated how the idea of direct payments took hold at CI, I now examine how it was converted into a policy model for global implementation. To do this, I consider three distinct phases of policy operationalization that I witnessed at CI: *definition, deployment,* and *validation* of the conservation agreements model. Together, these processes generated a sense of global coherence and control around the model, which ultimately served organizational needs (see Mosse 2005). The analysis below shows how the policy model became an organizing principle, a source of purpose, and a blueprint for action—"the ghost in the machine" (Shore and Wright 1997) of CI's global CSP program. Studying the role and function of policy models in this way also reveals how they emerge from and serve corporate-style organizational processes.

DEFINING THE MODEL WITH ECONOMIC THEORY

To transform an idea into something implementable requires a detailed policy design. This process has long been observed in conservation and development practice: theoretical ideas validate projects and help to establish causal linkages between activities and outcomes (Blaikie 2006; Mosse 2005). What emerged in the case of CI's conservation agreements, however, was a uniquely corporate and neoliberal version of this process. Enormous emphasis was placed on defining the core policy model, which eventually appeared to acquire a power of its own. For example, the CSP director claimed that the donor had "invented the model" in collaboration with two of CI's top economists. Collectively, she said that their motivation was now to "test the model" at pilot sites so that they could learn "what worked." This process began in earnest after the official launch of the CSP in 2006.

To achieve the donor's and CI's aspirations, the model required a precise, hypothesis-like definition, which was theoretically informed and globally applicable. Initially, a broad and practical definition was provided by one of CI's head-office economists in a policy brief: "Under a conservation incentive agreement, national authorities, communities, or individual resource owners agree to protect natural ecosystems in exchange for a steady stream of structured compensation from conservationists or other investors." Of key importance here was the notion of exchange, to imply that the agreements should be quid pro quo, or that benefits depended upon conservation performance. This language ensured that the conservation agreements would conform with widely accepted definitions of PES: the key underlying policy innovation being tested by CI.

To minimize potential controversy, however, the model was expressed in relatively neutral terms. This meant that the language of community choice was used to define the model, without any reference to payments or market mechanisms. By 2007, this was reflected in formal statements of "the program idea," cited widely in CI project documents, presentations, and proposals as follows: "The . . . program idea is to conserve biodiversity as a *community choice*, by building agreements that provide communities with benefits and capacity building in exchange for delivering effective conservation of high priority areas and species. Hence conservation agreements are the main tool to implement the . . . idea."

This emphasis on "community choice," along with the program's self-declared "guiding premise" that "people will conserve if the benefits outweigh the costs," reflects a core assumption from neoclassical economics, shared by members of the CSP team: that local people in conservation areas are rational and are inclined to "maximize utility." Such economic jargon was usually avoided in practice, but it did come up in conversations among team members and in program documents.

Economic theory was also implicit in the concept of win-win agreements, which found its way into CI's policy documents as follows: "[Agreements] must benefit biodiversity *and* local people . . . both parties can still decide to stop working together if a win-win agreement cannot be designed." What is being referred to here is the "willing buyer, willing seller" model of market transactions, which was the original theoretical basis for direct payments (Ferraro and Kiss 2002; Wunder 2005). This theory says that PES contracts are voluntary, with both parties engaging on the basis of mutually beneficial, negotiated outcomes. A key assumption here is that both parties in the transaction have sufficient capacity and information to make decisions that are in their best interest. However, community-level decision-making in practice rarely conforms to this ideal in economic thinking, as I show in chapter 5.

DEPLOYING THE MODEL AT SCALE

Apart from providing a theoretical basis for intervention, the model also needed to be replicable or scalable across field sites and countries. This aspect of the model—as organizational device or corporate technology— emerged in CI's policy documents that articulated how the model would enable the "CSP idea" to be "replicated at scale." The model's purpose was therefore to enable global policy to be transferred systematically to country programs. This implies an inherently top-down process, following age-old patterns in global conservation (Brosius, Tsing, and Zerner 2005).

To enable replication, the model was defined precisely and generically by the head office using flowcharts and a step-by-step "procedures manual" to be followed by field staff. Funding to field offices was contingent on their adherence to the model, and if they wished to deviate from the procedures manual, they had to ask the head office for permission.[10] The rollout of the policy model was also carefully managed through annual workshops, monthly reporting, and frequent visits by head-office staff to the field. This

---

10. This was clarified at the 2007 CSP workshop in China, which I attended. All field offices receiving CSP funding were obliged to use the model. The model specifies steps to take every six months, and the procedures manual describes steps for project development in a flowchart. The manual states that field programs must consult with the head office in cases where "the implementer wishes to modify the model."

strategy produced an apparently coherent "global program." For example, within the first six months of the CSP's operations, the model was being "tested" in four countries; by late 2008 it was operating in eight countries, with another eight in preparation.[11]

One distinctive element of CI's "scaling up" process was the emphasis on testing and refining the model. Indeed, what was referred to in program documents as "the portfolio" of CSP projects was chosen by the head office for its range of "distinct elements," so that data could be gathered to "determine if/how agreements work under different conditions." The program's quasi-experimental design was in turn reflected in its monitoring systems, which were designed to "test the premise in a methodical way," as conveyed in a CSP concept paper: "The program is looking to methodically test which incentives are most effective and under what conditions. . . . Therefore, we are building a global, but manageable, portfolio of projects that will allow us to test the premise while advancing the achievement of country/regional conservation outcomes."

A parallel process of refining the model was in turn initiated through a "Learning Network" for field programs. Here, field staff attended annual meetings to discuss their experiences and to provide input into the model. I participated in the first of these in China in June 2007, as a PhD student. I then joined the 2010 meeting in Cape Town as CI's social development director. These were the CSP's signature events, requiring participation by all grantees and field programs, whose purpose the director explained was to "contribute to improving the model globally." At the outset, she insisted that "implementer input is critical to completing the model," as though the model were a grand unifying theory for global action, to be refined through experimentation. Reflecting this belief, field staff at the inaugural CSP workshop were told, "If it's not working, then we can redesign the model!" As a result, the program's investment in testing and refining the model was substantial, easily exceeding US$100,000 per year in the first few years.[12]

Ultimately, these organizational practices and investments were driven by CI's faith in the model and its power to effect change. The premise of the CSP program was that conservation solutions could be achieved through good

---

11. The first four countries were Cambodia, Ecuador, China, and Madagascar.

12. For example, the China meeting was attended by over forty staff from fourteen countries, and a similar meeting was held in Ecuador in 2008.

The Policy Idea as Corporate Product **75**

policy design—and this led to the logics of testing and refinement. However, policy making of this kind reflects a deeply policy-centered view (Mosse 2004; see also Lea 2008), which factors out contextual data that do not fit the model. The consequences of this narrow thinking had serious ethical implications in the Cambodian context, as later chapters show.

VALIDATING THE MODEL WITH QUASI-EXPERIMENTAL METHODS

Consistent with the policy-centered view, CI's technical staff believed that the model's effectiveness could be tested using quasi-experimental methods. Ultimately, they said that their intention was to "prove the model" to donors and the conservation community. Monitoring methods were therefore adopted so that the conservation agreements' impacts could be measured with reference to baselines and controls, following an influential paper at the time on impact measurement, by two economists with connections to CI (Ferraro and Pattanayak 2006). The CSP donor was also very keen for CI to use quasi-experimental methods to test the model's effectiveness. As a medical doctor, he was well versed in clinical approaches to gathering evidence, and he was an advocate of methods developed by the Poverty Action Lab at Massachusetts Institute of Technology—the latter's founders being recipients of the 2019 Nobel Prize for their work.[13] These ideas have profoundly influenced conservation practice, as seen in the rise of "evidence-based conservation" (Adams and Sandbrook 2013; Sutherland et al. 2004), which also purports to test "policy tools" using clinical methods.

In its pioneering way, CSP therefore required field programs to implement rigorous monitoring systems for impact measurement. Baselines and controls were established, along with quantitative indicators to measure change over time. Field programs received written guidance from the head office on the matter, stating: "The monitoring system should be as cost effective as possible while providing the necessary level of quantitative information . . . and socioeconomic monitoring should include indicators in at least the following categories [below], all of which help to improve delivery of the agreement, and demonstrate results." This strong guidance on monitoring in

---

13. See Peter Dizikes, "MIT Economists Esther Duflo and Abhijit Banerjee Win Nobel Prize," *MIT News*, October 14, 2019, http://news.mit.edu/2019/esther-duflo-abhijit-banerjee-win-2019 -nobel-prize-economics-1014. Jeffrey Sachs's "clinical economics" is another close relative of this (2005).

effect dictated what could officially be seen and known about CI's field practices and their effects. Apart from enshrining the importance of the policy tool, this approach also signaled a corporate capacity for institutionalized myopia with regard to field realities, which is a recurring theme in this book.

THE MODEL AS CORPORATE DEVICE

My account of the definition, deployment, and validation of the CSP model shows how it provided a script or blueprint for global conservation action. In a powerful way, the model enabled communication between the head office and the field by providing a single framework for thinking and talking about conservation agreements. It also enabled the head office to track the progress and performance of its investments in the field. Yet, the model's strict format and authoritative deployment created a uniquely top-down organizational environment—one that structured knowledge about the field and filtered local voices. For example, at the CSP's global workshops, each country program was required to present its activities with reference to the model's step-by-step guide. To enable this, staff were asked to use preformatted PowerPoint templates. In this way, staff from diverse and complex field settings were enlisted into a globally articulated mission: they were provided with a song sheet, so that they could sing along with the choir.

This adherence to the model apparently gave the head office a sense of control and accountability with regard to the field programs. As one CSP officer commented: "They could be doing anything out there . . . but the model gives us a way to show and know what's happening. . . . [Now] we can demonstrate results and actually say to donors and the public what we're doing and show how it works." Thus, the model was used to structure knowledge about the field to serve the needs of the head office. This use of the model to filter *what is seen* also reinforces the power of global expertise: that is, experts measure what they deem to be important or valid. As a result, the complexity and richness of the field became *unknowable* by the head office. This illustrates how the model works: by simplifying the world, intervention and global governance become possible (see Li 2007; Merry 2011).

The model was also used to reinforce the authority of CI's global expertise, justifying the place of expatriate advisors. Here, the model acquired symbolic power, as though it were an embodiment or instrument of expert knowledge. For example, one junior CSP officer explained to me how the

Ecuador program had encountered "implementation difficulties" in the early days, which he attributed to their failure to follow the model, saying: "[In the end] they filled out the model and found that they had left out a step in implementation, which had caused them trouble . . . this is proof that the model is good." Not all head-office staff had such blind faith in the model, but they *were* conscious of its power to bring order to the field. As one seasoned observer from the head office explained to me, CI's primary motivation in using the model was for "credibility." For him, the model's ability to offer a neat solution made it a "political tool" for engaging governments and donors.

In sum, the CSP model heavily influenced language and action at CI, including its communications with external audiences. In this sense, the model functioned both as a corporate device, by scripting organizational action, *and* as a corporate product, by providing a conservation solution that could be marketed. Furthermore, the model made global action possible, as it could be scaled up or replicated around the world. The beauty of the model for CI, therefore, was that it enabled globally standardized problem-solving and management, in large part through the simplification of local complexity and context. From here, the politics of the model emerge.

The Politics of the Model

Given that the CSP model shaped and enabled intervention at a global scale, its discursive and political dimensions demand scrutiny. As I have suggested, the model became a "political technology" (Foucault 1977) in practice: a discursive formation, able to disguise the workings of power through neutral, objective, rational, and technical language (Shore and Wright 1997). These power dynamics were most keenly felt in relation to "the field," which was discursively constructed as a realm of intervention where policy tools could solve problems (Ferguson 1994; Li 2007). I now examine how this worked in the case of the CSP model, which mobilized particular assumptions about local communities, human behavior, and environmental change.

PRODUCING AND IDEALIZING THE FIELD

The CSP model carefully stipulated what kinds of field sites and scenarios were best suited for the conservation agreements. Initially, this occurred through "feasibility assessments" that field staff conducted at potential CSP investment sites. These assessments all followed a set of "general feasibility criteria," outlined in CSP documents. There were nine criteria covering issues like the "stewards' rights," "biological priority," "project cost," and capacity of the steward to be an "effective conservation partner."[14] Each criterion had to be ranked by staff on a scale from most to least favorable. Where conditions were not necessarily favorable, then an indication of "how easy it would be to make the status favorable" was required. Thus, the model demanded a simplified account of the field, according to a scorecard that measured only what the head office deemed to be important or wanted to see. The feasibility assessment criteria therefore enabled CI to make the field "legible" for intervention (Scott 1998).

The feasibility assessments were also complemented by a set of "enabling conditions," articulated in the CSP model, which apparently needed to be in place before conservation agreements could be negotiated. These enabling conditions were like an ideal scenario against which field sites would be judged, and to which field sites should aspire. These conditions included the existence of an "identifiable steward"; property rights that could be "secured and enforced"; conditions for "good governance"; "capacity for technical implementation"; "buy-in from relevant actors"; a "supportive policy environment"; and "interest from potential stewards to engage in a partnership." When the head office made its initial call for conservation agreement proposals in 2006, it said that it would invest only in field sites that conformed to these conditions.

I draw attention to these "enabling conditions" for two reasons. First, they reveal the theoretical assumptions, mainly derived from neoclassical economics, that underpin the policy model. Second, for most field sites in postcolonial settings, they are inherently unrealistic and unachievable. This means that the implementers of conservation agreements are inevitably drawn into a game of representation, where they produce favorable feasibility assessments for field sites that apparently meet the enabling conditions. There is little incentive for honesty, given the dire need for conservation funds at most sites, nor is there an appetite at the head office for unstruc-

---

14. The criteria were: (1) steward's rights; (2) biological priority; (3) threats to biodiversity; (4) legal options for protection; (5) policy context; (6) project costs; (7) capable implementer; (8) ability of the steward to be an effective conservation partner; (9) overall stability.

The Policy Idea as Corporate Product

79

tured assessments sensitive to the local context. Thus, even before implementation, the field is socially produced for global consumption, according to a specified ideal. This is how the erasure or denial of local realities begins — a process that becomes far more entrenched and elaborate as implementation proceeds.

Another effect of the enabling conditions is that they provide a subtle mandate for intervention or improvement at the local level. For example, in cases where the enabling conditions did not yet exist, "the implementer" in CSP's policy model was prompted to make local adjustments. Investments could therefore proceed if property rights were "easy to secure or enforce" or if "governance" could be "easily improved." This simple policy language implies that the implementer can somehow rearrange local governance as required. In this way, the theoretical needs of the model created a basis for intervention into the social and political affairs of the steward. Effectively, field sites were asked to conform to the model's ideal type, through an apparently easy set of bounded and technical actions.

This played out in Cambodia, where concerns were raised about whether the proposed field site met the enabling conditions for investment. A senior manager from the head office therefore visited the field for a few days to make an assessment. He then cautioned the Cambodia team via email: "If community stewardship [CSP] is to be the approach, there is a great need to strengthen governance by the local [commune] councils." He identified a need for "formalized land title" and for the councils to be strengthened as "representative local institutions." This was the guidance that came with the head office's conditional support for the CSP in Cambodia. Yet even the most cursory effort to gather background information on the site would have revealed locally fraught governance conditions and property contests, which have only deteriorated over the last decade. No one in Cambodia pushed back, however. This had the effect of propelling the project into a virtual realm: the head office asks for the impossible, while field staff are tempted or pressured to misrepresent what they know in order to secure funding.

The ability of field sites to attract funds was even covered in the CSP policy guidance. For example, additional conditions were specified to encourage potential projects to be not just feasible but also attractive. The guidelines stated: "The agreement has to be attractive to potential funders, in terms of its area, the community commitment, and the cost. . . . [I]t's like bringing something to market. People will buy the one that is the best quality and the lowest cost." In this sense, each field site became a product, which the head office would "sell" to donors. Furthermore, special support was offered to projects that could, in CSP's language, "pilot a valuable new part of the market" through innovations in local partnerships, funding sources, or legal mechanisms. Additional support was also given to field sites where the agreement design could be "easily replicated at scale." Thus, a marketing mindset was encouraged, as the CSP director pronounced at the 2007 China meeting: "We're selling your products to these donors. . . . That's why we're here. . . . We can give you the concepts and get the word out."

This conscious embrace of the market analogy—that conservation products can be made and sold—reflects the entrepreneurial spirit that gave rise to the CSP. It also resonates with notions of "spectacular" production in neoliberal conservation (Igoe 2010) and "Nature Inc." (Büscher et al. 2014), which points to global conservation's use of commodified and marketable products.

ECONOMIC FORMATTING OF PROBLEMS AND SOLUTIONS

In addition to producing field sites that were legible and marketable, the policy model also powerfully framed problems in the field so that they could be solved. Here, the head office devised what it called an "agreement matrix" for all field programs so that their ideas could be expressed in terms of the model. The matrix design (see figure 2) included categories for the "conservation target" and the "opportunity cost," among other things. All elements of the matrix had to be measurable in either quantitative units or simple indicators. For example, the default measure for "conservation target" was hectares protected, while "opportunity cost" was expressed in monetary terms. These narrow metrics in turn framed conversations in the field, which meant that community members could not readily define conservation goals and costs on their own terms. Conservation problems were therefore conceptualized as "hectares of forest cleared," while solutions took the form of monetary compensation in exchange for "community obligations" to conserve.

The abstraction and problem formatting required by the agreement matrix also subtly changed how local actors conceptualized conservation. For example, in Cambodia, the task of setting the conservation target as the number of hectares protected initially created confusion for field staff and villagers, because the target did not apply to the local situation, where res-

Conservation target (has)	Threats	Community obligation	Opportunity cost of doing conservation	Benefits proposed	Cost of benefits	Enforcement required (patrolling)	Risks
ha	...	...	$	...	$	...	...

Figure 2 Conservation agreement matrix for Cambodia.

idents lacked formal land and resource rights (Milne 2012). Nevertheless, the conservation agreement format prompted a rethinking of relationships between people and the forest. With inputs from advisors, villagers and the CSP team eventually settled on the construct of "avoided deforestation" to quantify and value their conservation target, anticipating what is now a prominent concept in climate-change mitigation strategies (Milne 2012). They defined "avoided deforestation" as land not cleared for shifting agriculture that would otherwise have been cleared. This enabled a neat calculation of the opportunity cost of conservation in terms of "rice yield forgone," and thus provided the basis for the conservation agreement and its benefit package.[15]

This concept of hypothetical land clearing was new for villagers, and so was the idea that they could seek compensation for what they did not do. Entrepreneurial villagers latched on to this, seeing the potential for negotiation: Could they hold the forest to ransom, so as to extract financial value from CI? This new thinking encouraged a capitalist vision of the forest, which had never been fully articulated in the area, given that land-use dynamics until then were based on shifting cultivation and subsistence production (Milne 2012). In other words, by presuming a relationship between people and nature that can be articulated in financial or economic terms, local and Indigenous perspectives are subtly obscured. Nonfinancial values for forests and nature are factored out of the equation.

Lastly, with the idea of opportunity costs came a monetary understanding of the impacts of conservation among CI staff, along with notions that negative impacts could be offset with financial compensation. Indeed, there was limited discussion of the potential for *nonmonetary* negative impacts of conservation.[16] For example, the opportunity cost calculations in Cambodia were derived from the market value of lost rice yields as a result of constraints to shifting agriculture. This meant that land-use benefits other than rice—vegetables, forest products, customary user rights, and the Indigenous way of life—were not included in the calculation. There was primarily

---

15. The first calculations of payments for avoided deforestation in Cambodia occurred in 2007, through conversations between one field officer and the commune chiefs. Together they estimated rice yields that would be lost if forest clearing stopped, which they converted to a dollar amount based on the local price of rice.

16. CI's socioeconomic monitoring protocols did attempt to measure "social impacts," but only quantitatively and not explicitly for purposes of compensation.

The Policy Idea as Corporate Product

83

a preoccupation with calculating the *amount* of benefits forgone, rather than a broad consideration of costs and implications of land-use change for local people. This illustrates the local effects of economistic thinking: a preoccupation with monetary compensation, which distracts from the wider social and political processes of conservation.

DISCOURSES OF OVERSIGHT

Ultimately, the conservation agreements' logic and language influenced how CI staff conceptualized their work. Their problem-solving and analysis of human–environment relations in the field soon became framed mainly in economic terms. Indeed, after the initial success of the agreements in Cambodia, program staff seemed to believe that the new tool could be crafted to fit any kind of village-forest scenario, or any kind of conservation problem. This meant that the agreements were soon structured to incorporate other project activities where possible, like land-use planning that was formerly a separate community-based initiative. The expatriate biologists also soon requested that various behavior changes be added to the "community obligations" component of the agreements in order to address hunting and poaching.[17] Thus, the presence of the agreements encouraged staff to see the field according to the CSP matrix of economic costs and incentives. The implicit assumption was that villagers' behavior could be adjusted with the use of incentives and disincentives, as though the field were a system to be crafted, subject to design and control.

I regularly heard these discourses of economic oversight as I interacted with CI's expatriate and head-office advisors over time—typically alongside fieldwork, travel, and staff meetings. One topic of conversation, for example, was how to lower the "perceived opportunity cost" of conservation in the village so that the agreements would be less expensive. As one senior manager asked, in relation to the compensation payments in Cambodia, "Do you think the perceived opportunity cost can be reduced? Perhaps we can we try for US$2500. . . . We don't want them to expect US$3500 every year, to have a sense of entitlement . . . or we'll go bankrupt due to rising opportunity costs."

17. For example, the biologists amended the 2007 agreements so that (1) villagers cannot take their dogs into the forest, as an anti-hunting measure; and (2) villagers must report "intelligence" on wildlife poachers and traders to the FA. I attended staff meetings on this subject in Phnom Penh in March 2007.

Along these lines, discussions also focused on how to set up appropriate incentives in the village so that the stewards would be "satisfied," without making unreasonable financial demands. Here, the CSP policy guidelines made specific reference to neoclassical economics, citing "Consumption Theory and the Revealed Preference Axiom" (Samuelson 1948), as the basis for establishing whether the incentives were sufficient, as follows: "If local communities are freely choosing to stop the destructive behavior that jeopardized biodiversity, or are willing to protect that biodiversity from outsiders that could destroy it, it is because it is more beneficial to them . . . [this] reveals their preference of maximizing utility." Accordingly, CSP policy allowed benefit packages to increase, if necessary, to "pair to inflation processes and maintain the level of incentives for the stewards."

Overall, I argue that the application of these economic theories in the CSP model reframed communities as single actors who make rational choices. Engaging communities in this way was even seen to be more *efficient*, as the CSP's planning documents for Cambodia stated: "Working through the councils (rather than individual households) would decrease transaction costs and could increase compliance through group pressure." The consequence of this thinking was that community engagement in the field soon emulated a business transaction rather than a participatory process (see chapter 5). This signals an inherent danger in economistic views of human motivation: they obscure the moral, cultural, historical, and political factors that also influence how people behave (Cleaver 2002). Furthermore, the practice of economic reductionism denies the agency of local actors and their potential for "irrationality" (Brohman 1995). We should therefore be cautious about economic discourses of oversight in global conservation, which now dominate how social issues are framed and treated.

Concluding Remarks on CI's Neoliberal Turn

This chapter has recounted how the PES idea caught hold at CI, eventually to become a corporate device and product: a new policy model, ready to be rolled out across the globe. The initial discursive and persuasive work that underpinned the birth of PES or conservation agreements at CI was highly effective, but not uncontested. This reveals how enacting policy change within the NGO-donor establishment requires concerted effort by entrepreneurial actors, along with the blessing of leadership. In CI's case, the steady privileging of neoliberal and economic thinking at the head office enabled the powerful idea of payments-based approaches to gain the status of conventional wisdom among staff. CI was a trailblazer in this domain: it helped to convert the PES policy idea into what is now a mainstream approach for global conservation.

The fact that PES as a policy concept has achieved such eminent status, largely in the absence of evidence about its effectiveness in practice, is remarkable. Its discursive power and appeal—achieved largely through its ideological alignment with notions of market efficiency, rational choice, and effectiveness—has much to answer for here. With the mobilization of such powerful ideas and neoliberal assumptions in practice, however, we must ask after their implications for people and nature. My analysis of CI's operationalization of the conservation agreements in this chapter points to some key implications, which I shall now summarize.

The first implication relates to how the model reframes local communities in neoliberal terms. Through the implementation of the conservation agreements, community participation in conservation is reworked into a contractual or market transaction—what CI called "community choice." CI also used the notion of stewardship to name and brand the whole program, since the agreements were considered as a "mechanism" to ensure "community commitment" to the stewardship of nature.[18] The problem is that, as communities are transformed into stewards by contract, they are subtly denied agency as custodians and potential owners of their natural resources: instead, they become caretakers of the world's biodiversity. In the context of conservation agreements, this is problematic because those who are making the payments are likely to become those who dictate the obligations and caretaking functions of stewardship.

The second implication of the PES model emerges from the power dynamic of NGOs paying for behavior change—something that is neatly disguised by the persistent framing of communities as rational actors, acting voluntarily. This discursive framing implies that the responsibility for doing conservation now rests with local communities through their contractual obligations. Neoliberalism has long encouraged this mode of governing through

---

18. From CSP policy documents in 2007, original quote: "the mechanism is a *commitment* by the community to protect those areas."

community, as "regimes moved away from the idea that they had the responsibility or the capacity to define the good life and shape the citizenry according to an overall plan" (Rose 1999, 135). Here, the task of government is not to plan or control but rather to enable and facilitate community action (Li 2007, 234). This thinking was clearly present in relation to CI's conservation agreements, as one advisor explained: "It's up to the community to find the solution . . . the program will build the project and people will build their own capacity as a response." And so, a powerful neoliberal subjectivity of communities as willing service providers and market actors emerged. This market analogy is incredibly appealing because it portrays field activities as organic products of market forces: in this way, the politically and morally loaded processes of global intervention in nature-society become a "market masquerade" (Milne and Adams 2012).

Finally, by portraying communities as capable partners and stewards[19] in the context of payments-based approaches, CI could quietly avoid the need to engage with the real complexities of project implementation on the ground. This was aided by the discursive positioning of global conservation as an investor, which enabled the head office to distance itself from the practical details and consequences of delivering conservation services. There is no relationship to place here, nor any need to delve into *how* conservation is achieved or *who* benefits in the process: these concerns are effectively delegated to the partner or service provider, who implements and monitors the conservation agreements. Ultimately, this is an outsourcing of responsibility, as "the how" of conservation is put into a black box. This corresponds closely with processes of commodification, which disguise the conditions of production, even for virtual commodities like ecosystem services (Büscher et al. 2012). It is the role of the ethnographer, then, to look inside the black box of apparently neat market-based solutions in global conservation.

---

19. CI's website refers to "partner communities" and their "innate capacity" for conservation. For example, "our partner communities have shown that it's possible to live in harmony with nature . . . communities are the natural stewards of their surroundings." CSP website, accessed June 2020, https://www.conservation.org/about/conservation-stewards-program.

Chapter 3
Situating the Field in Cambodia

December 2003, Cardamom Mountains:
After more than a year in the field, I fancy that I have found my feet as an NGO worker. Plans are afoot to realize the dream of our Australian country director, which is to restore old rice paddies that became impossibly overgrown during the post–Khmer Rouge chaos of the 1980s and 1990s. For CI, the logic is simple: enable paddy rice production for villagers in order to prevent so-called "slash-and-burn" agriculture in the protected forest. I buy into this, and with fresh donor funds in hand, we begin project planning.

To this end, I excitedly trot off down a narrow village track behind the ranger station, led by my Khmer colleagues. Along the way we come upon a grove of ancient and very tall durian trees, planted generations ago by Indigenous villagers. I look up nervously at the enormous spiky fruits, seemingly ready to drop. They could easily impale an unsuspecting visitor. Looking down, I see the characteristic blue sign of our partner, the Forestry Administration, nailed into one of the old fruit trees: "Forest Estate, keep out." I pause, uneasily.

Continuing on, we arrive at a vast round, grassy field, surrounded by forest. These are the old paddies that we will restore! We are talking logistics: how to get the tractor in to plow it up; how to set up a buffalo bank for villagers to continue the work. Then I ask, "When was the last time that these paddies were plowed?" The answer is matter of fact but chilling: "These paddies were made by the Khmer Rouge." I immediately think of The Killing Fields *and the program of forced peasantization run by Cambodia's Maoist regime of 1975–*

1979.[1] Lost in the horrifying imagery, I stare out across the overgrown paddy, my feet sinking into the mud.

In this chapter, I develop a situated and historical account of "the field" in the Cardamom Mountains, where CI's project was implemented. I draw inspiration from Nancy Peluso's "situated political ecology," which emphasizes the importance of telling critical histories and narrations of place, because they "continuously articulate with and shape stories at work in the present" (2012, 80). In bringing this perspective to light, the implied or assumed "socio-natural relations" of new green constructs like "parks, forests, wildlife, carbon and water" can be critically examined (Peluso 2012, 82). The NGO-sponsored tractor, disturbing long-dormant paddy fields in pursuit of yet another utopian vision, is a rich metaphor for this. Memories and meanings are literally unearthed, recalling not just the Khmer Rouge's murderous projects but also a prior timeless era of Indigenous connections to land. The field, therefore, is necessarily intertwined with and contingent upon multiple historical layers of culture, identity, and past regimes.

In global conservation practice, the field is typically an ahistorical and acontextual construct. The field is an artifact of urgent work and a global mission: it is where the biodiversity is, where projects happen, where ideas and strategies are enacted. It is the subject of log frames, mapping exercises, surveys, funding proposals, and donor reports. Expatriates talk about the field over a beer or in the office: "I just got back from the field"; "I'm going to the field"; "When I was on fieldwork . . ."; "How was your field trip?" The field is therefore a passionate raison d'être for conservationists, but it is also often simplified and "rendered technical" (Li 2007, 7) through their professional practices. In other words, the field is constructed as the realm of intervention for global conservation: it is the space in which the governing of "men and things" takes place (Li 2007, 9).

The construction of the Cardamom Mountains as a field site for global conservation provides an archetypal example of these governing processes. In the late 1990s, when Cambodia's civil war had subsided sufficiently for foreign biologists to access remote areas, what they found was, for them, a cornucopian wilderness. For example, the first biological survey of the Cardamom

---

1. *The Killing Fields*, released in 1984, is a film that depicts the story of Dith Pran, who survived the Khmer Rouge regime.

Mountains in the year 2000 created a flurry of excitement (see Appleton, Bansok, and Daltry 2000). The survey results confirmed the "global value" of the area's biodiversity, measured in terms of the presence of species that featured on the internationally recognized IUCN Red List of Threatened Species. This enabled funding to be mobilized and NGO projects to begin. In this chapter, I describe these processes: I show how the Cardamom Mountains became a realm of intervention for CI in Cambodia, with its efforts focused on what was then known as the Central Cardamoms Protected Forest (CCPF).

Before I describe the makings of CI's field site, however, we must situate ourselves in Cambodia. To do this, I begin with a broad overview of the interplay between society and environment in Cambodia, focusing especially on the role of forests and natural resources in the making of contemporary politics and government. The contours of colonial rule, civil war, socialism, donor intervention, and authoritarian state making are all visible in the way that forested land and biodiversity have been annexed and are now governed in Cambodia. By situating the field through historical political ecology in this way, the true dynamics of global conservation come into view—especially how selective knowledge or blindness to the local context enables powerful green intervention while also limiting its possibilities.

A Kingdom Shackled to Nature

Contemporary Cambodia, known affectionately in tourism campaigns as the "Kingdom of Wonder," is nestled between large and crowded neighbors in mainland Southeast Asia. Cambodia has a small and predominantly rural population, and only one major urban center around the royal capital Phnom Penh. The role of its natural endowment therefore cannot be overstated. Rivers, floodplains, and forests are intertwined with Khmer culture and identity (Chandler 1991). Furthermore, the country's political economy has been fundamentally shaped by recent patterns of exploitation of forested land and fisheries, which have enriched elites at the expense of rural and Indigenous people (Amnesty International 2022; Le Billon 2002; Milne and Mahanty 2015).

Cambodia's geography consists of the central lowlands, surrounded by upland border regions. At the heart of the nation is Tonle Sap Lake. Considered to be one of the richest freshwater fisheries in the world, the lake's remarkable floodplain is the country's food bowl (Roberts 2015). For good reason, Tonle Sap was the bedrock of the ancient Khmer empire. Beyond the vast floodplains are Cambodia's forested uplands—so extensive that the country still claims the highest forest cover in mainland Southeast Asia (RGC 2017). Since 2005, however, the forests have been under significant pressure, with a wave of extractive development leading to industrial-scale forest clearing and land grabbing backed by elite interests (Milne, Pak, and Sullivan 2015; Neef, Touch, and Chiengthong 2013). This contemporary transformation has served Prime Minister Hun Sen's regime well, to the extent that the state must be seen as "shackled to nature" in every sense (Milne, Pak, and Sullivan 2015). To decipher this, I shall now trace the recent history of rule in Cambodia.

THE FALLEN KINGDOM

Cambodia is known for its glorious and mythical past. The Khmer empire produced phenomenal architectural and artistic achievements, most evident in the famous temples of Angkor, now a World Heritage Site. From the ninth to the thirteenth century, the empire exerted cultural and political influence far beyond present-day Cambodia.

By the nineteenth century, however, French colonists encountered more humble circumstances. In 1860, the French naturalist Henri Mouhot claimed "discovery" of the "lost city of Angkor," consumed by jungle. Over the following hundred years of colonial rule, the French developed a paternal affection for Cambodia as a "gentle land of smiling people" (Bit 1991, xiii). The Khmer were often portrayed as simple and gracious, living self-sufficiently from the bounty of their lands (Bizot 2003). Yet Cambodian peasant life as the rural idyll was also a dangerous fantasy. For example, the nationalist "father of independence" King Norodom Sihanouk was fond of his rural subjects, but his ideals and affections soon intermingled with Communist sentiments. The subsequent Khmer Rouge movement, which emerged from the countryside, elevated this peasant ideal to the extreme, with disastrous consequences (Kiernan 1996).

Most of Cambodia's modern history is wrought by conflict. Independence from the French came in 1953, after a series of patriotic struggles that enabled King Sihanouk to become the head of state in 1960 (Kiernan 1996).

By the late 1960s, however, Sihanouk could not contain the effects of the Vietnam War, despite his public efforts to remain neutral (Chandler 1991). With Vietnamese communists active in northeast Cambodia, Sihanouk was ousted by a right-wing coup d'état in 1970, and a period of chaos followed. Sihanouk then retreated to China, eventually to side with the Mao-inspired Khmer Rouge movement (Kiernan 1996). The Khmer Rouge gradually increased their control over rural Cambodia, eventually taking full power in April 1975 with the dramatic fall of Phnom Penh.

The resulting regime of the Communist Party of Kampuchea, popularly known as the Khmer Rouge, lasted from 1975 to 1979 and is now recognized as a genocidal tragedy. At least one million Cambodians, or one in eight, died from warfare, starvation, execution, overwork, or disease (Chandler 1991; Kiernan 1996). The Khmer Rouge attempted to transform Cambodian society through a utopian program in which money was abolished, intellectuals were murdered, and social institutions for religion and education were dismantled. The entire population was made to wear matching peasant clothes and forced into unpaid agricultural labor on collective farms. The regime also attempted to break down traditional social norms and family ties by making mealtimes communal and enlisting children to spy on their parents (Chandler 1991; Kiernan 1996).

The horror ended in 1979, when Vietnamese forces entered Cambodia and installed a new regime with their Cambodian allies, a dissident former Khmer Rouge group. Cambodians are still divided as to whether this constituted an invasion by the Vietnamese or a liberation (Gottesman 2004). This history is contested in part because much of Cambodia's current leadership was installed by the Vietnamese—including current Prime Minister Hun Sen. In the 1980s, nation building by the Vietnamese created a Socialist-style administrative foundation and a political culture that persists to this day (Gottesman 2004, 335; Hughes 2003). With ongoing armed resistance against the Vietnamese, fueled by Cold War dynamics, Cambodia's civil war wore on for another decade. Eventually, as communism fell in Europe, the Vietnamese withdrew, leading to the installation of the United Nations Transitional Authority in Cambodia (UNTAC) in 1990. An uneasy peace was then established with the signing of the Paris Peace Accords in 1991, heralding Cambodia's apparent "triple transition" to peace, democracy, and economic liberalization (Hughes 2003).

HUN SEN'S SECOND KINGDOM

Cambodian politics is dominated by one man and one party: Prime Minister Hun Sen, leader of the Cambodian People's Party (CPP). In power since 1985, Hun Sen now bothers little with the pretense of democracy. Under his rule, wealth and resources have become concentrated in the hands of a powerful and entrepreneurial elite with strong party ties (Global Witness 2016; Hughes 2006). Cambodia is still officially a constitutional monarchy and a liberal democracy, according to its 1993 constitution, which gave rise to the "Second Kingdom" (Norén-Nilsson 2016). However, with Hun Sen increasingly using symbolic imagery and narratives that hark back to the Angkorian kings, he has crafted the Second Kingdom in his image—not as the constitution intended (Norén-Nilsson 2016).

The CPP's dominance is due in part to its skillful manipulation of economic and political reforms introduced by the UN and other foreign advisors in the 1990s (Hughes 2003). For example, the processes of economic liberalization provided a number of opportunities for political gain. The privatization of land, and the introduction of forestry and fishery concessions in particular, enabled the CPP to establish networks of protection and patronage that facilitated the accumulation of wealth by loyal officials. The party embraced these reforms to facilitate the flow of Western aid but also to consolidate its control over Cambodia's resources and institutions (Hughes 2006; Le Billon 2000). Today, the state apparatus is considered to be held together by "entrepreneurial activity, rent-seeking and crime" (Hughes and Conway 2003, 27), with much of this activity focused on wealth extraction from Cambodia's natural resources (Milne 2015; Un and So 2009).

The CPP has managed to fend off political opposition with terrifying effectiveness over the years. Flourishes of opposition do occur, but the pattern remains the same. For example, after Cambodia's first elections in 1993, the CPP and the royalist FUNCINPEC party were forced to form a coalition.[2] But Hun Sen could not tolerate sharing power, so he staged a coup d'état in 1997, after which the opposition party was gradually co-opted and dis-

---

2. FUNCINPEC stands for the French Front Uni National pour un Cambodge Indépendant, Neutre, Pacifique, et Coopératif, or National United Front for an Independent, Neutral, Peaceful, and Cooperative Cambodia.

mantled (Sullivan 2016). After 2012, with a new and credible political threat emerging in the form of the Cambodian National Rescue Party (CNRP) the same occurred: opposition party members and their leaders have been variously exiled, jailed, threatened, and put on trial (Croissant 2019). In what amounts to a constitutional coup, the CNRP was disbanded ahead of the 2018 election (Un 2019). There is now little room left for peaceful political opposition, while impunity and authoritarian rule pervade. Assassinations of political activists like Chut Wutty in 2012—whose murder I described at the beginning of this book—and Ley Kem in 2016 serve as stark warnings to would-be critics of the regime.

This most recent disintegration of democracy in Cambodia, after the groundswell of opposition that ignited the populace's political imagination through the CNRP, corresponds with long-held narratives about Khmer political culture. Some argue that Khmer culture is antithetical to the establishment of democracy, with its tendency to produce social hierarchies, extreme power differences, and submissive peasants (Bit 1991; Martin 1997; O'Leary and Meas 2001). Blunt and Turner observe that the democratic movement in Cambodia must compete with "extremely powerful values which are mobilized to support the organizational principle of hierarchy" (2005, 78). In this view, democratic potential is effectively constrained by cultural and historical conditions. Others have been more optimistic about the possibility of nurturing civil society and popular agency in Cambodia (Milne and Mahanty 2015; Öjendal and Sedara 2006), but recent events have sobered most hopes for democratic change.

Cause for hope is often derived from the historically significant civil society sector in Cambodia, which thrived with inputs from international organizations in the 1990s and 2000s. Compared to neighboring Laos and Vietnam, the possibilities for nongovernmental organizations to deliver services and push for change in Cambodia have been multiple and robust. For example, with the huge influx of aid during UNTAC, NGOs virtually formed a parallel system of governance (Curley 2004; Devas 1996). Occasionally, too, they enabled grassroots concerns to be expressed (Hughes 2003; Prum 2005). But a key ongoing question relates to whether Cambodian civil society has ever truly been able to maintain political space that is free from state influence (Frewer 2013; Hughes 2003). This book shows just how hard it is for NGOs to resist pressure from the CPP-controlled state—especially when it comes to interventions around land, forests, and natural resources.

Furthermore, the government's passing of a carefully crafted "NGO law" in 2015 now makes it even more difficult for civil society to disrupt the ruling elite's interests (Curley 2018).

STATE AND SOCIETY IN THE RURAL DOMAIN

While Hun Sen's government is top-down, with political power concentrated in Phnom Penh, rural areas remain of fundamental importance to the ruling party. With 75 percent of the population still reliant on farming and other natural resources for their livelihoods (UNDP 2019), the countryside *needs* to be a CPP heartland, if only to maintain a veneer of popular legitimacy. The countryside is also fundamental to state territorial control over resources, which is a key ingredient in the CPP regime (Beban 2021; Milne, Pak, and Sullivan 2015). The processes of CPP-backed state-making therefore give rise to a complex and multiscalar rural politics, the dynamics of which shape how natural resources are used and governed.

A core dynamic is the party-controlled state's influence in rural areas, even in remote forested regions like the Cardamom Mountains. The notion of a socially embedded state helps to explain this (Migdal 2001), as traditional forms of social organization have mixed with contemporary political practices and structures. For instance, village life is still shaped by the classic patron-client relations of rural Southeast Asia, in which villagers are tied to their leaders through unequal exchange relationships (Scott 1976). Yet these old patronage institutions have transformed since the early 2000s, with new political and resource dynamics in play. The CPP in particular has cleverly manipulated local institutions to integrate village leaders into the state apparatus: this has enhanced CPP power but eroded the traditional obligations of patrons to protect their clients (Hughes 2003; Marston and Chhoeun 2015). Local leaders are now connected to sources of power beyond the village, such as government and party budgets. They are also subject to pressure when it comes to the facilitation of elite interests—especially extractive agendas like logging and land grabbing (Mahanty 2022; Marschke 2012).

Many of these political dynamics occur through the commune councils, which are the primary institution for local government in Cambodia. Based on the old French colonial administrative unit, each rural commune (*koum*) contains a cluster of villages, or a population of around 200–2,000 people.

Commune councils were democratically elected for the first time in 2002, under Cambodia's donor-backed decentralization and local democratization program. International advisors and donors at the time suggested that Cambodia was starting from scratch, or building the foundations of a new democratic society through the commune councils (Blunt and Turner 2005; Prum 2005). But they failed to consider historical patterns.

In fact, local-level government institutions have a long legacy in Cambodia, and this partly explains the facility with which commune councils have been perverted by the ruling party over the last twenty years. For example, the Vietnamese-backed regime of the 1980s relied heavily on what it called village committees, used by the central government to control the population (Ledgerwood and Vijghen 2002). These committees implemented Socialist-style programs of collectivized agriculture, education, and even local militias to maintain security: in effect, they established a local political system that has been reborn through today's commune councils (Prum 2005; Slocomb 2004). Accordingly, the commune councils have tended to replicate past practices, whereby top-down party pressure and upward accountability prevail. In remote and more traditional areas like the Cardamom Mountains, this leaves commune councilors pulled between being answerable to "their people" and being controlled by the regime—a balancing act that usually falls in favor of elite interests, at the expense of local social cohesion (Milne 2017). With the party's tentacles reaching deep into rural society, village resistance to state control has been difficult to sustain.

Natural Resources and the Contemporary State

The governance of Cambodia's forested land—whether for exploitation or conservation—has been fundamental to contemporary state-making. Since the 1990s, the country has seen various modes of government enabled extraction and enclosure through logging, land concessions, and protection. These processes have generated revenue for the state and elite actors, but they have also alienated and dispossessed Cambodian peasants and Indigenous people. I shall now describe key cycles of resource control and exploitation in contemporary Cambodia, illustrating how they have bolstered state-making and simultaneously shaped conservation practice.

FORESTS AND STATE FORMATION IN THE 1990S

With the chaos of civil war, Cambodia's forests were relatively unexploited until the late 1980s. At that stage, forests provided refuge and illicit resources for dispersed guerrilla factions and remaining Khmer Rouge along the Thai border, where an illicit timber trade thrived (Le Billon 2000). With the onset of peace, however, Cambodia's rulers turned to the forests as a key source of revenue and power—in part consolidating extractive strategies and networks of the 1980s (Gottesman 2004). With forest covering about two-thirds of the country, the new government was able to declare a vast Forest Estate as public land (Cock 2016), in spite of the presence of peasant farmers and customary resource users throughout (Diepart and Sem 2018). This was the first in what has become a series of postwar, post-Socialist land enclosures in service of the Cambodian state.

Following the creation of the Forest Estate, a period of rapacious logging began. This occurred as competing factions in the new government jostled for access to logging rents (Le Billon 2002). The incipient state in Phnom Penh wanted to control the logging, so it initiated a system of Forest Concessions throughout the Forest Estate, with support from the International Monetary Fund (IMF). These concessions enabled senior officials to capture forest rent for themselves while also using the proceeds to cement patronage ties and party loyalty (Cock 2016; Le Billon 2002). By 1997, all of Cambodia's productive forests were under concession, and from 1991 to 1998 approximately US$2.5 billion of timber was exported. Most of the proceeds escaped formal taxation, leading to a parallel economy or shadow state, in service of the new leaders (Le Billon 2000).

International outcry over the logging and corruption soon prompted changes. Donors expressed alarm about the large portion of timber revenues that were "off the books," with the IMF stating: "The diversion of public resources has probably reached the same amount as actual budget revenue collections . . . We consider illegal logging to be the single most critical issue in Cambodia" (Boyce 2003). In a form of "environmental adjustment," the IMF eventually suspended its support for the Cambodian government until it demonstrated efforts to curb illegal logging (Seymour and Dubash 2000). This led to sweeping reforms, driven by conditional donor funds. For example, all logging was suspended in 2001, with its resumption dependent upon an overhaul of forest governance, including adherence to international management standards (Cock 2016). Yet the standards were so stringent that no legal commercial logging has ever resumed. Millions of hectares of former forest concessions were therefore left suspended as Forest Estate, to be managed under the new Forestry Law of 2002. This created a blank slate of apparently unmanaged and empty state property. The conditions were ripe for global conservation to engage.

THE RISE OF CONSERVATION IN THE 2000S

The Cambodian government has made bold commitments over the last two decades to conserve its forests and ecosystems, fueled in part by the engagement of international donors and NGOs. Early foundations were laid in the 1990s, when the Ministry of Environment (MoE) was created and charged with managing a new protected area system, covering 18 percent of the country (Paley 2015). Cambodia also signed the United Nations Convention on Biological Diversity at this time, which prompted the adoption of national benchmarks for biodiversity management. The MoE was responsible for this nascent environmental mandate, but it was not considered to be a very lucrative or strategic ministry at the time (Milne 2009).

Real power and territory lay with the management of the Forest Estate, controlled by the Forestry Administration (FA) (formerly the Department of Forestry and Wildlife), under the Ministry of Agriculture, Forestry, and Fisheries (MAFF). The paradigm in MAFF was one of production and extraction, given its past management of the logging concessions. With the demise of commercial logging, the new task of conserving forest territory took hold from 2001 onward—and global conservation organizations were poised to help. This led to the creation of several new protected forests: former forest concession areas, designated for conservation under special legal orders or subdecrees. These protected forests were all created with the involvement of international conservation NGOs, including the CCPF, which was backed by CI.

A two-track conservation system therefore emerged in the 2000s, in which MoE and MAFF competed for donor funding and NGO partnerships. The interministerial dynamic was also shaped by party politics, dating back to the early 1990s, when Cambodia was governed by the CPP-FUNCINPEC coalition. Under the coalition, patrimonial control over each ministry was divided along party lines, with Hun Sen ensuring that the most powerful and lucrative ministries went to the CPP. Thus MAFF, with its resource rents, went to the CPP, and MoE went to FUNCINPEC. This legacy of weak and strong ministries, and their party-patronage alignments, was felt for at least a decade after the 1997 coup, which signaled the end of multiparty power sharing. NGOs therefore considered MAFF to be the most competent government partner—one that had political clout and authority to implement projects. On the other hand, MoE was seen as weak and unable to stand up to elite interests, such as the military, which sought to plunder the protected area system (Paley 2015).

The ensuing period of 2000–2010 was like a golden decade for conservation, when significant donor funds flowed into protected area management across Cambodia. Most projects involved NGOs working alongside government counterparts, in a capacity-building type of relationship. In effect, conservation funding became a source of revenue for MAFF, akin to the creation of environmental concessions. Some protected forests were arguably created arbitrarily in response to funding opportunities from overseas—such as in the case of Hollywood actor Angelina Jolie's conservation project on the Thai-Cambodia border, allegedly the homeland of her adopted Khmer son (Sam 2003). The geography of Cambodia's protected areas was therefore underpinned not necessarily by scientific biodiversity assessments but rather by government opportunism in response to international funding.

Conservation NGOs also enjoyed considerable influence and autonomy in Cambodia in the early 2000s. This led to inconsistent implementation of national laws, as each protected area or protected forest was managed according to the preferences and style of its international NGO sponsor—a truly transnational governance situation (see West 2006). This was the case in the Cardamom Mountains, where three international conservation NGOs jostled over the management of five different yet connected protected areas.[3] There was a strong sense of purpose and urgency at this time, driven largely by expatriate NGO staff. There was also jovial rivalry between individuals and projects, as each compared whose conservation strategy or territory offered the greatest possibilities for saving Cambodia's forests and wildlife.

---

3. These NGOs were CI, Flora and Fauna International, and Wildlife Alliance (formerly WildAid). Map 1 shows the extent of the protected area landscape in question.

ENVIRONMENTAL ENCLOSURES AND RESOURCE EXTRACTION

Time has revealed a more cynical interpretation of the Cambodian government's enthusiasm for securing protected areas and the Forest Estate. By 2010 it was clear that the embrace of conservation was not necessarily about biodiversity but rather about the objectives of a ruling elite that saw potential gains from Cambodia's vast environmental enclosures. International NGOs had apparently been engaged by the government to serve its strategic and territorial interests, which involved controlling valuable land and timber resources (Milne 2015). Hun Sen's enactment of the subdecree on Economic Land Concessions in 2005 had unleashed the consequences of this state territorialization: "state public land" could now be converted into "state private land" and leased out for long-term agricultural use by private companies. The land-grabbing boom that followed saw over two million hectares of arable land enclosed by the state, then handed out to a range of concessionaires, including for mining exploration and plantations, among other things (see Diepart and Schoenberger 2016; Lamb et al. 2017; Loughlin and Milne 2021; Neef and Touch 2012). As a result, hundreds of thousands of peasants have been displaced from their lands and resources, leading to an array of conflicts (Neef, Touch, and Chiengthong 2013).

The land-grabbing crisis has a direct relationship with Cambodia's state-backed environmental enclosures. This is because many of the land concessions overlapped with protected areas and Forest Estate or were located directly next to these forested areas. The concessions therefore gave rise to a new and largely informal logging boom, which included extensive illegal logging in protected areas, orchestrated by powerful elites and tycoons (Amnesty International 2022; Milne 2015). The same occurred around major government-backed developments like hydropower dams, roads, and transmission lines, which cut through protected areas. During this boom period of 2005–2012, Cambodia recorded the third highest national deforestation rate in the world (Hansen et al. 2013). This led to speculation over whether the government's infrastructure projects and concessions were really just a front for lucrative illicit resource extraction (Milne 2015). The Cardamom Mountains were not immune to this phenomenon, as illegal logging took hold in the area from 2009 onward in association with hydropower development. Chapter 6 explains how this happened.

Faced with grassroots and international pressure, Hun Sen eventually announced a moratorium on new land concessions in 2012 and a new ban on timber exports in 2016. However, these reforms have entailed government secrecy and antagonism toward international environmental actors (Loughlin and Milne 2021). The position of conservation NGOs is now somewhat insecure, with their influence significantly diminished. That said, government overtures to conservation are bolder than ever: reforms in 2016 enlarged and consolidated Cambodia's protected area system to cover over 40 percent of the country's land area (Loughlin and Milne 2021). The role of international NGOs and donors in this new set of government-led environmental enclosures remains ambiguous.

Cambodia's Southwest Forest Frontier

A key focus for global conservation in Cambodia has been the Cardamom Mountains. I shall now situate and contextualize this forested, mountainous frontier—a site of contested claims and multiple imaginaries—before describing how the region became a realm of intervention for CI. The area is known as Phnom Kravanh in Khmer, after the treasured cardamom spice: a ginger-like plant that was cultivated and traded by local Indigenous people for centuries.[4] The Cardamom Mountains form a rugged, ancient boundary between Cambodia and Thailand, where invading armies came to grief and where the usurped could take refuge. Testament to their remoteness, the mountains remained sparsely populated by mainly Indigenous villages until around 2010, when lowland settlers started to arrive alongside new roads and hydropower dams.

Biogeographically, the Cardamom Mountains are of great significance. They contain Cambodia's four highest peaks—the highest of which is Phnom Aural at 5,948 feet above sea level. The region is the wettest in Cambodia, with annual rainfall approaching thirteen feet, and a dry season that lasts only four months. Correspondingly, the mountains provide essential water flows to Cambodia's main hydrological systems: the Tonle Sap floodplain to the north, which drains into the Mekong, and the coastal mangroves and fisheries to the south, which drain into the Gulf of Thailand. The region is covered predominantly by tropical evergreen rainforest. Indicatively, CI's

---

4. *Phnom* means mountain, and *kravanh* refers to the cardamom plant (genus *Zingiberaceae*).

website estimates that the "annual value" of the Cardamom Mountains' "ecosystem services" is over US$1 billion.[5]

THE ORIGINAL INHABITANTS

Although the Cardamom Mountains are remote and wild, they are not a "pristine wilderness" as early media reports claimed (Sustainable Forestry Initiative 2002). Missing from the media hype was an account of the region's Indigenous people, who had maintained rice paddies, harvested food and medicine from the forest, and practiced shifting agriculture in remote settlements for centuries (Martin 1997). Their presence in the area seemed to have been forgotten amid the chaos of the late twentieth century and the NGO-driven hype of the early twenty-first century.

Only one researcher described the Indigenous people of the Cardamom Mountains before Cambodia plunged into civil war. From 1968 to 1970, French ethnobotanist Marie Martin conducted detailed studies of the villages that today fall within CI's project area. Her book, *Les Khmers d'origine* (1997), provides detailed descriptions of local livelihoods, customs, plants, and plant use in the area. In the most remote areas, these livelihood activities have been maintained in spite of disruption, with subsistence rice production, fishing, hunting, and the collection of wild nontimber forest products being foundational to the Indigenous way of life. When I first arrived in the area, I encountered local livelihoods very similar to what Martin described in the 1960s (Milne 2002). In addition to subsistence production, villagers also traded high-value nontimber forest products such as resin, cardamom, and *krisna* or agarwood. Before the war, elephants had carried these valuable goods out of the mountains via well-trodden "elephant roads" (Martin 1997). Back then, villagers also maintained agroforest groves for the cultivation of cardamom; for this, they chose the richest volcanic soils, where huge and ancient trees provided shade. However, agricultural expansion, forest degradation, and market integration have now taken their toll on this Indigenous way of life.

The origin and ethnicity of the first people in the Cardamom Mountains is unclear, with various labels and theories at play. Local legend suggests

---

5. See CI's online material, accessed June 2020, https://www.conservation.org/projects/cambodias-central-cardamom-protected-forest.

that the people are descendants of the royal family of Angkor, who apparently fled into the mountains hundreds of years ago, escaping Thai invaders.[6] Ancient funerary urns from around this time are present on exposed rock ledges in the mountains, but they reflect "highland burial rituals" rather than lowland Khmer culture (Beavan et al. 2012, 1). Given the mysterious origins of people in the Cardamom Mountains, they are sometimes referred to as Khmer Daeum, or the "original Khmer." This term was probably invented by Marie Martin to cope with the fact that the people of the Cardamoms did not easily conform to conventional notions of an ethnic minority. That is, they did not readily self-identify as a particular ethnic group, and they spoke what appeared to be an ancient dialect of Khmer. Martin notes that French administrators assigned some ethnic labels to people in the area (Pear, Samrey, Chong, Sa'och), but by the 1960s these identities were not readily used by local people. One reason for this was King Sihanouk's introduction of the homogenizing nationalist term Khmer Leu, meaning "upland Khmer," to refer to all ethnic minorities in the hills. This term was promoted aggressively in the 1950s, after independence from the French.

Identity debates in relation to the villagers of the Cardamom Mountains continue. These days, when prompted, villagers refer to themselves either as ethnic Chong, in a form of identity reclamation, or they use the official term for Indigenous people adopted by NGOs and the Cambodian government: *chunchiet daeum piektec*, which literally means "original ethnic minority" (see Baird 2010). For example, villagers used this term recently to assert their ancestral claims to the Areng Valley, which is now threatened by a proposed hydropower dam. Local resistance to the dam, on the basis of Indigenous claims to land, was also bolstered by remarkable support from urban and international activists but not conservation NGOs (Milne 2021). Thus, a new identity politics is at play in the mountains, which has its roots in the language and sensibilities of pro-Indigenous international actors.

Identity politics aside, the lifeworlds and cosmology of people in the Cardamom Mountains *are* different from the Cambodian mainstream. A key aspect of this relates to local religious beliefs and practices: people of the Cardamom Mountains combine Buddhism with animism in a deeply place-

---

6. This was suggested by villagers. At the eastern foot of the mountains is a place called Roleak Kang Cheung, "casting away the anklets," where the royal family apparently cast off their jewels before heading into the forest.

Situating the Field in Cambodia

based way. They pay special respect to local forest spirits such as *yey mao*, the revered "black lady," and *neak ta srok*, the "spirit guardians" or "ancient ones" (see Work 2019). These beliefs are reflected in the presence of sacred forests or *prey arak* throughout the area, where the spirits reside and where burials take place. In some areas like the Areng Valley and Veal Veng marsh, powerful beliefs in the crocodile spirit, known as *arak kropeu*, also prevail. It is no coincidence that these areas hold the last remaining wild populations of the Siamese crocodile (*Crocodylus siamensis*)—a critically endangered species of great interest to foreign biologists working in the area.

GOVERNING AND CLAIMING THE MOUNTAINS

Although the Cardamom Mountains may appear remote and ungoverned, state presence in the area has long been felt. Regular encounters between Indigenous villagers and government officials have occurred since the colonial era. Initially, governing processes occurred through mapping, with ancient and remote villages appearing as small dots on French maps. The full extent of village lands and shifting agriculture, however, was never properly mapped, reflecting a prevailing view of the Indigenous presence as merely informal or mobile. Ironically, it was the 1950s French maps that CI's conservation project used in 2002, as it tried to make sense of the chaotic, post-conflict landscape that had just been declared a protected forest. There were no other maps available at the time.

With Sihanouk's post-independence nation building, the tentacles of state and modernity began to penetrate into the area. Martin (1997) described this process as *encadrement modern*, or modernization. It involved government agents introducing the Khmer Daeum to institutions such as legal marriage and formal property rights. In turn, government agents became "the personalities of the district," including the commune chief, the forestry officers, the military personnel, the doctor, the teacher, the clerk, and the monks (Martin 1997). Alongside this state-based ordering of village life, militarization of the area also occurred as soon as independence was gained. By the 1960s, King Sihanouk had placed entire military battalions in the Cardamom Mountains in an attempt to consolidate territorial control over the new nation. This even involved a personal visit from him: older villagers still speak of "the day the king came." It apparently rained furiously as the king landed his plane on a gravel airstrip at the southern end of the Areng Valley. The airstrip is still visible, and when it rains hard, elders look to the sky and recall the day the king came.

But the newly minted Cambodian state and its troops were no match for the Khmer Rouge, who began operating in the remote forests of the Cardamoms in 1970. Local villagers initially attempted to resist them, but this resulted in a series of brutal encounters, followed by submission (Martin 1997). The Cardamom Mountains then became a Khmer Rouge stronghold until the mid-1990s.

Under the Khmer Rouge regime (1975–1979), great social and ecological changes were wrought. Cambodians from urban areas and other provinces were brought into the Cardamom Mountains to farm paddy rice collectively. At the same time, Indigenous villagers were forced to abandon their swidden plots and join the new Khmer Rouge settlements in their homelands, which were based on the lowland practices of permanent agriculture. Irrigation dams and channels were built using forced labor in an attempt to establish large-scale wet-rice paddies, which were not well suited to the area. The physical traces of this activity are still evident today in the landscapes of the Areng Valley and Thmar Bang. There are also countless small traces of the past: in one village, large and very alien eucalyptus trees now stand tall, having been planted by the Khmer Rouge at their former health post. These trees remain as living ghosts in the village main street—reminders of a terrifying time that villagers simply refer to as "the three years."

The relatively short-lived Khmer Rouge projects were followed by more terrible upheaval. When the Vietnamese took control in 1979, all villagers living in the remote mountains were forcibly evacuated, apparently for security reasons. As a result, for nearly twenty years, the Indigenous people of the Cardamom Mountains remained in consolidated settlements at the foothills. Only in 1997 did repatriation begin, with people gradually returning home to rebuild their lives. This was an enormous task, for in the villagers' absence everything had been consumed by jungle: schools and temples lay in ruins, wooden houses had rotted away, and land that was formerly cultivated had become overgrown with forest. Furthermore, villagers' domesticated elephants, once used for transporting goods, had run wild, and their precious herds of water buffalo had also disappeared, apparently eaten by Vietnamese soldiers. Yet the imprint of generations of belonging to homelands, plus the memory of village life in the 1960s, served as template and motivation for reconstruction.

Perhaps the greatest tragedy of the displacement and repatriation process was what happened to people's property rights. Villagers returned home to find their swidden plots entirely regrown with forest, with little left to indicate prior use—at least to the untrained or willingly blind eye. This meant that the Cambodian government was able to declare most of the area as Forest Estate, or state public property—and later, in 2001, a protected forest for the purposes of conservation. In one fell swoop, involving a map and a government-held pen, the customary rights of the Khmer Daeum were subordinated to the Forestry Law. As a result, fundamental conflicts over property rights persist in the area, as they do across forested zones of Cambodia (see Beban 2021; Diepart and Sem 2018; Mahanty 2022).

Alongside Indigenous repatriation came others, in search of resources and land: logging companies, demobilized soldiers, a military battalion, and ex–Khmer Rouge groups. This led to a period of intense timber extraction, mainly focused upon tropical hardwoods. Initially, military actors controlled the logging, and they profited handsomely from timber sales to Thailand. But in 1997, the government's new forest concession system allowed five different logging companies to operate in the area, with two Malaysian groups dominating the game (SCW 2006).[7] The companies took as much timber as they could while the opportunity existed: roads and bridges were built in haste, and huge logs were floated down the rivers to collection stations. This continued until the 2001 suspension of commercial logging. Today the rivers of the Cardamom Mountains remain clogged with logging debris and abandoned timber, reflecting the rapid departure of overly zealous loggers.

The logging not only made the area accessible to newcomers but also eroded key aspects of Indigenous livelihoods. A particular grievance was the removal of resin trees (*Dipterocarpus alatus*), from which villagers regularly harvested the oily sap, from a permanent hole in the trunk, for local use and for sale. Villagers often told a story about when they complained to the logging company about the destruction of their precious trees. Apparently, the loggers said, "We will only cut the top part of the tree, we'll leave the resin hole for you." One village leader had then replied angrily, "If you cut off my head, do you think I'll still be alive?" Villagers laughed about this story over rice wine, but this was the only way for them to cope with the tragedy of losing their ancient resin trees, called *cher teal*.

---

7. The Malaysian companies were Grand Atlantic Timber and Samling.

The exploitation of wildlife was also rampant at that time. Poachers sought tigers, elephants, and other rare or valued species for the lucrative wildlife trade to China and Vietnam. When foreign biologists arrived in 2000 to conduct the first wildlife survey of the area, they encountered a highly militarized but lawless place, where threats to biodiversity were high (Appleton, Bansok, and Daltry 2000). The setting was ripe for a conservation intervention. However, as I explain below, conservation would become just another layer of territoriality laid onto already complex and unresolved circumstances.

Becoming a Field Site for Global Conservation

The story of CI in the Cardamom Mountains shows how global conservation in Cambodia has generated and emerged from a mêlée of post-conflict resource struggles. After a decade (2002–2012) of NGO intervention in the Cardamom Mountains, which I describe below, perhaps the most significant observable outcome was state territorialization. I use the term *territorialization* to refer to the spatial, bureaucratic, and technical processes used by state actors to produce and secure territory—processes that in turn bolster state power (Vandergeest and Peluso 1995). In the Cardamom Mountains, NGOs have also been involved in these territorialization processes variously as managers, donors, advisors, partners, puppets, or bystanders (Milne 2012; Paley 2015). By examining how global conservation produces new territorial dynamics in places like Cambodia, we gain a window into its wider implications and potentially insidious side effects.

As with most global conservation projects, this story begins with the discovery of biological value. In 2000, a wildlife survey conducted by British biologists from Flora and Fauna International was the defining moment (Appleton, Bansok, and Daltry 2000). An excerpt from the report conjures the image of children in a candy shop:

> By the mid-point of the survey, the biologists' checklist already contained at least 30 species of large mammals, well over 100 birds, 64 reptiles, 30 amphibians, 30 small mammal species and numerous plants and insects; many of which have never previously been recorded in Cambodia. A wide range of globally threatened species were shown to be present in relatively high numbers, including tiger (*Panthera tigris*), Asian elephant (*Elephas*

maximus), Asiatic wild dog (*Cuon alpinis*), gaur (*Bos frontalis*), pileated gibbon (*Hylobates pileatus*), Siamese crocodile (*Crocodylus siamensis*), elongated tortoise (*Indotestudo elongata*), various hornbills and green peafowl (*Pavo muticus*).[8]

The report generated great excitement, and its findings were soon echoed by other conservation actors. For example, the World Wildlife Fund described the Cardamom Mountains as a "virtually intact forest; the best location for biodiversity conservation within the forests of the Lower Mekong Complex" (WWF 2001, 7–8). This view was then reflected in an international press release that hailed the area as "the largest, most pristine wilderness in Southeast Asia" (SFI 2002).

These declarations quickly made the area a global conservation priority. By 2002, there were commitments from six international organizations to provide financial and technical support for conserving the area. In particular, funds were secured from the Global Environment Facility (GEF) to enable a major collaboration between CI and FFI and their government counterparts, MAFF and MoE, respectively (UNDP 2007). The GEF contributed US$998,000, which was then complemented by over US$3.3 million in "cofinance" from international donors (UNDP 2007). The new initiative was to focus on the protection and management of nearly one million hectares in the Cardamom Mountains within three protected areas. CI's focus was on the central part of this landscape (see map 1).

SECURING THE TERRITORY

Even before the GEF money was in hand, CI had begun operating in the Cardamom Mountains using discretionary funds from the Moore Foundation.[9] Operations began after head office staff from CI managed to "secure a deal" with Cambodian officials, in which logging would be halted and early conservation activities could "build justification" for the area's permanent

---

8. Interviews with expatriates in 2007 indicated that many of these wildlife records have not been verified since the survey. Scientists have now revised down their estimates of some wildlife populations in the area.

9. As explained in chapter 1, the Moore Foundation awarded CI the largest ever grant for conservation in 2001 (over US$261 million). See https://philanthropynewsdigest.org/news /moore-foundation-awards-261-million-to-conservation-international.

protection (SFI 2002). This effort was led by the retired Australian Army Colonel David Mead, who was a Vietnam war veteran and former defense attaché to Cambodia with the Australian embassy. His political connections were instrumental in getting a memorandum of understanding signed between CI and MAFF to provide a formal basis for the conservation program in the Central Cardamom Mountains.

During the first two years of the conservation program (2000–2002), operations were dangerous and highly militarized. Security in the Cardamom Mountains was fragile, and the logistics of running remote ranger stations were seriously challenging. There was no road from Phnom Penh into the southern mountains at that time, so project staff operated from the coastal town of Koh Kong, which could only be accessed by boat from Cambodia's coastal provinces. From Koh Kong, staff traveled on degraded logging tracks for hours, and sometimes days, to reach the ranger stations that were located deep in the mountains (see map 2). All travel was conducted with at least two armed military policemen, who were hired as park rangers for security reasons.

One of the most significant achievements of CI's Australian director at this time was his successful negotiation with the Royal Cambodian Armed Forces to have its soldiers relocated out of Thmar Bang in the southern Cardamom Mountains. This meant that the soldiers' illegal logging and wildlife poaching activities ceased immediately—for CI, this was seen as a major conservation outcome. Ironically, when the soldiers left, the new park rangers took over the former military headquarters in Thmar Bang. For villagers, this was like a changing of the guard, as the rangers were also uniformed armed men whose main task was to patrol the area and control the use of natural resources.

These early conservation efforts were notably protectionist in style. CI's country director told me that the project's main purpose was to "hold the line" to prevent encroachment into the Forest Estate. To achieve this, the project's recently recruited rangers and forestry officials implemented Cambodia's new Forest Law with gusto, often targeting innocent villagers with arrests and fines, as though they were criminals. For many, this was an improvement on the past, as the director explained to the press: "Even though [our] team denied local villages the forest products they were accustomed to harvesting, the villagers . . . told [us] they preferred protection to Grand Atlantic Timber's rapacious logging" (Barron 2003). Ultimately, these bold efforts paid off with the declaration of the CCPF in 2002.[10] This occurred through a subdecree signed by the prime minister—a major victory for international conservation. Indeed, the CEO of CI at the time said that the creation of the CCPF was an "excellent example of how the conservation movement is supposed to work" (SFI 2002). Never mind that local villagers and Indigenous people were not consulted over the new protected forest. That would supposedly come later, as part of the CCPF management process.

CRAFTING THE INTERVENTION

CI's management of the CCPF became known as the Cardamom Conservation Program, referred to by staff as the CCP. The acronym's close resemblance to the name of Hun Sen's ruling party, the CPP, was noted by some Khmer staff in a lighthearted but nervous way. None of CI's expatriate staff could then have anticipated the poignancy that this association would acquire with time, as the conservation project slowly transformed into a Trojan horse for the ruling party. I explore how this happened in chapters 4 and 5. For now, my purpose is to introduce the conservation project's original design and intervention logic.

For CI, project design was a technical matter, in which strategies were developed to address perceived threats to forests and wildlife. Log frames were produced with support from the head office, in which the Cambodia program's objectives, assumptions, outputs, activities, and indicators were compiled. The resulting project design followed typical protected area management formulas, with three programmatic components: (1) law enforcement, to be implemented by government park rangers hired into the project; (2) community engagement, which was mainly an NGO function, arranged ultimately around the PES-like conservation agreements; and (3) biological research and monitoring, which involved regular surveys by field biologists, including Cambodian students and foreign volunteers.

CI's project logics therefore reflected established global approaches to protected area management. Here, interpretive power over the field lay with CI's leadership in Cambodia, who then worked with head office staff on what they called "pressure-state-response" analysis to address the key "threats to

---

10. Renamed the Central Cardamom Mountains National Park (CCMNP) in 2016, with the jurisdictional reforms that saw a switch over to MoE control.

biodiversity" in the Cardamom Mountains.[11] Widely used in conservation planning, this toolkit for threat analysis derives from managerial approaches to risk assessment (Hummel et al. 2019), while its companion "log frames" originate in military planning techniques (Kerr 2008). Thus, the conservation intervention was crafted using a hybrid toolkit from biodiversity and management science, with key information inputs from Cambodian informants. One of these informants was the young KGB-trained ex-soldier Chut Wutty, who was the CI country director's right-hand man in the early days.

The "threats to biodiversity" that were identified in CI's early strategy process were diffuse and diverse. They included small-scale illegal logging of luxury timber; wildlife poaching by professional hunters; hunting by local residents for either local consumption or the wildlife trade; and agricultural expansion, driven by both local residents and newcomers. Another threat was the occasional appearance of well-organized, almost industrial, efforts to extract valuable forest products like yellow vine and safrole oil—both alleged to be ingredients in Asian Ecstasy or *yaba*.[12] The key point about these threats is that they had an easily identifiable culprit or enforcement target—a villager engaging in illegal activity, a criminal to be caught, a local problem to be suppressed. Thus, they prompted technically achievable and well-bounded actions for conservation. In other words, the formulation of threats and responses *was* the intervention logic: it *enabled* government (see Li 2007).

The technical focus on local threats in turn meant that the project was not well equipped to deal with political or systemic *external* threats to forests and biodiversity, which began to appear from about 2005 onward. For instance, CI never questioned the proposed construction of five hydropower dams by Chinese companies in the Cardamom Mountains, which had Hun Sen's blessing. Rather, CI adopted a politically neutral stance, choosing to see the hydropower operators as potential buyers of ecosystem services, who could be conservation partners (Killeen 2012). This regime-friendly stance also emerged through the park rangers' behavior: their tendency was to enforce the law selectively, leaving powerful government interests untouched. As a result, resource grabbing by provincial and district governors,

---

11. I attended many strategy meetings that used this language.

12. This illicit industry still comes and goes from the Cardamoms, as trafficking networks, enforcement efforts, raw materials, and demand vary (see Otis 2014).

business tycoons, and party officials started to take hold in the CCPF, generally unhindered, while local villagers' customary resource use was curtailed through conservation measures (Milne 2012). This dynamic ultimately led to the conservation project becoming complicit in illicit logging operations from 2009 onward (see chapter 6).

Before these aberrations, CI's project in the Cardamoms ran an annual budget of about US$500,000, derived from a range of donor sources. CI's annual report for the year 2006–2007 indicates the spending levels: there were around 100 employees, 60 percent of whom were government staff engaged on law enforcement. These staff included military police and Forestry Administration officials who effectively worked as park rangers, based at six ranger stations across the area. There were also six expatriates employed by CI Cambodia, along with a range of consultants and volunteers from countries including the United Kingdom, the United States, New Zealand, Denmark, Philippines, the Netherlands, and Australia. Their tasks were mostly technical, and they advised on a range of matters such as law enforcement, biological monitoring, community engagement, and legal compliance. The remaining Cambodian staff worked with the biological research team (twenty people), the community engagement team (six people), and in administration and support (around five people). While this may appear like a large allocation of effort, the budget was in fact thin for the task at hand—fundraising was a constant source of worry for NGO staff in Phnom Penh.

Resource allocation within the project also reflected donor priorities and head office interests. Consistent support for fundraising came from CI's head office, where staff noted: "It's easy to raise money for community work . . . what's hard is raising money for law enforcement!" These circumstances meant that any available discretionary funds were spent on the park rangers' running costs. Meanwhile, the community program gradually mobilized a variety of donor funds, which at times caused the park rangers to become jealous. Apparently, the rangers saw community engagement work as a potential threat to their authority and power in the field—an issue that increasing government and party influence eventually rectified (see chapter 5).

Finally, the biologists developed a number of species-specific interventions, focusing mainly on the monitoring of globally threatened species, including pangolin (*Manis javanica*); dragon fish (*Scleropages formosus*); Malayan sun bear (*Helarctos malayanus*) and Asiatic black bear (*Ursus thibetanusi*); otter (two unknown species); turtles and tortoises (eleven species); and Siamese crocodile (*Crocodylus siamensis*).[13] Their activities involved deploying camera traps, conducting surveys, and removing snares from the forest, among other things. These efforts reflected CI's scientific focus upon biodiversity, a core priority of CI's global leadership at the time. It is no coincidence that the expatriate biologists running this work later went on to run the entire CI Cambodia and Greater Mekong operation, from 2007. For example, the herpetologist Luke became CI's most senior expatriate in Cambodia, responsible for overseeing the Cardamom Mountains project from 2007 to 2010.

EARLY COMMUNITY ENGAGEMENTS, 2002–2006

With CI's emphasis upon law enforcement and biological values, local residents of the Cardamom Mountains were initially seen as "threats to biodiversity" that required management. Early community engagement was therefore ad hoc and top-down, leading to strained relations with local people. For the program's first two years, local villagers mainly encountered CI through its law enforcement activities: villagers witnessed armed patrols and were often prosecuted for conducting subsistence livelihood activities, like shifting agriculture. Even though government park rangers implemented national laws, villagers attributed the conservation program to what they called "*aungkar* CI." Aungkar is the Khmer word for "organization" or NGO, but it is heavily loaded because it was also the vernacular name used for the Khmer Rouge. The presence of a new aungkar in the village was thus the subject of thin laughter. Alongside this were jokes about CI being like the CIA—a key enemy of the Khmer Rouge regime, and a favorite subject of its deadly interrogators.

I entered this scene in late 2002 as a naïve volunteer, working under the job description "winning hearts and minds." I did not know at the time that this phrase came from the Americans' strategy in Vietnam—a direct expression of my boss's wartime past. I simply followed his instructions, which involved public handouts of rice and salt in every target village. This practice, too, had historical precedents in the post-conflict hunger-alleviation strategy of the United Nations in Cambodia. Thus, from war-torn threads of the past, CI's new Community Engagement Program was woven into being.

---

13. This list derives from the program's 2006–2007 annual report. The main threat against these species was, and is, illegal wildlife trafficking and trade.

From the outset, CI's community engagement efforts were affected by conflicts over land and resource rights. A core problem was that, when the protected forest was created, there were no consultations with local residents and no explicit provision for customary resource rights. The only legal basis for customary rights came from the 2002 Forestry Law, but this was never consistently implemented on the ground. Instead, local rangers saw the villagers' use of forest products and their practice of shifting agriculture as illegal. Villagers were permitted only to retain land under cultivation at the time of the creation of the CCPF. This was a blatant denial of villagers' legitimate and customary claims—a situation not helped by two decades of forest regrowth on their pre-war swidden lands.

Villagers therefore contested the conservation agenda. Countless Forest Estate and CCPF boundary signs were removed or battered by villagers over time. Furthermore, villagers were adept at outsmarting rangers, as they opened new swidden plots in pockets of forest that could not be seen from the road. Later on, more acts of outright noncompliance were observed. For example, in 2005 and 2007, there were large and vocal protests by villagers at the main ranger station in Thmar Bang, in which strong demands for land and forest demarcation were made. These were important events, but several local observers quietly speculated that the protests were in fact organized by a powerful local businessman who had his own anti-conservation agenda and land claims to push.

In response to these circumstances, CI's nascent Community Engagement Program initiated a range of conflict-resolution and rights-based interventions. I led this process, drawing from my experience in Indigenous Australia, along with advice from like-minded expatriates in Cambodia working on similar things. To advance this work, CI received some technical and financial support from the head office, but there was not a top-down transfer of policy ideas. Rather, the policy guidance came from Cambodia's then recently adopted participatory land-use planning, or PLUP, program. This had been endorsed by the Ministry of Land Management Urban Planning and Reconstruction as part of Cambodia's massive donor-backed land reforms. There was even a "PLUP manual" (Rock 2001) for NGOs and land-use planning practitioners to use in rural Cambodia.

The aim of PLUP was to enable communities across Cambodia to map their customary lands and resources, with the goal of achieving formal rights recognition from the government. With this in mind, CI implemented

PLUP across the CCPF from 2003 onward, leading to detailed maps of community land use, including shifting agriculture areas, in six communes. But the process ultimately suffered from a lack of government support, especially from ministries like MAFF. This meant that none of the PLUP maps were ever formally recognized, in spite of NGOs pushing on behalf of villagers. After a few years, the government moved on to other things, leaving the draft PLUP maps to become lost in the system.[14] Unfortunately, this was not just a case of rapid policy change and weak institutional memory. The PLUP maps were inconvenient because they represented formal Indigenous and villager land claims that the government preferred not to see (see Biddulph 2014).

Nevertheless, the PLUP process *did* imprint upon local imaginaries and ambitions in the Cardamom Mountains. Apart from seeding the idea of Indigenous land rights, PLUP also involved the creation of local representative organizations called Commune Natural Resource Management Committees (CNRMCs)—a radically bottom-up intervention at the time. These committees were elected in six communes of the CCPF, in a nominally democratic process, sponsored and facilitated by CI from 2003 to 2005. The committees were to oversee the PLUP process, but they also became vehicles for community participation in the conservation project more generally, and an entry point for CI in local villages. Relationships soon formed between committee members and CI's community engagement team, and the committees were also engaged in crafting the conservation agreements that came later. With time, however, the committees became more politically complex, as NGO resources began to flow and as committees played an increasing role in discussions over land and resources in the area. The ruling party took notice of this, and responded accordingly, as I show in chapter 5.

Finally, CI's early community engagement also involved support to local livelihoods, in a way that resembled a traditional integrated conservation and development project (ICDP). Financed mainly through a USAID population and environment grant in 2004, this entailed a distinctly Malthusian combination of family planning, "alternative livelihoods" activities, and "environmental awareness-raising." Following a predictable NGO formula,

---

14. In 2010, CI and FA staff told me the PLUP maps were lost. Other NGOs were told the same thing. Villagers, however, did retain their copies of the maps—they were important for new looming battles over land, especially related to the Areng dam.

women's groups were created for growing vegetables and raising chickens; a healthcare post was constructed; and school outreach programs were initiated. This program also supported the rehabilitation of old rice paddies, which had last been used during the Khmer Rouge period. For CI, the idea was to boost local paddy rice production so as to reduce pressure on the surrounding forests—a classic conservation logic of "land sparing" (Phalan et al. 2011). Poverty-afflicted villagers were initially hesitant about this, but were eventually happy to have support in the form of a CI-sponsored tractor and buffalo banks.[15] In this way, paddies last cultivated in the name of a Maoist utopia were plowed again, following a new logic of global conservation—one cause as alien as the other.

THE CONSERVATION AGREEMENTS (2006 ONWARD)

Once CI's Community Engagement Program in Cambodia was well established, the head office sought to extend new ideas and opportunities to the field. Visits from head-office staff in 2005, who were promoting the newly formed Conservation Stewards Program, led to brainstorming sessions in Phnom Penh about how to implement direct payments in the Cardamom Mountains. A concept paper was then developed, which proposed that community-based direct payments could build on existing project activities. A field trip by the CSP director in March 2006 then sealed the deal: Cambodia would become one of CI's early pilot sites for the conservation agreements. In this way, the CSP built on what was already there: relationships and structures, but also a tangle of conflicts over territory, memory, place, identity, and resources.

The new conservation agreements were implemented from 2006 onward. They built on the draft PLUP maps and also mobilized the project's existing logic of land sparing to form an early version of payments for avoided deforestation (Milne 2012). The first set of conservation agreements was signed between CI, local communities, and the Forestry Administration in 2007: five agreements for the five communes of Thmar Bang district (see table 2 and map 2). The agreements have since been renewed annually, with

---

15. One cause for hesitation among villagers was lack of clarity over ownership of the paddy fields, given post-war disruption. The "buffalo banks" were managed collectively, in each commune, for breeding and plowing fields (see Milne 2009).

Table 2 Summary of Conservation Agreements, 2007–2010

Commune	Conservation Services	Annual payment (2010)	Sanctions
Thmar Dan Peuv 113 families	Protect **dragon fish** spawning pools and no harvesting of fingerlings; Assist FA to combat illegal hunting and wildlife trade; No forest clearing	**US$17,050** Included purchase of mechanical tillers; wages for community patroling; and support for schoolteacher	Sanctions depend on number of transgressions. If 10 transgressions occur, the agreement is suspended.
Chumnoab 76 families	No forest clearing for farms; Protect **crocodile** and its habitat along the river; Assist FA to combat illegal hunting and wildlife trade	**US$8,788** Included mechanical tillers for paddy restoration; wages for community patroling; support for schoolteacher	Sanctions depend on number of transgressions. If 10 transgressions occur, the agreement is suspended.
Roussey Chrum 272 families	Assist FA to combat illegal hunting and wildlife trade; No hunting, snaring, logging, or wildlife trading	**US$7,160** Support for schoolteachers; wages for community patroling; individual cash incentives for all households	If 5 transgressions detected, cash bonus is suspended and patroling canceled for following year.
Tatai Leu 135 families	No forest clearing for farms; No hunting; Assist the FA to combat illegal hunting, logging, and wildlife trade	**US$8,588** Included $3,200 cash to community fund; wages for community patroling; and support for schoolteachers	If 5 transgressions detected, payments are suspended and patroling canceled for next year.
Prolay 182 families	No forest clearing for farms; No hunting; Assist the FA to combat illegal hunting, logging, and wildlife trade	**US$18,360** Included mechanical tillers for paddy rice; construction of school and support for teachers; patroling wages	If 5 transgressions detected, payments are suspended and patroling canceled for next year.

Source: Milne and Adams (2012).

relatively little variation.[16] Consistent with the PES concept, each agreement articulates: (i) conservation services to be delivered, such as protection of critically endangered species like Siamese crocodile and dragon fish, and forest conservation; (ii) benefits paid to communities in exchange for the conservation service, such as buffalo banks and tractors; and (iii) sanctions in the case of nonperformance by community members, usually removal or reduction of benefits. Park rangers, local community rangers, and CI's community engagement team were also involved in agreement monitoring, to ensure compliance and to administer sanctions if necessary.

A final aspect of the CSP program in Cambodia involved monitoring the agreements' socioeconomic impacts over time. This was implemented from 2007, after baseline surveys that I helped to implement as a consultant. These efforts showed, among other things, the distribution of costs and benefits in local communes resulting from the conservation agreements. Rather predictably, the poorest families bore many of the costs of conservation, due to their subsistence reliance on forest products, and their inability to fully utilize the benefit packages for farming, due to land and labor shortages (Milne 2009). These data pointed to intracommune complexities, and they also signaled key policy debates over distribution and equity in community-level PES that would come (Milne and Niesten 2009).

Conservation's Entangled Territories

In this chapter, I have illustrated how a postcolonial, post-conflict, and anthropogenic landscape in the Cardamom Mountains became a field site for global conservation. This process began in the year 2000 with the discovery of global biodiversity values in an apparent forest wilderness—a process that subtly paralleled how the French "discovered" and acclaimed the "lost city" of Angkor in Cambodia's mid-nineteenth-century jungle. Global conservation investment then flowed into the Cardamom Mountains, with the Cambodian government acting as a willing partner.

---

16. CI's 2021 profiles for the Central Cardamom Mountains National Park and the Conservation Stewards Program both mention the conservation agreements in Cambodia. See https://www.conservation.org/about/conservation-stewards-program and https://www.conservation.org/projects/cambodias-central-cardamom-protected-forest.

A key part of the conservation action that followed was the crafting and construction of "the field" as a realm of intervention (see Ferguson 1994; Li 2007, 7–9). For most conservationists I worked with, the field was a category to which strategic tools or survey techniques could be applied. The field was where "threats to biodiversity" were addressed, as points on a map or activities in a log frame, or where "tracks and scats" were detected on transect walks through the forest. In this way, biological and technical expertise determined what was valuable and what counted in the new realm of intervention. Here, too, the bewildering complexity and potentiality of interactions between conservation activities and local village life were essentially left undiscussed, even unnoticed, by CI's foreign project proponents. CI's discursive construction of the field therefore involved a degree of calculated blindness to the project's potential entanglements and knock-on effects in Cambodia.

This failure to situate the field, or to attribute agency to the field, is one of global conservation's fundamental weaknesses. In Cambodia, the result of this failure was a dangerous combination of well-meaning transnational policy ideas, like the conservation agreements, and local processes of state territorialization and government control. In the following chapters I shall explain how this unfolded.

Chapter 4

Brokering and Transforming the Idea

March 2007, Thmar Bang Ranger Station:
I am reaching the end of a two-month period of fieldwork, based in the Car-
damom Mountains. It feels like an age of village immersion and isolation from
my usual cultural reference points—something I have enjoyed immensely, as my
purpose is to collect data for my PhD thesis. Nonetheless, it is with some excite-
ment that I welcome CI's foreign biologists, a young couple, to the station that
evening. They arrive at sunset in the NGO truck, after a full day's travel, carrying
equipment and their handsome dog. I was eager to speak English, my own lan-
guage, and to download about my field experiences. We decide to eat together.

As per usual practice at the ranger station kitchen, foreigners are served
first, to eat separately in the dining area. Having been served, we eat very
well, and take our time. We talk about conservation strategies, project chal-
lenges, and the next visit from CI's head-office staff. Crickets and frogs animate
the tropical evening, along with occasional hushed Khmer voices outside. I
have the sensation of being watched. The Khmer cook—a local widow and
mother—stands observantly, waiting for us to finish. She has a small son to
feed, and kitchen leftovers typically go to her family or to others in need. The
Khmer custom of serving food on communal plates facilitates this sharing. It
is a practice that I have grown to love, in a country where meals feel sacred.

As we wrap up, the female biologist asks, "Has everyone finished eating?"
We nod. She then grabs the remaining plate of beef, and places it on the
ground for her dog to eat. The cook and I exchange glances, both of us wit-
nessing this excruciating moment. Villagers in the area almost never have

money to buy meat. Furthermore, the conservation project prevents villagers from subsistence hunting—even for common species like wild boar and deer. Such moments never go unnoticed. From then on, I would overhear jokes at the ranger station about the chkai barang—*the foreign dog or the French dog—who ate better than the Khmers. Somehow, these jokes insinuated that the foreigners were like dogs too.*

This anecdote is uncomfortable for many reasons. It exposes colonial baggage, the ignorance and potential arrogance of foreign expatriates, structural inequalities within the conservation project, and deep cross-cultural divides. In the setting of the ranger station back then, I also recall wrestling with my own foreignness, and how I compensated for that by striving to be as Khmer as possible—as any young student ethnographer might have done. Yet my striving could not fix the awkwardness that occurred so regularly in the practice and indeed the *performance* of the conservation project. It often felt as though, if we were all to stop going through the motions of NGO project implementation, we might find ourselves suspended in midair, suddenly exposed. Imagine the stage lights being turned off during a performance, leaving actors to face an impossible abyss of history, complexity, and difference before them.

This awkward sensation of performance, which also points to a certain hubris or selective vision on the part of project actors, offers insight into the dynamics of transnational project implementation in conservation and development (see Long 2001; Mosse 2005; Rottenburg 2009; West 2006). In this chapter, I offer a fresh account of these dynamics by examining how CI sought to enact and maintain its project in Cambodia—in particular its conservation agreements in the Cardamom Mountains. What I begin to reveal, therefore, is how corporate nature functions when it hits the ground. The result is inevitably messy, because corporate nature is an institutional form that does not want to be situated or emplaced: instead, it is utterly wedded to its policy ideas and their supposed ability to achieve conservation outcomes, regardless of the location. This chapter shows how the fantasy of corporate nature begins to unravel in the field.

Inside Transnational Policy Implementation

To interpret transnational project processes, I take inspiration from ethnographies of conservation and development. For example, Paige West (2006) tells us how BINGO-backed conservation projects *are* the transnational. Meanwhile, David Mosse (2005, 9) describes international development as a never-ending process of "creating order" or "maintaining coherence" in the face of fragmentation and confusion. In these contexts, project "brokers" are those who continually make links between policy goals and the various practical interests at play (Mosse 2005; Lewis and Mosse 2006). This insight draws from Bruno Latour's groundbreaking ethnography of a French engineering project (1996), which showed how project managers must constantly juggle competing interests to maintain conceptual and operational order. Latour called these processes "translation."

This chapter explores translation in the context of global conservation by asking: How do policy ideas from the head office get translated across scales to become projects in the field? What happens to policy ideas when they are translated into practice? What forces or factors shape the processes of translation in Cambodia, and hence policy outcomes? I explored these questions empirically during my doctoral fieldwork, when I observed CI's project in Cambodia from 2006 to 2007. At the time, I had privileged access to the project, and I was in regular dialogue with key project actors. In parallel, I spent extended periods in the field doing project ethnography. This enabled me to observe how CI's policy ideas were brokered across scales.

In retrospect, this period of participant observation in the field was also unique because it captured a key transition moment in CI's project trajectory. This transition involved a shift away from foreign control and NGO influence, alongside an embrace of Khmer leadership in the project, which ultimately led to an increased government say over CI's decision-making. My observations therefore trace the early patterns of what may now be recognized as a contemporary era of more explicit or formalized control over international and local NGOs in Cambodia (Curley 2018). While Cambodia has a sovereign right to manage the influence of NGOs on its soil, it is the gradual erosion and curtailment of civil society that is of real concern here. For NGOs like CI, this closing of civil society space presents real challenges for ethics and accountability, which play out through transnational projects. This chapter illustrates just how hard it is for international NGOs to know, let alone control, what happens within the transnational governance spaces that they create—spaces that are by definition contingent, ephemeral, political, and negotiated (Wells-Dang 2010; West 2006). Casper Bruun Jensen (2016) likens this space in Cambodia to a gray zone between worlds.

To navigate this gray zone, I return to my characterization of CI's project in the Cardamom Mountains as a transnational system or "project system" (Mosse 2005; see chapter 1). The system includes connected or networked actors such as donors, CI staff, government staff, local administrators, commune chiefs, villagers, researchers, and others. Money, ideas, and instructions flow down through the system so that conservation action can be realized on the ground. Reports from the field are then sent back upward, to the head office and donors, to become "results" or "outcomes." Importantly, these two-way flows are productive processes, through which field conditions and project impacts are socially produced (Appadurai 1996) and strategically represented (Mosse 2005). For this reason, the project system may also be considered as an assemblage (Anderson and McFarlane 2011; Corson et al. 2019) in which conventional notions of scale, hierarchy, and direction collapse into a networked web of interconnection and knowledge production.

To analyze CI's project, this chapter examines two key fault lines or "interfaces" (Long 2001) within the project, across which the translation of ideas and knowledge was problematic. The first interface was that between CI and the Cambodian government, a partnership between two organizations with separate and often incompatible "system goals" (Mosse 2005). The second interface was between foreigners and Khmers working on the project, in which linguistic and cultural differences gave rise to awkward and sometimes serious misunderstandings, as illustrated by the tale of the foreigner's dog. I explore these project interfaces and their effects in this chapter. My account especially focuses on the role of "skilled brokers" (Lewis and Mosse 2006) in the project, who regulated and enabled information flows across interfaces: between field site and office; government and NGO; Khmers and foreigners.

There were four key brokers involved in implementing CI's conservation agreements in Cambodia, all of whom were charismatic, multilingual, and at home in the transnational project space. They were (see table 1, chapter 1): Maria, the director of CI's conservation agreements global program; Kiry, CI's first Khmer country director in Cambodia; Chung, the government manager of the protected area, from the Forestry Administration; and Nhet, CI's Community Engagement team leader, based in the field. These brokers were constantly negotiating an array of competing perspectives and interests, as they juggled the demands of CI, donors, government officials, field staff, villagers, and others. Yet their communications about the project were necessarily partial, being crafted to suit the audience or political dynamics at hand. This corresponds with the work of translation in projects, which requires ongoing effort and performance (Latour 1996), as brokers work to stabilize interpretations of events or to establish apparent project coherence (Mosse 2005). As this chapter shows, project outcomes often depend on *who* is authorized to do the interpretive work and *how* certain versions of events gain precedence over others.

With these dynamics in play, the final part of this chapter explores the consequences of strained or partial translation processes within projects. I show how CI's neatly defined policy idea of conservation agreements was transformed into a locally contingent hybrid form—something that CI's head office could not comprehend or control. These observations call into question the power of global conservation to determine field outcomes. They also challenge conventional views of policy instruments as implementable products whose effects stem from design. The ways in which policy is distorted by field realities will vary between places, but in Cambodia the two most prominent factors driving transformation were NGO–government relations and Khmer–foreigner interfaces, as I shall now illustrate.

The Role and Influence of Government in an "NGO" Project

The most problematic interface that I observed within the project was the relationship between CI and the Cambodian government. In the project's early years (2002–2005), this was largely a relationship of mutual dependence. CI had power because it provided funds and technical assistance, which the government desperately needed at the time. Government actors were also adept at making the NGO expatriates feel good about their contribution and potential influence, although everyone knew that CI could not operate in the Cardamom Mountains without the government's blessing. Government actors therefore retained great discretionary power over the management of the protected area, and their confidence grew with time. By 2010, CI's capacity to exert influence over the conservation program on the ground was significantly diminished.

The formal basis for the relationship between CI and the government was through a memorandum of understanding with MAFF, signed in January 2001 (Ouk and Chay 2013). This document provided little guidance on how

CI and the FA should interact on a daily basis, other than vague allusions to capacity building and technical support that would be provided by the NGO. Practical authority and influence over the conservation project was therefore an ongoing juggle: a product of daily negotiations. By the mid-2000s, this had stabilized with a nominal division between the "government-run" law enforcement component, and the "CI-run" community engagement and biological research components. This partly related to financial flows, because CI provided an annual subgrant to the FA to finance the park rangers, who fulfilled the state function of law enforcement. All other activities were financed by so-called "NGO money," for which CI was responsible.

In the analysis below, I illustrate the gradual penetration of Cambodian government interests into the ostensibly nongovernment realm of CI in Cambodia. The government's influence was primarily exerted through FA staff working for the project, but these staff were in turn subservient to other higher-level government and Cambodian People's Party interests, well beyond the project's boundaries. Eventually, this dynamic affected all Cambodian staff working on the project, whether they were government officials or not. The implications of this shift would only become apparent much later, when the project became subject to powerful illegal logging interests (see chapter 6). As Diane Vaughan famously illustrated (1996), the subtle beginnings of "organizational deviance" often go unnoticed but are important to recognize because they can normalize and accumulate over time, until critical failure occurs.

STRUGGLES FOR CONTROL OVER THE PROJECT

Tension between CI staff and their government counterparts was a defining feature of the conservation project. Initially CI enjoyed significant influence, due mainly to its first country director—an Australian retired colonel and former defense attaché. In 2002, I saw how the rangers would salute him and stand to attention, solider style. With the colonel's departure in 2003, however, CI's expatriate leadership in Cambodia changed multiple times in the face of increasingly assertive government staff. From 2007 onward, the conservation project therefore transitioned to Cambodian leadership, to become something like a CI-housed government entity. I now explore how this transition occurred because it portrays the early workings of CI's ethical compromises and eventual loss of control over its project in Cambodia.

A key way in which the NGO–government struggle for control over the project played out was through the position of country director. This CI position, reporting to the head office, underwent seven leadership changes from 2003 to 2007, involving three locally recruited Australian directors, and four periods of leadership by head-office staff deployed to the region on an interim basis. The conspicuous and repeated departure of expatriate directors points to a key difficulty: that of foreign directors winning the support of Khmer staff. An underlying reason for this emerges from Cambodian organizational culture, in which Khmer staff are forced by their superiors to make their loyalties clear (see O'Leary and Meas 2001). Constant pressure from senior government staff pushed all Cambodians in the project to choose between "following the foreigners (*barang*)" or "following the government." Furthermore, if nongovernment Khmer staff resisted this pressure, then they would be accused of "working for the barang," as though they were traitors.[1] CI's foreign directors therefore found themselves constantly undermined, as Nhet observed through an old Cambodian saying: "an army of bucks led by a lion is to be feared, but not an army of lions led by a buck."

At the time, few foreigners employed by CI recognized these dynamics. Fewer still paused to consider the fraught experience of their nongovernment Khmer staff, who were employed to advance CI's interests but were also subject to government pressures. As Nhet explained: "What the government wants, the Khmer staff must facilitate. . . . [If not] government staff can make a problem for NGO staff until they leave." Indeed, Nhet had been unwilling to accommodate government demands in 2006, and so he was gradually ostracized: "They do not value me. The [government] office staff just tell me what to do now. . . . They want to put their own people in the forest, not me. I am independent, and harder for them to control."

Thus, the Khmer nongovernment staff were trapped in a constant struggle between the competing interests of CI and the government. This led to moments of dissonance in the project, which left many expatriate managers bewildered as to why "Khmers never do what we say." I recall countless expat conversations on the subject: "Why don't they do their job? Why don't they report the problem? Why don't they have initiative? Maybe they are lazy?" These questions led to a preoccupation with how to "incentivize" the Khmers to do their jobs. Yet the fundamental problem went unrecognized:

---

1. This dynamic was explained to me in late 2006 by Nhet, along with other Khmer NGO staff.

given the need to save face, Khmer staff would never decline their foreign managers' requests, even if government pressure made their jobs impossible to complete.

This government-instigated resistance to NGO activities played out vividly in the field. For example, the CI-led community engagement activities of 2002–2005 were constantly targeted and criticized by government staff within the project—apparently because the community engagement team consisted almost entirely of NGO staff. This manifested in unfortunate ways. For example, Nhet alleged that FA staff spread rumors around the villages in 2005 that CI's community program was an opposition political party. These rumors provoked threats of violence against the community engagement team and made some villagers reluctant to participate in their meetings. It was therefore effectively impossible to maintain a true nongovernment space within the project without ongoing conflict.

Conflicts dissipated by mid-2007, however, once the government had consolidated its control over the project through informal channels. This new era was made possible by CI's appointment of a Cambodian country director, Kiry, who was the former community engagement team leader. Kiry formed a close working relationship with his FA counterpart, Chung—with both men emphasizing to me the need for strong leadership and internal discipline in the conservation program. This created a typically Khmer hierarchical management culture (see O'Leary and Meas 2001), which government interests could easily manipulate. This also meant that new NGO staff, hired by the Cambodian leadership, were generally government compliant. CI could now "run" the conservation project in a relatively stable way.

Not all CI staff in Cambodia were comfortable with this leadership transition. For example, prior to Kiry's appointment, there had been ongoing disputes over whether CI's new country director should be Cambodian. Some expatriates were concerned about whether Cambodian control would cause a loss of transparency, while others worried that a Khmer leader would not be able to withstand pressure from powerful interests. Comments were made in reference to Kiry's candidature: "He's just not ready," said one of the foreign biologists. Even some Cambodian NGO staff expressed doubts: "It's too soon to have a Khmer director," they said, alluding to the risk of corruption. Emails were sent to the head office from dissenting staff, pleading for ongoing expatriate leadership. But the head office was driven by other concerns.

At the global level, CI had just adopted a new strategic emphasis on working with partners, including being a "trusted advisor" to governments.[2] Empowering Khmer leadership in Cambodia therefore made sense from a global perspective. This stance in the head office was made abundantly clear when CI's president and senior vice presidents visited Cambodia in late 2007. I attended their strategy meetings in Phnom Penh, which allowed me to ask about the problem of transparency in CI–government partnerships, especially in places where authoritarian control and corruption were the norm. One of them replied, "Well, even if it's opaque, it's OK if it works!" Echoing this, CI's then president encouraged staff to "work with heads of states" and "to push at the highest levels of government." It seemed that CI's global leadership was not concerned about potential ethical compromises it may face in embracing a Cambodian-run, government-aligned project.

THE CONSOLIDATION OF GOVERNMENT CONTROL

As the conservation project matured, the level of government control over project activities increased, even when these were ostensibly NGO-run. Project activities simply could not happen without informal, high-level endorsement from the FA and sometimes even higher echelons of government, including the prime minister. As one experienced legal consultant to the project explained to me in 2007: "It's all trickle down here. . . . They've never seen grassroots. . . . You can't do anything without top-down intervention." This was echoed by CI's field logistics manager, Sok, who said to me earnestly, "If the government wants the forest to stay, then the forest will stay." Nothing more needed to be said, as the distribution of power was clear.

Management of CI's government collaboration was therefore left to CI's savvy and well-connected Cambodian staff. This task mainly involved Kiry and Chung, who used their high-level relationships to solve problems and get things done. Each described their regular interactions with provincial governors, ministers, and the FA director while running the project.[3] An ad-

---

2. A recent version of this CI policy is at https://www.conservation.org/priorities/working-with-governments (accessed May 15, 2020).

3. For example, the program relied on high-level government connections to avert a murder investigation against it in the case of a woman who was allegedly shot by park rangers (see Soenthrith and Maloy 2007). This apparently enabled CI to pay an out-of-court settlement to the victim's family.

ditional complication was that government connections had to be the "right" ones. As Sok explained: "If you choose the wrong FA staff to work with, then this may be a problem. . . . He must have links to the top." Sok's comment also shows that it was almost always men involved in these brokering processes. Ultimately, the need for government approval empowered the project's government staff; they knew that NGO staff could be worn out and demoralized without their backing. As one ranger explained: "Without government support, it's difficult to work. If you are just an independent NGO, and work with just local authorities, many people ask you about your permission from government, like the letter from high up. . . . They ask where you are from, and it wastes your time, and finally your emotions are not good."

Despite the pervasiveness of these local protocols, many expatriates remained puzzled and frustrated when their plans could not be implemented. For example, a persistent stumbling block for foreign conservationists was the weak legal basis for prosecuting wildlife crime, such as poaching. By 2007, expatriate staff had been asking for legal clarification on this matter from their FA counterparts for two years, but without progress. Eventually, a Filipino lawyer explained the blockage to me, while expressing amazement at the expatriate staff's inability to understand: "I've been telling them that the trouble with the wildlife [law] is that Hun Sen didn't state 'no hunting' in his declaration." For this reason, the FA rangers were reluctant to prosecute wildlife crime, even though CI had hired them to do so. Countless similar examples occurred over time, including one that frustrated me greatly: the government's refusal to sign off on villagers' land-use plans. Even though government policy for participatory land use planning (PLUP) was in place at the time (Rock 2001), Hun Sen never backed it, meaning that the FA would not sign off on any community-made maps. In this way, senior political figures determined how conservation policies and laws were implemented in Cambodia.

For conservation NGOs, this meant compromise: an ongoing balancing act between maintaining vital government support, on the one hand, and upholding NGO ideals and principles, on the other. CI learned early on about the nature of this dynamic. For example, when CI sought to renew its memorandum of understanding with MAFF in 2005, to cover project operations, the ministry took two years to sign off. Furthermore, the result was considered a significant compromise by some expatriate staff, one of whom said in 2007: "It took so long [to sign] because it had to go to Hun Sen . . .

and now we are giving everything to the FA, all the money, but the FA is giving us nothing. It's watered down now, with no commitment to World Heritage listing and no map." This was only the first of many compromises that would follow.

Indeed, over time CI was forced into a classic Cambodian power play, in which NGOs must choose between doing "advocacy" or working "normally" with the government. Advocacy in Cambodia implies risk and moral hazard, as it is taken to mean "anti-government" action (Milne 2017). Cambodian project staff frequently used strong disciplinary narratives to caution those considering advocacy as a strategy. What happened to Global Witness in 2003 was used as a prime example of the consequences of advocacy, as Sok explained: "The role of Global Witness is to complain issues to the government, so the government hate them." For this reason, their staff were attacked, and the NGO was expelled from Cambodia. Thus, CI had little choice but to cooperate with the government, meaning its activities had to comply with the ruling party's wishes.

CI's post-2007 pragmatic and compromising stance had various effects. For instance, it became harder to demand good performance from Khmer staff, according to Western professional notions of following a job description or being motivated. This was particularly an issue among the rangers, who remained beholden to the government agencies from which they had been seconded. Patronage norms and hierarchy governed their behavior, with many staff employed through friendship or kinship networks. This entailed arrangements in which jobs were purchased, alongside staff obligations to provide ongoing payments "up the chain" to one's superiors or patrons.[4] As one Cambodian staff member explained of the rangers: "Many FA get sent here because of their boss. . . . They come here and sleep. . . . They care more about money than conservation." Thus, CI had trouble controlling the behavior of government staff in the program, even though it financed their wages.

Struggles over rangers' performance had been an issue for CI from the outset, resulting in periodic NGO-led overhauls and program restructures. I witnessed one of these in early 2007, which explicitly aimed to boost the "ac-

---

4. Two of my informants explained in detail how one must take out a loan to buy one's position in a government department through a payment to the boss. The loan is then repaid through expected earnings from corruption. FA jobs are expensive because revenues from illegal timber are high. See Paley (2015), for similar accounts of the MoE. See Scopis (2011) on Cambodia's "string economy" more generally.

countability" of rangers. Or, as the CI regional director explained at the time, "We got rid of those rangers who were past their use-by date." He was referring to CI's push to remove some key high-status rangers who had apparently become complacent and lazy on the job. However, this reform was delicate for the FA director Chung, who was under pressure from his superiors to retain certain staff in order to secure government interests within the project. The result was that CI was forced to retain some FA staff it did not want.

Tensions over government accountability therefore remained, and CI soon learned that even corrupt or incompetent government staff were not easily removed from the program. This lesson was dealt to CI in late 2007, when a foreign advisor attempted to fire his government counterpart for suspected dealings in illegal timber. A dramatic conflict then ensued with the counterpart's boss in the FA, who threatened to have the foreigner removed from the conservation program. This moment signaled what was effectively a government takeover of the project, as one expatriate lamented: "If we say to the FA that we will pull out, then maybe there will be some changes, but CI would risk losing its investment. The FA have us wrapped around their little finger." Thus, by the end of 2007, it seemed CI was having to dance to the government's tune.

Of course, a key risk of government control over the project was corruption, especially the abuse of state authority and control over natural resources. No one imagined the scale at which this would unfold by 2009, but there were some early warning signs as the machinery of government gathered strength. Part of the problem emerged from the 2003 restructure of Cambodia's forestry sector (see Forestry Administration 2008), with the formation of provincial forestry cantonments (*khan*). This donor-backed reform created more points for bribe collection, as well as new yet diffuse lines of authority that undermined CI's Phnom Penh–led conservation efforts. In particular, the cantonments began to facilitate illegal logging, backed by powerful elites, and this placed the CI-sponsored rangers under new pressures. For example, when one ranger commander in the northern CCPF reported illegal activity to the FA cantonment in 2007, he was intimidated by them. He told me that he became "scared" to report cases that "the khan did not prefer." Similarly, in Thmar Bang, trouble ensued when CI rangers confiscated a car associated with illegal activity. Apparently, the offenders enjoyed protection from the FA cantonment, which then issued threats against the CI rangers and eventually forced them to release the car.

Brokering and Transforming the Idea 131

These 2007 incidents signaled a new modus operandi, in which state appropriation of resources in the conservation area would be the norm. Cases began to multiply. For example, a company from the distant province of Kampong Thom arrived in the area, without prior warning, yet with a permit in hand for the commercial harvesting of rattan from the protected forest.[5] The company apparently had links "high up" in the government, meaning that its activities could not be curtailed. As one ranger explained: "We cannot stop them because they have a letter from FA. . . . It is too hard to inspect their vehicles. . . . We cannot monitor the company." Thus, the company's destructive and illegal activities, which included industrial harvesting of rattan and other resources like wildlife, proceeded under the noses of the rangers and the villagers.[6] At the same time, Chinese engineers also began appearing in the area, ahead of the construction of three major hydropower dams, which would bring unprecedented environmental destruction (Milne 2015, 2021). By this stage, it was clear that CI's head office had little ability to influence high-level Cambodian government plans for the Cardamom Mountains: the global strategy of a government "partnership" was beginning to unravel.

Despite these developments, CI pursued its organizational interests and investments in Cambodia without pause. For example, CI's conservation agreements were publicly celebrated as a success in 2007 and "scaled up" to all communities in the protected forest by 2009. CI also pursued its goal of creating a conservation trust fund for the Cardamom Mountains, for which a "business plan" was developed (see Starling Resources 2008)[7]. These policy ideas fitted neatly together: a sustainable financing mechanism would allow ongoing payments for the conservation agreements and other conservation costs. Thus, CI held on strongly to its policy vision, in the face of increasingly sinister government-backed resource exploitation. CI's ability to succeed

---

5. According to park rangers, the company was well enough connected to acquire a permit from the FA. In March 2006, the company apparently came to the CCPF, accompanied by CI's former FA manager. The group met with local leaders and got their thumbprints on a consent form to allow the company to operate.

6. Villagers said that if the rattan-harvesting company could not be stopped, then they should at least be employed as laborers to cut the rattan. Instead, the company brought in workers from outside, claiming there was not enough local labor to employ.

7. The trust fund was eventually established in 2016. One quarter of the US$10 million financing goal has been achieved so far. See https://www.conservation.org/projects/cambodias-central-cardamom-protected-forest (accessed February 16, 2022).

would therefore depend on its ability translate its policy ideas into practice. Success would require skillful cross-scalar and cross-cultural brokering, to which my attention now turns.

Brokering the Project Across Cultures and Scales

A major implementation issue for CI's conservation program was the cultural and linguistic divide between foreigners and Khmers. At a basic level, this entailed an encounter between Western ways of doing things, which purported to be meritocratic, individualistic, and rational; and Khmer ways, which were said to be imbued with the cultural practices of hierarchy, face, relationality, and patronage (Bit 1991; Jacobsen and Stuart-Fox 2013; Ledgerwood and Vijghen 2002; O'Leary and Meas 2001). In practice, the interface between Khmer and foreigner worlds was a productive social space, in which contrasting and changing worldviews came together, and in which new identities and meanings were forged (see Long 2001; Tsing 2005). For project purposes, this space involved efforts to translate global policy ideas into field-level actions, on the one hand, and interpretations of project effects, on the other, so that "impacts" or "outcomes" could be demonstrated to the head office and donors. I will now explore how these processes operated within CI's Cambodian project; or, more accurately, how these processes went wrong, leading to disjuncture and dissonance in relation to project intentions, actions, and effects.

Perhaps the most significant issue that shaped project brokering was that none of the CI expatriate staff spoke functional Khmer. For these staff, learning Khmer was a personal choice, given that CI did not require language skills per se. The situation was summed up by the comment of one foreign biologist, who had lived in Cambodia for five years and was still incapable of the most basic exchanges: "I've almost given up learning Khmer."[8] Thus, most interactions between expatriate and Khmer staff occurred in English. As a result, the English-speaking Khmer staff in the project became the primary mediators and brokers between global and local realms. They facilitated nearly all aspects of the foreigners' fieldwork, meaning that the foreigners

---

8. Similarly, another expatriate staff member complained that CI didn't pay for Khmer lessons. The expatriates were apparently happy enough to operate through Cambodian translators.

Brokering and Transforming the Idea

only received information about the field that the brokers deemed necessary or relevant. The foreigners' understandings of the field, therefore, could only ever be partial—being a product of the brokers' discretion. Furthermore, the brokers were the foreigners' mouthpiece, responsible for translating CI's global policy ideas and intentions into Khmer.

This work of Khmer-English language translation was also complicated by the demands of Cambodian hierarchy and the cultural imperative to "give face" to foreigners.[9] With expatriate advisors usually treated as superiors in organizational terms, Khmer staff were often reluctant to provide suggestions or ask questions of them. Indeed, there was an underlying colonial dynamic in these interactions, as one government staffer told me: "Cambodians are very respecting of the barang face. . . . We have a long story with the French." This tradition also accorded status to the Khmer staff who were responsible for facilitating the work of foreigners within the program. Non-English-speaking Khmer staff were in turn unlikely to interact directly with foreign staff unless they were invited to do so by the English-speaking Khmer brokers. This face-saving and respectful treatment of foreigners was highly performative, however, as Nhet explained: "The Khmers respect the foreigner's face only." Indeed, as time progressed, I became aware of the multitude of funny but derogatory nicknames used by the Khmers for each expatriate staff member at CI.

Certainly, some resentment came from the expatriates' high status yet utter dependence upon Khmer translators and counterparts in the field. As one ranger quipped, "Foreigners cannot work without Khmer," even though the foreigners typically earned about ten times more than their local counterparts. This dynamic led to all kinds of absurdities, often occurring when Khmer counterparts lacked either capacity, status, contacts, or motivation to complete the tasks that foreigners asked of them. For example, on one occasion, a foreign biologist complained that there were no bananas to buy in the village. Apparently, her university-educated counterpart from Phnom Penh was unable to work out how to obtain bananas locally, and help was not forthcoming from bemused rangers and villagers. It was a cultural impasse, which was later revealed to me in private when Nhet said, "Give me a truck, and I will return in one hour with a full load of bananas for free!" Although

---

9. While Khmer-English translations are usually language translations, I consider them also to be translations in the Latourian sense (1996), described at the outset of this chapter.

apparently trivial, this example shows how the navigation of cross-cultural spaces—including the establishment of respectful relationships—is a critical factor in determining how transnational conservation happens in practice.

Ultimately, the Khmer brokers whom CI chose to hire and empower determined how cross-cultural navigation occurred, and how the project took shape in the field from 2007. The leading Khmer brokers were Kiry and Chung: their role was to interpret the foreigners' guidance and convey this to Khmer field staff as instructions to follow. As a result, the park rangers and non-English-speaking field staff rarely interacted with CI's expatriate staff, whose roles and function remained a mystery. For one ranger, the foreigners were "scientists who came to see the wildlife," without much concern for protected area management. For another, CI's role in the project was unclear: "I am not sure who makes the plans, but I think maybe the ideas come from Washington." These comments show how Kiry and Chung began to form a closed circuit with the Khmer field staff.

Eventually, CI's utter dependence upon these two brokers led to a rift between Khmer and international realms within the project. Events that I witnessed in early 2007 were illustrative: tensions were high because, at the time, park rangers had not received their salaries for over two months due to administrative delays at CI's US head office. The rangers were surviving on borrowed food from villagers and skimping on basic equipment. Yet, in the midst of this, the rangers had to facilitate two lavish field visits from DC-based technical advisors, some of whom arrived by helicopter. The rangers were outraged, but they did not voice complaint. As one said: "The head-office advisors don't know that we have no salary . . . and we do not dare to ask barang for our money. . . . We asked our Khmer boss, and they said, 'Please wait!'" Thus, the Khmer program managers carefully controlled and mediated all interactions between foreigners and the field, especially to save face and give a good impression. This gave rise to an intricate and multiscalar project politics, in which the head office's inability to obtain information about field operations became a conspicuous element.

THE POLITICS OF BROKERING AND TRANSLATION

Brokering is inherently political because it involves knowledge production and control over information (see Lewis and Mosse 2006). For CI in Cambodia, the two Khmer brokers, Kiry and Chung, were effectively accorded interpretive authority over the program from about 2007 onward, with Kiry remaining at the helm after Chung's departure in 2009. Once the pair assumed their new positions—Kiry as CI country director and Chung as FA Protected Forest manager—they worked hard to control information that circulated through the project, especially interpretations that English-speaking Khmer staff provided to foreigners. Soon, these intermediary Khmer staff realized that they should not share information with foreigners that might be controversial or embarrassing for their new Khmer bosses. In short, Kiry and Chung sought to control all official accounts about the field that circulated through CI. This in turn provided them with the means to control project activities.

Kiry and Chung's strategy in part was to avoid past experiences when the program had suffered from troublemaking brokers and interpreters. For example, during the period 2002–2005, one powerful broker was said to have undermined CI's relationship with the government by deliberately misrepresenting CI's motives and actions. Kiry used this example to emphasize the importance of his brokering role between CI and the government, which he likened to being a "middleman" in the Khmer style: "The rangers never hear directly from barang, only from the middleman. . . . He is the one who represents the NGO to the field. But before [in 2005], the middleman created conflict and blamed barang to make his own power. . . . Conflict comes from the individual, not the institution." Thus, Kiry understood well his interpretive and political power as CI's main broker in Cambodia. Concomitantly, he understood CI's vulnerabilities in the face of powerful government interests.

As I have indicated, the chief source of the brokers' power was that CI's expatriate and head-office staff depended on them for essential information and connections with the Cambodian realm of the project. This included interfacing with villagers, rangers, government staff, and other influential stakeholders: a Cambodian milieu generally inaccessible to foreigners. This dynamic was particularly pronounced in the field, where project meetings were held in Khmer and foreigners were reliant upon selective and minimal translations. Some Khmer staff resented the foreigners' dependence, but they were willing to share information when good personal relationships existed. Most of the foreign staff instinctively knew this, but they found it difficult to establish relationships based on trust, especially with their government counterparts. CI's expatriate regional director expressed frustration about this: "We just need an FA person who will listen to us and tell us what's going on." He was referring to ongoing struggles over access to information and field knowledge in the project.

Indeed, it was difficult and sometimes risky for CI's foreign staff to discover what was really happening in the field, beyond Kiry's and Chung's official interpretations. For example, in 2007, one foreign advisor attempted to establish his own set of Khmer informants within the project so that he could monitor the rangers' performance independently from formal project channels and investigate corruption allegations. Apparently, the foreigner had secretly enlisted informants from each ranger station, with the assistance of his own English-speaking counterpart. When Kiry discovered what was going on, he took swift disciplinary action. When explaining this to me, Kiry accused the rogue translator of disloyalty: "He is the man who always relates to foreigners, but never to Khmer. Foreigners like him because he gives them information, but he doesn't participate on the Khmer side, the Khmer way." Thus, the Khmer directors were vigilant in their efforts to present a coherent view of field activities to CI's foreign staff.

This vigilance eventually determined who was engaged to do Khmer-English language translations within the project. Kiry and Chung knew that the personal views of a given translator could critically shape the information that foreigners received, which had implications for their control over the project. Thus, they began to insert their preferred translators into project processes, especially when there was head office involvement, such as in the implementation of the conservation agreements. Furthermore, at critical interpretive moments—such as when the global Conservation Stewards Program director Maria visited the field—they were present themselves to ensure that translations matched their official version of field realities. In this way, the head office's view of the field was sanctioned by Kiry and Chung. Together they ensured that controversy, complexity, or failure were hidden, with problematic information being filtered out.

REINTERPRETING AND SIMPLIFYING THE LOCAL

In the churn of communication between CI's head office and the field, which included emails, Skype meetings, field visits, and the production of shared documents, the Khmer-English translations that became habitual also worked to establish particular understandings of the field. That is, the dominant translations used about villagers, communities, livelihoods, farms, landscapes, and forests all combined to "produce the local" within the project realm (Appadurai 1996). As implementation proceeded, these translations also began to respond to project needs by emulating CI's policy language. For example, the conservation agreements model demanded certain highly bounded forms of information about the field, usually in response to questions directed at villagers from the head office, like: How many hectares of farmland do you have? How many hectares of forest do you clear each year? Is the community happy with the agreement? Achieving simple answers to these questions, when each was potentially a Pandora's box, entailed a range of judgments, simplifications, and representations, all carefully controlled by the key project brokers.

Another factor in these knowledge-making processes, from 2007 onward, was the rise in prominence of government translators, inserted into the project by Kiry and Chung. This meant that Nhet, who was formerly the foreigners' translator of choice in community engagement matters, was replaced by a new FA officer, Aung, whose compliance and discipline better suited the new Khmer directors. With this embrace of government functionaries in the project, the local relationships and field knowledge of CI's original nongovernment community engagement team were sidelined. As Nhet observed, lamenting the new top-down, government-friendly style, "Aung and Kiry take information and ideas from us. . . . They take it to the office to make a plan . . . then they tell us to implement their plan." This dynamic was a source of great frustration for him and like-minded others.

This project transition, from expatriate to Khmer control, also enabled government-led interpretations of local landscapes and people in the Cardamom Mountains to dominate CI's knowledge and practice. This meant that certain field complexities were erased, while villagers' voices were simplified or misunderstood (see Li 2002; Sachedina 2010). This problem was most acute in the domain of community engagement. For example, *sahakoum*, the Khmer word for "community," does not translate into English in a way that matches usual Western concepts of communities as self-evident or cohesive groups of local people (Agrawal and Gibson 1999). Rather, sahakoum refers to a more formal organization of people, like the Communist-era cooperatives that villagers remembered painfully well. Indicative of this interpretation in Khmer, villagers regularly said that CI had "come to make the community here," referring to the formation of NGO-backed committees, as noted elsewhere in Cambodia (Pasgaard and Nielson 2016). The Khmer translation for "participate" (*choroam*) was also problematic because it usually referred to attendance at meetings, rather than participation in the Western democratic sense. Thus, what the head office imagined to be "community participation" in the field was something else entirely.

Important nuances about local land use were also left out of communications with the head office, which impacted the design of the conservation agreements. This especially came into play with notions of "farm" and "forest." With government logics dominating the translation process, the landscape soon became interpreted according to a binary of forest and farmland. This occurred despite local villagers' rich descriptions for a range of landscape gradations between farm, fallow, and different forest types in the context of shifting agriculture, including scrub (*prey bos*), old forest (*prey chas*), newly regrown forest (*prey thmei*), fallow shifting agriculture plot (*chamka chas*), fallow regrowth with grass (*songrai*), and so on. Unfortunately, these local words were ignored in official project translations and maps. As a result, the conservation agreements effectively reproduced the FA's simplified view of the landscape: a singular category of forest as Forest Estate was used, while villagers' rights became restricted to permanent paddy land.

These examples illustrate how language translation and knowledge filtering can have political and material consequences in the field. Translations that simplify landscape and community participation are not trivial. Rather, they are implicated in struggles over property and resources—especially when conservation measures activate conflicts between state claims over forest and local customary use of forested land (Milne 2012). It is unlikely that CI's head-office staff ever reflected on the translation politics that they activated. Rather, in their drive to see the conservation agreements implemented successfully, they readily consumed and legitimized the knowledge that was provided to them by Aung, Kiry, and Chung. Unfortunately, this knowledge privileged government agendas, while also serving superficial and authoritatively produced accounts of project success in the field.

THE PRODUCTION OF PROJECT SUCCESS

The final aspect of knowledge production that I observed within CI was concerned with the portrayal of project success. This mainly involved interpretations of field impacts for external audiences, such as donors, various stakeholders at CI's head office, other NGOs, and the public. In this sense, CI's project brokers were not just translating across cross-cultural and cross-scalar interfaces, they were also producing knowledge to meet organizational or corporate needs (see Mosse 2005). For the conservation agreements, CI's carefully controlled and curated knowledge production was led by Kiry in Phnom Penh and Maria at the head office. Kiry provided regular information to Maria, including monthly reports of successfully completed field activities. These reports typically included pictures of villagers participating in project activities and short summaries that omitted controversy or discussion of challenges. This pattern was apparently true across CI in general, as one expatriate biologist noted: "The field's reporting to head office is glossy, like reporting to a donor."

However, the presence of glossy reporting also led to moments of dissonance, when unofficial information from the field reached the head office through nonroutine or informal channels. For example, in late 2006, a significant instance of forest clearing was not included in Kiry's monthly report to Maria, even though it was a major violation of one of the conservation agreements and should have been dealt with under the agreement sanctions (see table 2, chapter 3). Instead, the clearing was detected by two foreign biologists during a CI surveillance flight, after which the data were reported to Maria—an embarrassing incident for Kiry, which he eventually deflected. Similar problems occurred when an expatriate law enforcement advisor observed illegal electric fishing at the Areng River crocodile sanctuary in 2007, also protected under a conservation agreement. These findings, too, were reported directly to Maria, and Kiry again had to defend his implementation of the conservation agreements, which were meant to involve monitoring and penalties for nonperformance.

For Kiry, these incidents were examples of recalcitrant foreigners who had bypassed him in their communications with head office. He complained to me that they had used "unofficial" sources in their reports to Maria. In relation to the land-clearing incident, he said: "Why do they report to head office before they report to me? They see burning, but they never check on the ground . . . maybe it's an old farm? Maybe it's in the PLUP [land-use] map? But they never check. This is very hard . . . sometimes I want to kill myself when they do like that." To be fair, Kiry's frustration over the foreign biologists' lack of knowledge about local land-use and farming practices was legitimate. The ignorance of foreigners had caused unfortunate false alarms in the past, when villagers sought to reclaim their old swidden fields, only to be accused of forest encroachment. Nevertheless, Kiry's chief concern was in controlling the information about project performance that reached the head office.

After these incidents, honest information flows that might have revealed flaws or weaknesses in the project were further restricted by the Khmer leadership. Meanwhile, those who destabilized official interpretations quickly found themselves in conflict with Kiry and Chung. In this context, Nhet commented on the Khmer directors: "They are always reporting good news. . . . This is not really transparency in relationships." Yet, as Nhet explained, this practice is typical in Cambodian organizations, where staff always try to look good as a way to save face and sometimes to advance their own interests. An infamous historical example of this was during the Khmer Rouge period, when field commanders drastically overreported local rice yields to Phnom Penh—enhancing their own power but leading to local starvation in the process (Bashi 2007). While the case of the conservation project is not as extreme as this, it entailed similar practices of information filtering up the chain to serve the interests of powerful individuals.

Information, however, is always produced with an audience in mind, and this is where CI's head office became complicit in the social production of success that I have described. By not scrutinizing Khmer-English translations, or seeking alternative accounts of the field, CI's foreign and expatriate staff also participated in what became a highly politicized and undemocratic form of knowledge production. It was CI's technical advisory staff who exercised choices here: they chose which translator to believe; they empowered some brokers over others; and they ultimately privileged certain versions of events over others. In this way, they obtained an interpretation of the field that met their organizational needs, being aligned with CI's project imperatives and policy ideas like the conservation agreements. Just as Mosse observed in international development, this project was a "system for the production and control of information" (2001, 176). Yet it was also a system that involved selective listening and knowledge filtering at all levels, meaning that the production of non-knowledge (McGoey 2012) was also at play. I shall now describe how these messy knowledge-making and translation processes led to the transformation of CI's conservation agreements model in practice.

Transformation of the Policy Idea in Practice

Having illustrated rising government influence over CI's project in Cambodia, as well as the contingent and political nature of project brokering across cultures, languages, and scales, I now examine how this affected the conservation agreements. Ultimately, the conservation agreements were transformed in practice so that they no longer resembled the original PES-like policy model, which I described in chapter 2. The agreements acquired a life of their own in Cambodia, never to become the policy instrument envisaged by economists at the head office, who remained largely oblivious to what was happening in the field. I shall now illustrate four key dynamics that produced these field-level distortions of the policy model: state territorialization of forested land; coercion of local communities; flexibility in agreement enforcement; and absorption of CI's policy ideas into local development visions.

STATE PROPERTY, NOT COMMUNITY RIGHTS

The first distortion of CI's policy was due to strong government influence in the project. This occurred as the conservation agreements were gradually subsumed into the underlying protected area management regime, which involved government control over the forest through territorialization and law enforcement. This meant that one of the original distinguishing features of PES—that it should be a market-inspired *alternative* to top-down regulation—was lost. Instead, the agreements were reframed as a complement to law enforcement. As Sok commented, "If law enforcement is strong, then we don't need an agreement with villagers." Similarly, his park ranger colleague thought that local people's participation in the agreements was only due to law enforcement: "If there is no law enforcement, then maybe the people will not join the community program. . . . It's like the fish in the river, we have to have something to chase them to go into the net, that's a Cambodian saying." These remarks reflect an underlying and distinctly Cambodian emphasis on state legal authority within the project.

As a result, government objectives like achieving control over the Forest Estate crept into the conservation agreements. For example, once the community commitment of "no forest clearing" was made, the FA soon rearticulated this as protection of the Forest Estate. This made the head office's notion of compensating communities for "avoided deforestation" almost nonsensical, even though Maria and Jan regularly used this REDD+ concept. Furthermore, as if to reinforce their control, the FA rangers went about demarcating the Forest Estate *during* the 2007 agreement negotiations in a separate CI-funded activity. The agreements therefore appeared to reward villagers for not breaking the law, rather than providing compensation for customary resource rights forgone—a problem that created subtle yet dispossessory property effects for local communities (Milne 2012).

This lack of common understanding between CI and FA over who owned the forest led to unresolved and frustrating exchanges about the conservation agreements in practice. For example:

> **Maria**: Is there a map? How do we know how much the villagers are cutting each year?
> **Chung**: Since the permanent state forest was demarcated there is no cutting.
> **Maria**: But how much forest are we protecting with the agreements?
> **Chung**: It's hard to answer this question. [silence]

Ultimately, the FA exploited this confusion and used the conservation agreements to expand and reinforce its claims. This meant that CI's investment in the agreements provided no additional benefit for conservation, other than to facilitate or legitimize the FA's law enforcement. In other words, while CI's head office and donors believed that they were paying local communities for forest protection, in practice they were paying villagers to comply with the Forestry Law while strengthening the government's territorial agenda in the process. Government manipulation of the foreigner's tools is a familiar theme in Cambodia (Cock 2016; Hughes 2003), and this case is just another example. A key factor here was CI's failure to engage with the complexity of local property relations, especially Indigenous and customary claims to forested land. Had CI championed local resource rights, pushing for full and correct implementation of the Forestry Law, then outcomes may have differed. For example, at the very least, local claims might have been heard or government officials might have had to pause and explain their actions. As it was, CI's silence enabled authoritarian conduct and state appropriation of resources.

COERCION, NOT COMMUNITY CHOICE

The second dynamic that transformed the conservation agreements policy idea related to the notion of "community choice." This was another critical element of the policy model, as the agreements are meant to be voluntary market-like transactions. However, agreement implementation in Cambodia was a top-down affair that involved mainly instrumental engagements with local villagers. For example, in March 2007, before the signing of five new agreements in five communes, CI held a series of "negotiation meetings" with the local leaders and committees. These meetings, which I attended as an ethnographer, led to decisions on the conservation commitments and benefit packages for each commune (see table 2, chapter 3). Yet much of the content of these rather formal meetings was based on prior *informal discussions* between CI's field staff and select commune leaders, particularly between Nhet and the commune chiefs. Thus, the apparently inclusive "negotiation meetings" really hinged on private prior negotiations between individuals, rather than any wider deliberation or consultation. This is a familiar scenario in Cambodia, where mainstream notions of participation in the development industry face a range of cognitive, cultural, and structural barriers (Knowles-Morrison 2010; see also Hickey and Mohan 2004).

Furthermore, the way in which the agreements were finalized and publicly signed in 2007 was far from participatory. After the signing ceremonies, I debriefed with villagers and learned that CI's Khmer team had drafted the conservation agreements themselves, without local consultation or circulation of drafts. This meant that the agreements were brought to the field in their final form on the very day of the signing ceremonies. Once proceedings had begun, local representatives were handed the microphone and asked to read the conservation agreements out loud, for all villagers to hear, for their information. No one in the village had seen the agreements' contents before this moment, nor was this an invitation to engage or negotiate: it was assumed that they had already heard of the proposed conservation measures and benefit packages on the grapevine. And so the ceremony was a scripted and formal public event, presided over by local government authorities and senior CI staff—a fait accompli.

Later, in field reports to the head office, the signing ceremonies were portrayed in glowing photographs of crowds of villagers clapping and smiling in front of the agreement signatories. These photos reached the CSP global newsletter and CI's website (see Milne 2009). Adjacent to the images online were links for viewers to donate to the conservation agreements, like paying for environmental services. This provides a stark example of the dissonance that can emerge between head office images of success and local field realities about which head office staff are largely unaware. No one sounded the alarm in Cambodia—perhaps this reflected the fact that "community choice," in a liberal or democratic sense, is generally hard to realize in Cambodian rural villages. More pertinently, no one in the head office was asking questions about what lay behind the photos that they received.

FLEXIBILITY, NOT CONDITIONALITY

The third area of misunderstanding in the conservation agreements related to the notion of conditionality. Again, this is an essential conceptual element in the policy model: conservation agreements reward conservation performance, and they sanction or penalize nonperformance. However, in the Cambodian context this was difficult to achieve due to the cultural norms of avoiding conflict, saving face, and respecting powerful people. These norms meant that the agreements could not be strictly enforced without straining field-level relationships between project staff, village leaders, and other influential local actors. The result was a degree of flexibility in enforcement, whereby the rangers and CI field staff charged with monitoring agreement compliance used a discretionary combination of strictness and accommodation, following classic Cambodian style (Jacobsen and Stuart-Fox 2013; Luco 2002).

This double standard in enforcement inevitably operated in favor of the rich and powerful. For example, in 2007, villagers alleged that the most powerful man in the district, the tycoon Lim Long, had blatantly violated the conservation agreements for crocodile and dragon fish protection. They alleged that he had commissioned a team of nonlocal fishermen to collect a large quantity of highly prized "black fish" from the Areng River for his own consumption. Villagers complained that the fishermen had broken all of the fishing restrictions stipulated in the agreements, taking over 200 kilos of fish. As one local elder remarked, "Long's men caught all of the fish, by lighting fires and using nets to close off the small streams." Although everyone knew about the incident, its powerful instigator was not confronted, and no one recorded the violation of the conservation agreement by powerful outsiders. Thus, agreement implementation was not rigorous, and this was unfair to villagers who abided by the rules.

Flexible enforcement of the agreements also occurred because CI's field staff wanted to maintain good relationships with local communities. Cambodian staff took a gentle approach to agreement compliance. As Kiry explained: "In the first year, maybe we can get 80 percent of people to agree, little bit, little bit, and then the next year they can start to change more. But we cannot ask everyone to change 100 percent with the first year of the agreement." Thus, agreement conditionality was notional only, and there was no strict expectation among project staff that villagers would comply fully. This illustrates how theoretical notions of contractual obligation and accountability in the PES model, which provided the basis for the conservation agreements, broke down in the context of complex field relations. Consequently, the policy model's stipulations of conditionality and performance-based payments were lost in translation.

TRANSFORMATION THROUGH CONTEXTUALIZATION

The final factor that transformed the conservation agreement model in practice was how it was integrated into Khmer visions of development and progress. Mosse (2005) uses the notion of "contextualization" (Latour 1996) to explore this phenomenon in international development projects. He proposes that the need to establish and maintain buy-in from project stakeholders leads to the production of locally appealing "project narratives," which are often far removed from donor or head office intentions (Mosse 2005). For the conservation agreements, this occurred as CI's Cambodian staff tried to comprehend the new policy model, and then explain it to government officials and villagers, whose buy-in they needed.

Various misunderstandings resulted as the complicated technical notions of sustainable financing and incentives-based conservation made their way into the local vernacular. For example, most community engagement staff appeared to interpret CI's new policy model through old narratives of integrated conservation and development. As one field officer said: "We should give money, to give villagers jobs, to change from slash-and-burn farming to modern agriculture. We can educate them on how to do that and provide equipment." CI's local community program staff also believed that they should help villagers to find "alternative and sustainable livelihoods" in order to conserve forest. Little did they know that the head office was trying to erase these ICDP-like notions with its new policy idea (see chapter 2). Field staff also expressed concerns about the sustainability of payments. As Nhet asked: "What will happen to the people when CI leaves? What about jobs for local people?" Thus, CI's Cambodian team expressed both doubt and misunderstanding about the underlying principles of the conservation agreements.

Furthermore, as these (mis)interpretations of the conservation agreements were translated into ground-level actions, surprising things happened. For example, Maria had agreed on a plan to "restore" the cardamom forest in Thmar Bang as the basis for one conservation agreement. Her idea was for the ancient forest patch of about 200 hectares to be protected and rejuvenated to its original state: an old-growth agroforest where cardamom (*kravanh*) grew for traditional harvesting. Yet local staff and some villagers interpreted this idea as "developing" the forest to "make the forest beautiful" by planting new cardamom in straight rows, as though it were a plantation. This misunderstanding existed for months before the head office realized the extent of divergence from the original plan. It seemed that CI's global idea of forest as a wild and natural space had been utterly reinterpreted.

Such distortions of the original policy model abounded, and the head office had little capacity to observe or even find out what was going on. As a doctoral student in the field, I often reported my observations back to CI's head office informally. This was welcomed at the time because there was an increasing sense that the Cambodian project leadership was filtering information from the field. The head office was aware of the knowledge gaps that it faced back then, but its appetite for detail would soon wane with time.

Conclusion: Project Deviance and Its Implications

This chapter has explored how CI pursued its goals in Cambodia, and how its policy-driven intentions were both constrained and transformed by local conditions. Having had privileged insider access to CI's work in Cambodia from 2002 to 2007, I was able to observe how the project evolved over time. I especially saw how the project relied on key brokers who "translated" (Latour 1996) policy ideas and information across scales and between cultures, languages, and organizations. In short, the project became a multisited system of knowledge production, in which the usually discrete categories of NGO and government, or global and local, were hard to distinguish. Processes of brokering and translation therefore maintained project coherence, especially through brokers' control over information flows and project narratives (see Lewis and Mosse 2006 for a similar account of global development).

For CI, two key challenges made the translation of its policy ideas highly problematic in Cambodia. First was the rising influence of government in the project from 2007, and second was the cross-cultural context, in which foreign staff depended heavily on Khmer brokers to interpret local project realities and translate their ideas. These conditions meant that the processes of translation within CI's project were highly political and partial, resulting in a transformation of policy ideas and NGO intentions in practice. For example, the theoretical underpinnings of CI's PES-like policy idea—to use community-level agreements as voluntary, performance-based mechanisms for biodiversity conservation—broke down in the field to become something else. This is because, through implementation, the agreements became enmeshed in state agendas, local development narratives, and endemic Cambodian tendencies to bypass community participation and favor elite interests.

While such policy transformations may be anticipated and even mitigated by savvy transnational operators, the problem here was that CI did not fully or formally recognize how its global ideas had become distorted in Cambodia. This in turn meant that CI could not address the looming and insidious implications of the transformations that were under way—especially for the rights of Indigenous people and ecosystem conditions in the Cardamom Mountains. At fault here was not a handful of poor decisions or inaccurate reports but a systemic and institutionalized preference for not knowing about the social and political dimensions of what was really happening in the field. In other words, CI's inability to acquire information about field activities was a fundamental weakness, caused by organizational decisions about who to hire, who to empower, and who to believe. Thus, what I observed in 2007 was a situation in which two skilled Khmer brokers routinely translated CI's policy ideas to the field, and then filtered information back up the chain, to ensure an image of project success and coherence for head-office audiences.

While convenient for most project actors at the time, these circumstances exhibit what Diane Vaughan called the "normalization of deviance" (1996). In this case, CI's organizational culture and transnational practices led to a profound disconnection between the head office and the field site in Cambodia. Over time, this meant that CI had limited control over the outcomes of its project in the Cardamom Mountains, mainly because it possessed only fragmented knowledge of what was happening in the field. For this reason, illegal logging was able to take hold in the project area from 2009, building to a crisis point in 2012 (see chapter 6). In short, the conditions for crisis were established through long-term underlying institutional patterns, described in this chapter.

Finally, having illustrated CI's transnational project processes and their unintended outcomes in Cambodia, I turn to what this means for global conservation practice. In terms of epistemology, this case shows how an overreliance on knowledge that is thin, or rather not "thick" (Geertz 2008), can be dangerous in complex transnational projects. For instance, thin project knowledge can become "virtual" (Carrier and West 2009), meaning that it is disconnected from field realities and local voices. When this happens, and "non-knowledge" (McGoey 2012) begins to circulate within projects, an array of practical and ethical dilemmas arise. For example, it becomes hard to respond to potential problems in the field, like increasing government control or the erosion of community participation, when the institutional ability to "see" these things does not exist (after Scott 1998). The socio-nature that emerges from these conditions, which I call corporate nature, is therefore foundationally based on practices of disconnection, including knowledge making and project design that are purposefully not situated. The next two chapters illustrate how corporate nature, *as* disconnection, generates an array of risks and ethical problems for global conservation.

Chapter 5

The Idea in Village Life

Fieldwork break, October 2007, Thmar Bang village shop:
I am sitting with Nhet in the afternoon, debriefing quietly after our last round
of research interviews with village leaders. With some melancholy, he reflects
upon what has become of CI's Community Engagement Program—a suite of
activities that we had initiated together in 2002 but now no longer controlled.
He says to me, stirring his iced coffee and gazing off into the distance: "There
is one body but two hands. . . . Now community engagement is like this: in one
hand the pen and the other hand a gun. It means one face talks to the people,
but the other face is the Forestry Administration. It's like I build the house,
and now the government moves in."

This chapter examines the fate of CI's policy idea in village life through an
exploration of local perceptions and experiences of the conservation agreements. My focus here is on the encounters and engagements between CI and
local villagers in the project area—the two parties who, on paper at least,
entered PES-like contracts for the provision of conservation services. By examining the local social effects and village "imaginaries" (West 2006) associated with the conservation agreements, I complete my analysis of the life
cycle of CI's policy idea, having covered global policy making in chapter 2 and
transnational policy implementation in chapter 4. My aim here is to maintain
the line of inquiry around what happens to global policy ideas when they are
"contextualized" or "translated" (Latour 1996) into settings like rural Cambodia. We have already seen how CI's policy idea was transformed in practice,

through miscommunications, mistranslations, and government manipulation of project processes. Now I scale down further, to consider CI's policy idea in village life, where the full transformative power of place comes into view.

The simple version of this story is that village life—including the intricacies of Khmer political culture, Indigenous livelihoods, and post-conflict state formation—worked to produce local project effects that were a far cry from CI's original policy intentions. This perspective reveals how CI's global policy idea was utterly alien in the local context, and therefore unimplementable without a degree of performance or virtualism. Yet policy breakdown of this kind can still generate project "side effects" or unintended consequences that deserve serious attention, especially when the elaboration of state power is involved (Ferguson 1994). One way to consider this problem of side effects is through the notion of "environmentality" (Agrawal 2005; Bryant 2002), in which local people become environmental subjects for government. However, such interpretations often fail to allow for local agency and the productive power of "friction" in new governance processes (Tsing 2005, see also Cepek 2011; West 2006). Given this, I employ both perspectives to explore the side effects of CI's community engagements in the CCPF.

Importantly, when it comes to project side effects, mainstream global conservation is often poorly equipped to detect them. For example, conventional NGO ways to measure impact, like household surveys or rapid assessments, are far too structured to observe what is really happening (West, Igoe, and Brockington 2006). Moreover, as I have begun to show, there is a certain unwillingness to see complexity on the part of global conservation NGOs, whose actions tend to produce thin and simplified forms of knowledge. This chapter therefore delves further into the complexity of encounters between NGOs and villagers, which are so often hidden from view. In Cambodia, these encounters involved global conservation agendas interacting with authoritarian state making and pronounced power asymmetries on the ground. Such circumstances should prompt questions about the ethics of global conservation in practice. For example, to what extent can conservation NGOs detect and manage the outcomes of their activities in authoritarian settings? To what extent can NGOs be made responsible for the side effects of their projects, which may include the erosion of civil society and Indigenous rights? How can lines be drawn between what is and is not an NGO's business or moral responsibility in contexts like Cambodia?

To explore these questions, this chapter attends to CI's community engagement practices in the Cardamom Mountains. First, I examine how CI framed and managed its engagements with local communities, mainly through a set of commune-level committees. These committees were essential for CI's ability to map its policy model onto the local realm, to make "the community" a single actor, capable of entering a conservation agreement. Second, I explore how this work of committee making in rural Cambodia attracted the interest of local authorities and the ruling party, who were intent on controlling potentially subversive political forces. After some contestation, this dynamic ultimately produced a more closed political space for local villagers, and a series of ethical dilemmas for CI to navigate. Yet CI responded not with concern but with project practices that effectively ignored what was happening. In this light, the final section of this chapter explores villagers' perceptions of CI and the conservation agreements. Here I find a range of contradictory and strategic local responses: revealing, in short, a policy idea with a life of its own.

Project Logics for Engaging "the Local"

The design, intent, and practice of community engagement in conservation matters deeply for social and ecological justice (Brosius, Tsing, and Zerner 2005). Policy models, log-frame assumptions, hiring choices, and resource allocations for fieldwork are all political aspects of project implementation, which shape the productive interface between communities and conservation. For CI in the Cardamom Mountains, most community engagement action was focused on committee making, which enabled local land-use planning and conservation agreement activities to unfold. Committee making is rather like a necessary evil in mainstream conservation and development practice (Agrawal and Gibson 1999; Cleaver 1999). As a form of local participation it has the potential to be empowering, but it can also be "tyrannical" (Hickey and Mohan 2004), or it can even lead to environmental subject making (Agrawal 2005). Here I examine the origins and logics behind this instrumental form of community engagement in the context of CI's project in the Cardamom Mountains. Importantly, I show how the effects of committee making in places like Cambodia are often far deeper and more complex than one might anticipate.

EARLY COMMITTEE MAKING, 2002–2006

CI's initial community engagement efforts were ad hoc, focused mainly on resolving conflicts between communities and park rangers (see chapter 3).

As the Community Engagement Program began to grow, however, more formal arrangements were required for the sake of the program's visibility and credibility—especially to garner support from villagers, government officials, and CI's head office. Initially, the program gained momentum by piggybacking on wider policy processes in Cambodia at the time, the most prominent being the participatory land use planning (PLUP) initiative.

A key goal of PLUP was "to build up or use existing communal and village structures and committees as a frame for participatory processes" (Kirsch 2005, 24). In practice, this meant creating local committees for natural resource management that could function alongside the newly formed commune councils.[1] Instructions for committee making were provided in a "PLUP manual" that stated that the purpose of the committees was to represent "civil society" and enable "community participation" (Rock 2001). However, the PLUP manual was written mainly by foreign advisors whose key assumption was that, with strong NGO assistance, the PLUP committees would be able to represent local people's interests, without government interference. Ultimately, this idealized notion of democratic participation was unachievable.

According to the PLUP manual, each committee would be comprised of the following positions and functions, arranged hierarchically: a committee chief, two deputy chiefs, a secretary or treasurer, and others responsible for conflict resolution, community awareness raising, and patrolling. It was a predictable NGO formula. Each committee was to have around ten democratically elected members who were "ordinary villagers," without government affiliation, with one committee to be elected per commune. There was also a requirement for at least one or two women on each committee. For NGOs across the country, including CI, the PLUP manual was followed like a recipe book to elect what became known as the Commune Natural Resource Management Committees (CNRMCs).

This widespread implementation, however, did not give rise to a new civil society in Cambodia. While the PLUP manual promoted community participation, it was careful in stating that the new committees should "advise the commune councils on natural resource management . . . as its assistant."

---

1. Commune councils were first elected in 2002 as part of Cambodia's government decentralization program, backed by the United Nations Development Program, among other major donors.

The committees therefore had no official capacity or authority to implement land-use plans, but they were expected to represent villagers' interests in the planning process. At the time in Cambodia, with democratization through the commune councils being a fresh and strong possibility, this seemed like a reasonable idea.

Buying into this prospect, I led CI's early efforts to implement PLUP and elect CNRMCs in the five communes of Thmar Bang district, starting in early 2003. It was a major logistical undertaking, involving a team of five Khmer staff who worked tirelessly. For my part, I worked with the team to incorporate notions of community rights and empowerment into the process. Still rather naïve about Cambodia, I channeled notions of Indigenous co-management into the local context, imagining that one day communities of the Cardamom Mountains would be official custodians of their ancestral lands. Until I left my role with CI Cambodia in 2005, I made these ideals explicit in the project's community engagement strategies. It seemed worth striving for, even though the project was beginning to face challenging political realities.

By 2006, there were five committees operating in CI's target area for the conservation agreements. The committee members were more educated than most villagers, as they needed to be literate. In general, they were considered to be "good, ordinary people," as one local leader explained. Accordingly, committee membership remained quite stable, in part due to the potential benefits of being an elected member, such as NGO per diems, status in the community, and influence over local land-use decisions. Furthermore, a revolving door soon opened between the committees and the nascent commune councils, with several members of the former being elected to the latter in the commune council elections of 2007 and 2012. The committees, as leadership structures, therefore tended to reflect the underlying moral order and hierarchy of each village—a pattern seen in development projects elsewhere in Cambodia (Hughes 2003; Ledgerwood and Vijghen 2002).

ENTER THE GLOBAL POLICY IDEA

With the establishment of the Conservation Stewards Program in DC, and its substantial new investment in Cambodia in 2006, the community engagement team became increasingly responsive to its new and now primary main benefactor. This meant following a new set of guidelines for community engagement, which were provided to the Cambodian team by CI's head office as part of its global "procedures manual" for the conservation agreements. The manual gave instructions to field staff on how they should "engage" with communities, referred to as "the stewards." Avoiding the potential complexities of place and politics, the manual instructed staff as follows: "Begin community engagement by transparently *building a relationship* with the potential stewards or by selecting a partner who already has a good relationship . . . transparently design and *formalize an agreement* . . . punctually meet commitments and facilitate the steward in meeting theirs . . . ensure a relationship with the steward that is based on meeting a common objective rather than being adversarial."

If only community engagement could be so straightforward. Alas, the manual did not reflect international literature and experience on participation in conservation and development (e.g., Brosius, Tsing, and Zerner 2005; Hickey and Mohan 2004). Rather, the word "participation" featured only once in the entire document, as though it snuck in by accident.[2] A close reading of the manual instead suggested that participatory processes were not something that CI considered itself to be responsible for—this was apparently the domain of local "partners" and "implementers."

This subtle outsourcing of local facilitation work is akin to outsourcing the complicated work of building relationships to people and place—a key trope in the corporate form of global conservation. The CSP manual's references to how third-party "implementers" would "carry out support activities" for community engagement like "building the steward's capacity" and "building a solid relationship with the steward" are indicative of CI's view. In addition, the manual recommended that field staff identify a "community champion" or charismatic local leader, who could do "consensus building among community groups." This tactic subtly displaced the need for formal participatory processes, since community representation could apparently be achieved de facto through the "community champion." Thus, CI's policy model discursively outsourced relationship building with communities, along with potential responsibilities that might flow from this, such as ad-

---

2. The word "participation" featured as follows: "The management should consider the stewards' rights, culture, and skills . . . [the agreement] should be developed with the participation of the steward, as well as other relevant actors."

dressing local resource rights. While most CSP investments conformed to the model, the project in Cambodia was different because CI was already in the so-called implementer role, due to its preexisting Community Engagement Program. Even so, CI still failed to acknowledge or take responsibility for the complexities of community engagement, as I show below.

The arrival of the CSP in Cambodia was a turning point for community engagement in the Cardamom Mountains. With the prospect of negotiating conservation agreements, a suite of new staff were engaged, and project approaches began to change. In particular, the purpose of the committees came to be viewed differently: the committees were no longer institutions for community empowerment but instead were reframed as vehicles for CI to achieve its objectives. For example, CI Cambodia's 2005 concept note for potential CSP investments stated that the committees "have already provided the entry point for negotiating preliminary conservation incentive agreements." The proposal went on to identify the committees as CI's "institutional partners" for implementing the agreements, arguing that working through the committees would "decrease the transaction costs" of community engagement. In this way, the original intentions of CI's committee making were eroded and rephrased into the economics-based policy language of the head office.

In subsequent years, CI's instrumental approach only sharpened as the agreements became the primary mode of community engagement. Most notably, the committee's tasks became oriented toward *service provision*, following the contractual obligations of the agreements. For example, in the 2007 agreements, committees received a "terms of reference" statement from CI that described their roles and responsibilities. This included a list of tasks to be performed in exchange for a monthly administration fee, including allocation of the compensation package to villagers, running the community ranger program to help enforce the agreements, and reporting of "illegal activity" and "violations" back to CI. The contractual nature of the committees' work was further reinforced by conditionalities on the administration fee. That is, if the committees failed to deliver, then they would not be paid their monthly fee. This illustrates a narrowing of participatory space through the agreements, as the committees were not invited to define their role in the project, nor was there deliberation over how they might represent people and nature more broadly.

Over time, the committees became synonymous with project notions of "the local stewards" and "the community." This meant that the committees' willingness to sign the conservation agreements was interpreted by CI as "community choice," in line with the discourses of the policy model. Local circumstances, however, were far more complicated.

Committees in the Local Context

Although CI's engagement of the committees was ultimately instrumental, and not overtly designed for Indigenous empowerment, the creation of the committees *did* create a disturbance in the local governance context. This occurred because the new committees were perceived, by local elites and party officials, to have access to new kinds of power—as mediators of NGO resource flows or as potential influencers of local land-use decisions. The committees therefore represented a potentially new "political space" (Wells-Dang 2010) or a "stage" upon which political power could be enacted (Scott 1990). This was enough to provoke government interest in the committee making, and eventually interference, as I shall now illustrate.

COMMITTEES AS A POLITICAL DISTURBANCE (2003–2006)

The committees were initially the focus of complex political struggles between the conservation project and local elites, including businessmen and party officials. This is because, in the early years when CI's first country director was firmly in control (see chapter 3), the project would often directly confront elite actors responsible for deforestation—including the infamous tycoon Lim Long, who had land interests in Thmar Bang. With time, however, and with CI's transition to Khmer leadership, these conflicts were transformed into alignments and alliances. By 2007, for example, Lim Long had become a celebrated helper of the conservation project. I shall now describe how the local committees were embroiled in these struggles and changes. By examining what happened in the period 2003–2006, we also gain a window into the early tactics of domination used by the CPP to control potential political threats in rural areas.[3]

---

3. The period 2003–2006 is interesting because some scholars identify 2007 as a "turning point" in the CPP's consolidation of control over the state apparatus and the body politic (Morgenbesser 2019).

Overall, during my employment and subsequent field research in Thmar Bang district, I observed how local elites and party officials mobilized to challenge the legitimacy of the committees, seeking either to dismantle or dominate them. Each commune in Thmar Bang had its own version of the tale to tell. For example, the committee in Roussey Chrum commune was ignored by local officials for over a year after its election in 2005, eventually being forcibly dissolved and reelected under close supervision of the commune council in 2007. Likewise, in Tatai Leu commune, local officials initially engaged cautiously with the committee in 2003, but by 2007 the deputy commune chief was in the process of orchestrating the election of a new committee from a pool of his own handpicked candidates. Finally, in Thmar Dan Peuv commune in 2007, local businessmen attempted to dismantle the committee through the circulation of rumors and by pressuring the commune council. In this case, however, the commune chief fought to preserve the old committee in an effort to secure the conservation agreement and maintain good relations with CI. This time the challengers were not political elites but former dragon fish collectors whose income had been cut off by the conservation agreement's protection of the critically endangered fish.[4]

While these committee-related power struggles were diverse, the presence of party-political dynamics was a persistent feature. This was especially evident in Roussey Chrum, where business and party interests were most pronounced—this being the most populated and accessible commune in the area. At the time of the first committee election in 2005, local elites were disruptive. For example, Lim Long's bodyguards—who often rode in the back of a utility truck through the village, with AK-47 assault rifles on display—physically threatened CI's community engagment team, accusing them of playing political games. Nhet interpreted these events in terms of the CPP's desire for absolute power: "The party doesn't like anything better than them. . . . They accused me of being from an opposition political party!" Although shaken, the CI team pushed for the new committee to be inaugurated. But this prompted a dramatic "anti-committee protest," which was rumored to have been orchestrated by Lim Long and local party officials,

---

4. The conservation agreement in Thmar Dan Peuv commune involved the creation of a fish sanctuary on the Areng River to protect the vital spawning pools of this critically endangered fish (*S. formosus*). Its population was decreasing due to the aquarium trade.

using rice wine and other gifts as motivation for the protestors. The protest created a political impasse for the project and forced CI to suspend its community engagement activities in the commune. Later, when I debriefed with some members of the disbanded committee, they confirmed the underlying dynamic: there had been too many former opposition-party (FUNCINPEC) aligned members on the old committee.

Two years on, local elites began to reconsider their animosity toward the conservation project in Roussey Chrum. This change of stance may have been due to the benefit flows from conservation agreements in nearby communes, especially from the community ranger program, which villagers valued for its provision of cash wages to patrol teams (Milne 2009). The result was a meeting between Kiry, CI's new country director, and the two most powerful men in the commune: the district governor and Lim Long. As Kiry recounted to me, these local "power men" requested that CI arrange for a new committee to be elected for Roussey Chrum. Kiry agreed, but he insisted that they wait until after the commune council elections of 2007, so that the newly elected local authorities could also be involved in choosing the committee. In this way, high-level peace making between CI and local elites paved the way for a new and politically acceptable committee to be elected in late 2007.

Everything went to plan. The new commune council, now safely controlled by the CPP, helped CI to arrange the committee election in Roussey Chrum. For example, the new commune chief personally selected the candidates for election, and Lim Long and local party officials also cooperated willingly. Kiry explained enthusiastically how Lim Long had even offered his truck to transport far-away villagers, most of whom were laborers on his plantations, to the ballot boxes. Thus, the election of the new committee enabled local elites to assert themselves and effectively gain control over community participation in the conservation project.

SUBMISSION AND STABILIZATION (2007–2013)

By late 2007, all six committees in the Cardamom Mountains were apparently stable. This reflected the new political consensus, in which committees were expected to accommodate local elites. It now seemed that the committees represented a political opportunity for savvy local officials, keen to cooperate with the newly aligned, government-friendly version of CI. For example, one CI field officer explained to me that the local authorities "want to show to the provincial and district governors that they can work with NGOs . . . and bring resources into their commune." CI's new Khmer leadership was all too happy to facilitate this kind of cooperation, as it was in their interests too.

Under this new political order, my interactions with committee members revealed a conspicuous uniformity to their conceptions of how the committee should relate to the government.[5] This observation points to Hughes's notion of "state-sponsored political understandings" in Cambodia, deployed by the CPP to "attach notions of legitimacy to particular distributions of resources, and norms of decision making" (Hughes 2003, 11). In other words, the party-captured state was able to infiltrate the committees and control them through the deployment of apparently traditional social norms and protocols for state-society relations. For the conservation project, this meant that community participation could effectively be sanctioned by the state. Control was enacted mainly through bureaucratic protocols, which placed and kept the committees within local state hierarchies. For example, all the newly elected committees had to be officially recognized by the commune chief, who needed to sign off on the committee structure and its elected members. In addition, formal meetings between the committees and CI could no longer take place without the presence of the commune chief or one of his staff. Thus, the government was able to monitor and discipline most communication between the committees and CI.

Over time, this persistent state supervision led to new reporting practices in the conservation project. For example, every month, the committee chiefs were required to write a report about their activities to the commune chief. The commune chiefs would then pass these reports on to what committee members referred to as "the high level" (*khan leu*), meaning district and party officials. It seemed that little would escape the notice of the newly assertive CPP-controlled state. Furthermore, these new reporting protocols were never prescribed by CI, despite its close involvement with the committees. They were more like inherited or assumed practices, or artifacts of a political culture established during the Vietnamese-backed socialist era in Cambodia (see Gottesman 2004). The committees' reporting protocols

---

5. In 2007 I interviewed most committee members in all five communes of Thmar Bang district.

therefore reproduced wider logics of surveillance and discipline, with Cambodian characteristics.

In addition to the hierarchical reporting adopted by the committees, I also discovered a particular vocabulary being used to describe committee interactions with the state. For example, committee members and commune chiefs spoke in remarkable detail and consistency about the "rights" (*seut*) of the committees—"rights" being a way to signal appropriate actions and behavior. This indicated the committees' place in the local hierarchy, which was firmly below the commune council. For example, one commune chief said that the committees had only "the right to be curious" (*seut chngol*). By this, he implied that committee members could ask questions of the commune leaders, but that they could not pose direct challenges or make autonomous decisions. The committees' rights were also well defined in relation to their potential interactions with local villagers. For instance, committee members understood that they had no right to organize meetings or conduct awareness-raising activities without permission from the commune chief. This meant that the committees' potential to mobilize popular opinion or grassroots opposition to the government was kept in check. These findings reflect long-standing observations of how power works in Cambodia as a "zero sum game" (Bit 1991; Hughes 2003): the government was careful to ensure that the committees were tightly shackled, with power sharing *not* being a possibility.

Finally, if the committees' rights were not entirely clear, government officials were assertive in indicating their limits. This became evident in a handful of incidents when state officials disciplined committee members for perceived transgressions. For example, in late 2007, CI sponsored the three committees of the Areng Valley to attend an awareness-raising workshop in Phnom Penh about the impacts of hydropower dams. The trip was organized by CI's community engagement team because of the proposed Chinese-sponsored Areng dam—a major threat to the area (Milne 2021). However, when committee members returned home, their commune chiefs were angry that they had gone to the workshop without their permission, and they were told that they could not distribute any information from workshop. As one committee chief said: "I wanted to do extension (*psopsai*) about hydropower, and I told my idea to the commune chief, but he said no. . . . He is scared of politics, because the government supports the Chinese company."

Apart from being an ominous sign of oppression to come, this incident shows how the committees were subsumed into local state structures in service of party interests. This dynamic now defines much local governance in Cambodia, as commune chiefs are expected to fulfill top-down party demands while also maintaining a cooperative and submissive citizenry. Notions of a traditional "moral order" again featured here, as a way of constituting the commune chief's authority. For example, villagers would describe their commune chief as the "grandfather looking after his children and grandchildren." Or, as one commune chief explained in reference to the committee members who independently attended the hydropower workshop in Phnom Penh, "Children do not have the right to leave the house without their parents' permission." This use of "kinship terminology" appears across Cambodia (Ovesen, Trankell, and Ojendal 1996), and I found that it ordered political space in the early days. By 2015, however, there was much less political order in the Areng Valley due to emerging grassroots and activist resistance to the proposed dam. This divided communes like Chumnoab and made it impossible for commune chiefs to maintain authority in traditional ways (Milne 2017).

In describing the fate of CI's committee making in the Cardamom Mountains, I have revealed a critical moment in contemporary state formation in Cambodia, and I have also shown how the good intentions of global policy makers can be distorted by local context. In this cautionary tale, the committees eventually became nestled within local power structures, no longer able to fulfill their original goal of being local representative bodies with some independent political terrain. While the contextual constraints on community participation in Cambodia have long been observed (Öjendal and Sedara 2006; Prum 2005), the role that NGO-facilitated committee making can play in extending the state apparatus, and hence authoritarian control, is an important additional observation. Ferguson (1994) described this phenomenon in terms of the hidden "side effects" of international development projects, while Bryant (2002) showed how conservation NGOs too could be involved in the elaboration of government. As this case shows, CI's well-intended efforts to create governance structures mainly served to make local populations "legible" (Scott 1998) for state and party control. This problem of complex and insidious side effects raises questions about the ethics of global conservation practice. To explore this, we must look at

NGO behavior, which I shall now do by attending to CI's field engagements in the Cardamom Mountains.

CI's Practices of Community Engagement

CI's community engagement model was underpinned by the notion of "community choice" in the conservation agreements. This notion reflects an assumption that local representative bodies, in this case the CNRMCs, can be engaged in agreements as though they were the whole community. However, the fate of the CNRMCs in the Cardamom Mountains, of being utterly disciplined by the state, shows that this assumption was flawed. Here, I consider whether CI's project staff were aware of what was going on, and what role they played in it.

PROJECT-MANAGING PARTICIPATION

As the complexity of managing six conservation agreements increased, CI's community engagement team needed to find new efficiencies and pragmatic ways of operating. This was mainly achieved by aligning the conservation project with local power structures, as I have described. For Kiry, this meant increasingly working through the commune councils to implement the agreements, rather than the local CI-fostered committees. As he explained in 2007: "Our NGO role is to work with the community . . . but the community, they elect the commune council as their representative. So, if we . . . exclude the commune councils, it means you exclude the representative, and this makes the community feel unhappy . . . and [it means that] the representative can very easily break the bridge between your team and the community . . . and you cannot call the people for meetings."

In other words, the commune councils, as *government* representative bodies, had the power either to prevent or enable CI's community-engagement activities in the field. Kiry was apparently left with little choice other than to engage the commune councils as the "official representatives" of the community in the conservation agreements, rather than the committees. Yet his language also normalized this new mode of state-based community engagement. As a result, the commune councils became signatories

The Idea in Village Life **163**

to the conservation agreements from 2007 onward, while the committees were engaged only for negotiation and implementation.

Under pressure from the head office to implement the conservation agreements at scale, CI's field team soon worked only through the commune councils and the committees, rather than conducting wider community engagements. This practice became embodied in the agreement texts, which referred to "the commune and its members," as though the commune were a single actor, as follows: "[CI] has agreed to provide the following support to the commune to help its members uphold [the conservation commitments]." With this language in motion, CI could avoid having to address the internal political dynamics and complexities of each commune. Instead, CI focused on "the commune and its members" as a single entity.

The most convenient aspect of this framing was that CI could make "the commune" responsible for consulting and engaging with local residents to achieve their compliance with the conservation agreements. This became apparent when I observed the agreement negotiations in 2007. During the meetings, CI's Khmer negotiators stressed the need for the commune councils and committees to be responsible for local-level processes of consultation, saying repeatedly, "You must go and tell all the people, make them understand [about the agreement]." Kiry later explained the process to CI's head office staff: "First, we discuss with committee and commune council . . . then they go to talk with the people and see about rumor, informal discussion . . . and then after, we have another formal meeting with the committee and commune council." Thus, CI used the committees and commune councils to outsource potentially complex local-level engagements, which might have involved the facilitation of public meetings, discussion groups, or other deliberative processes in relation to local resource use and property rights. Instead, CI Cambodia pursued what Kiry called "smooth" (*pheaproluen*) implementation of the conservation agreements—a euphemism for government cooperation.

Under this strategy, CI's community engagement team also needed to deflect any involvement with intracommune politics or conflicts. In part, they did this by insisting that they would work only with committees and commune councils that functioned well. This meant suspending community engagement in conflicted settings, like Roussey Chrum, where CI paused its investment in conservation agreements for two years (2005–2007) due to local struggles over land and resources. Furthermore, when engagement did resume in Roussey Chrum, this was conditional on the committee and the commune council finding a way to navigate or contain local resource conflicts themselves. Kiry pushed this line during one heated negotiation meeting, when he threatened to withdraw from discussions over the conservation agreements if local leaders could not present a united front, saying, "We will wait for another meeting, we cannot do it now. . . . It's like a car: if one tire is broken, we cannot drive. . . . If the community program cannot work here, then the law enforcement team can do it." Thus, Kiry suggested that the alternative to the conservation agreements would be conservation by force, all the while demanding that commune councils themselves tackle local resource conflicts that arguably should have been the work of the conservation project.

Unfortunately, this became a recurring theme across all of the conservation agreements. During negotiations and implementation, CI consistently made the committees and commune councils responsible for stopping local land clearing and hunting, while avoiding difficult questions about *who* was to blame and *how* they could be stopped. Here, CI wanted simply to be able to state the "conservation services" that it sought from each commune, according to the policy model. But the commune representatives stressed that this would involve political and risky work. For example, during negotiation meetings in Tatai Leu, committee members tried to convey to CI that the resource exploitation happening in their commune was being driven by powerful outsiders, not "ordinary local people." The committee especially cited the case of a state-backed company that had begun operating illegally in the area, with a bogus permit to extract forty metric tons of rattan. But the company had taken one hundred metric tons of rattan, and worse, it had hired cheap laborers from outside the area, who had devastated local streams through illegal electric fishing. Being robbed of key livelihood resources, villagers were angry, but they could not tackle such a well-connected company. Rather than engaging with the problem, however, the CI team only deflected villagers' requests.

CI's unwillingness to act in these circumstances provoked a key local grievance, as villagers asked: How is it possible for powerful outsiders to take commune resources while local residents are constrained by conservation agreements? This was a vivid problem in relation to the rattan-harvesting company. As one committee member said: "Outsiders came and took all of

The Idea in Village Life **165**

our fish, they poisoned the fish. . . . We didn't say anything . . . but we should let villagers join this activity, too, if outsiders can." Similar comments were made about the issue of illegal land clearing by powerful outsiders in the protected forest. As committee members explained: "Here in the village, there is nowhere new to cut! Only outsiders and powerful people dare to cut new forest." Thus, committee members complained to CI about having to make villagers comply with the conservation agreements while powerful outsiders operated freely in the commune, beyond the law.

Faced with such complaints, along with villagers' requests for assistance to defend their homelands against outsiders, CI's response was telling of its new stance of avoiding conflict with powerful actors. As Kiry said in the Tatai Leu negotiation meeting, "We don't care about who is cutting the forest, we just want to know how much was cut." Kiry's words show how the demands of the policy model were front and center: CI's team was apparently most concerned with measuring the area of forest clearing per year in each commune for the purposes of calculating the opportunity costs of the conservation agreements and hence the value of the compensatory benefit packages (see chapter 2). But this flew in the face of expectations that had been raised earlier with villagers when CI facilitated the participatory land-use planning. As one Tatai Leu elder said in 2010, "We are still waiting for CI to come and help . . . to do land demarcation, as we planned to do in 2004." Elders in other communes expressed similar sentiments in private, saying that CI should "protect villagers from outsiders" and be "like a teacher" to show villagers the way and support them to secure their local resource rights.

Villagers' hopes were dashed, however, as CI chose not to contest the processes of dispossession and elite-backed exploitation that were gradually unfolding in Thmar Bang district. While villagers sought help to defend their resources, CI deflected their requests in the name of the conservation agreements that seemed to offer a contractual fix for the problem. For CI Cambodia, this approach was motivated by political pragmatism, as Kiry explained in his new government-aligned voice: "Our activity is conservation, and conservation is for everybody. It's for the government, not just for local people . . . so our work is easier than the work of [anti-government] advocacy NGOs." Thus, Kiry drew a clear line between what CI Cambodia did and did not do. When I raised my concerns about this with Jan from the head office, he said, "Well, we don't do social engineering." Thus, CI tried to position itself as an apolitical player, with project objectives that did not include advocacy. In practice, this meant that CI's community engagements began to silence villagers' voices, while also pretending not to see elite-backed resource appropriation in the project area.

THE COMMITTEES AS ENVIRONMENTAL SUBJECTS

While the conservation agreement negotiations generated a certain realpolitik, CI's routine project practices for community engagement soon normalized a suite of asymmetrical governance arrangements. I observed this ethnographically, through my attendance at an array of formal and informal project meetings with villagers over the years. In particular, I observed everyday interactions between project staff and local committees, since it is through such mundane practices that power relations are symbolically constructed and enacted (Bourdieu 1977). Thus, I observed how CI's project configured "governing relations" in the field, including who would be governed by whom and how (see Li 2007). Ethnographies of forest governance in Asia often describe these processes in terms of environmental subject making, which can lead to "environmentality" (Agrawal 2005) or "environmental rule" (McElwee 2016). The case of CI in Cambodia shows how international conservation NGOs can also be deeply implicated in these governing processes.

Before CI's community engagement became so routinized, most interactions between the project and villagers were based on personal connections and relationships of trust. These connections formed in the early days (2002–2005) with long project visits in villages, which afforded time for sharing meals and chatting. This often included drinking homemade rice wine and staying overnight in villagers' homes. By 2007, however, there had been personnel changes in CI's community engagement team, and the Forestry Administration officer Aung was now largely responsible for field operations. Furthermore, the field team was increasingly busy implementing six conservation agreements across six communes (see table 2, chapter 3). This involved administering the agreement benefit packages, which were delivered subject to each commune's conservation performance. The benefits included agricultural assistance in the form of "buffalo banks" and "mechanical mules," the latter being a small handheld tractor; and community ranger programs, which involved villagers being rostered onto forest patrol

The Idea in Village Life

groups in exchange for cash wages. While on patrol, the community rangers were asked to remove wildlife snares and report on illegal activity like forest clearing, with financial incentives to enhance their performance. Thus, CI's field team was stretched as it managed patrol plans, agreement compliance monitoring, monthly reports, and financial accounting.

The conservation agreements therefore led to a more structured and businesslike Community Engagement Program, with most village-level meetings being procedural or administrative rather than deliberative. According to committee members, these meetings were generally rushed and ad hoc. Furthermore, CI's field officers increasingly took the convenient approach of meeting only with the committee chief or the committee member responsible for the community rangers, so as not to have to call the full committee to a meeting. Indeed, most committee members said that they rarely met with CI's field staff personally after 2007. Rather, they waited for instructions from their committee chief about the work that they should do. With CI's focus on dispersing funds, giving instructions, and collecting reports, the opportunities for committee members to communicate back to the project therefore became constrained. Meaningful participation petered out.

These new managerial practices, enacted by the now very government-friendly field team, left some committee members feeling left out and frustrated. Female committee members, or those who lived in far-away villages, were most excluded. For example, one older woman in an outlying village of Chumnoab commune complained: "They only call me to meetings when an international visitor comes; otherwise I am not included." Her comment also points to the increasingly performative nature of community participation, in which her presence was required only at "staged" meetings for donors or head-office visitors. Similarly, in Thmar Dan Peuv commune, one committee member in an outlying village observed of CI's field officer Aung: "I only see him drive past, on his way to the main village. . . . I've never been to their meetings . . . it's too far away." Thus, CI's routine practices soon shaped community participation into a top-down administrative affair between CI's lead field officer and the committee chiefs.

If the achievement of meaningful community participation had been a priority for CI, then perhaps the project might have been resourced and administered differently. Instead, with the ambition and structure of the conservation agreements in play, field staff found themselves under significant pressure to implement complex yet rigid activities in multiple communes.

Strict timelines and small budgets also necessitated efficiency, meaning that field staff took shortcuts in community engagement: ticking boxes was now the main game. CI's head-office and expatriate staff were not necessarily aware of these developments, nor were they necessarily concerned about their implications. I raised what I perceived to be the erosion of community participation with various staff at CI in 2007 and 2010, but their priorities lay elsewhere. They opted to treat community engagement as something for the field staff to take care of.

Under these circumstances, CI's community engagement practices became increasingly confined to a Cambodian black box. A key aspect of this was the tendency for NGO and project staff to assume a position of high status with respect to ordinary villagers (O'Leary and Meas 2001). This dynamic was especially pronounced for more senior and office-bound Khmer staff, who visited the field only occasionally. For example, one Khmer technical advisor was known to insist on having a four-wheel drive truck, with a driver, to conduct his village visits. Meanwhile, field-based staff drove their old Honda Dream motorbikes to village meetings, often getting covered in dust or mud along the way. Thus, project hierarchies emerged, which subtly devalued the work and status of field-based staff, even though these staff were the ones upon whom project relations with villagers depended.

Another tendency of CI's Khmer staff in the village was to mimic the behavior of government officials, assuming that this would elevate their status and activate ingrained local practices of domination (see Hughes 2003; Öjendal and Sedara 2006). As Kiry explained to me: "The government is very clever in working with the people. We try to do like them. . . . The conservation program should do extension like the [CPP] party." Thus, some Khmer staff tried to emulate government techniques of engagement, which were presumed to be the easiest and most effective way of working with communities. In practice, this played out as though everyone was following a familiar script. For example, field officer Aung allowed villagers to address him as "Mr. Teacher" (lok kru), the term for a respected leader. He also asked local government staff to arrange his village meetings in advance, giving the impression that he was acting in a state capacity. Accordingly, he would arrive late for these meetings, having kept committee members waiting—behavior to be expected from a man of status. Thus, the local committees soon became seen as the "NGO version of the commune councils," as one Indigenous elder observed. Just like the commune councils, the committees

The Idea in Village Life

were subject to a state-like external power: they were no longer vehicles for grassroots representation.

The project's government style also prevailed in formal or ceremonial meetings held by CI in local villages. A classic example of this kind of meeting was the agreement-signing ceremonies, held annually in each commune. These meetings saw villagers sitting in rows, like students in a classroom, facing their teachers on stage—usually a lineup of NGO, government, and expatriate staff. The protocols for speaking at such meetings were strict, always involving an opening phrase that listed guests in hierarchical order: "Please, I pay respect to [*sohm garop*] the international visitors, the boss of CI, the district governor, the commune chief, etc."[6] CI would be acknowledged for its financial support, and the government thanked for its role in facilitating this, before any other words could be uttered. These formal meetings were therefore highly performative and rarely controversial. They were symbolic events that served to reinforce relationships and hierarchies between actors.

For Cambodians, this stiff and nondeliberative public atmosphere is familiar. Nhet recalled that this is how meetings were conducted during the Khmer Rouge time, saying: "If you don't pay respect in meetings like that, then maybe you have a problem." He was implying that one might face serious punishment or death for apparent noncompliance. Thus, older villagers were accustomed to a performative style of participation, influenced by memories of the past. For this reason, Nhet said that it was much easier to work in ex–Khmer Rouge villages, because "they obey and follow the boss, and you can do [projects] very quickly." These are challenging conditions for any NGO seeking to "do" community participation in Cambodia. The result in this case shows how NGOs can often end up replicating underlying power relations while also extending the practices of authoritarian rule.

Ultimately, these practices and cultures of community engagement led to the committees being framed as subjects of the conservation project and the state. This subject making was further sharpened into a neoliberal form by the conservation agreements, which contractually engaged the committees to perform specific tasks in exchange for what CI called an "administration fee." Effectively, the committees became service providers for CI, re-

---

6. "To respect" (*garop*) can also be translated as "obey," reflecting the power that status entails.

sponsible for local awareness raising and general running of the community ranger patrols, among other things. Or, as one commune chief explained, "The committee was formed to be responsible for natural resource management, to protect the forest and stop hunting, and to raise awareness among the people about reducing shifting agriculture and returning to the paddy field." I would hear this articulation of committee responsibilities countless times, from local leaders and committee members alike. A subjectivity had certainly been formed, even if it was only performed or recited to my face. Overall, it seemed that the committees had become mere instruments of the conservation project, like government-sanctioned service providers for the conservation agreements. By 2007, co-management and community representation were not concepts that I heard in local explanations of the committees' function and role.

This new neoliberal subjectivity, in the context of authoritarian state making, also meant that the committees had to behave as adjuncts or assistants to the government. This was most evident in discussions about the community ranger program, which always seemed to reinforce government authority. As one of CI's team members explained to me: "The community rangers have their own role: they can remove snares . . . but if they see people in the forest cutting or hunting, their role is not to catch them but to report this to FA." This meant that the community rangers could not directly challenge illegal forest clearing or timber extraction themselves. Rather, villagers passed information about illegal activity on to the FA, and then had to wait for action. Unfortunately, action rarely came—especially when powerful people were involved in the offending. The committees were therefore prevented from challenging unjust and illegal appropriation of resources by state officials and businessmen in the protected forest—a pattern that would continue with deleterious consequences from 2009 onward.

Similar dynamics played out with the other service that the committees provided for the project: awareness raising for villagers. The Cambodian version of this is "extension" (*twer psopsai*), which has strong governmental connotations as officials often spoke of "extending the law" (*psopsai chbap*) to villagers. For the conservation agreements, this extension process typically played out with reference to the Forestry Law. For example, as one of CI's government rangers explained to me, "The community program is to make local people understand about the law, protecting the forest, and not doing illegal activity." Accordingly, the committees fell into step with this legal-governmental regime. Committee members told me that their role was to convey information *from* the conservation project *to* the villagers, with permission from local authorities. Thus, the committees became instruments or mouthpieces for the law, rather than representatives of the people who were subject to it. Again, by defaulting to government-style practices in Cambodia, CI's local engagement was more like a form of *dis*engagement. Time and again, the potential political voice of the committees was substituted for top-down governmental control, in which the committees became project subjects.

Villagers' Views of the Conservation Project

Ultimately, to gauge the effects and outcomes of CI's community engagement, it is necessary to explore villagers' own experiences and understandings of it. This means going beyond the snapshot view of the village that an NGO worker might obtain during project meetings or monitoring visits. It means unstructured, longer stays in the village to observe project activities ethnographically, from the sidelines. This is what I did in 2007, over several months, then later in 2010 and 2015 with shorter visits. What I found underscored the transformative power of "contextualization" (Latour 1996) and its implications for global conservation. In short, I began to see that global policy is not implementable in any way that might be controlled or fully understood by so-called outside experts.

To explore the effects of contextualization, I especially asked villagers about the local committees. Their responses soon revealed that villagers did not understand CI's rather abstract committee-making process in any way that corresponded with the original policy intentions: it appeared as though the concepts of Western democratic thinking simply did not translate. When prompted, villagers could not articulate the purpose or structure of their local committees, but they *could* name the individuals involved in the conservation project. So it was through personal channels that villagers interacted with the project, seeking an informal village-style accountability from those elected to the committees. For example, committee members were often pressured by villagers to ensure that the conservation project would support their livelihoods. As one elder in Chumnoab remarked, reflecting on his role in the conservation agreement negotiations in 2007, "The people may accuse me of selling my head to foreigners [barang]! I must be careful [about what I agree to do for CI]."

Correspondingly, committee members described how they were sometimes lobbied by anti-conservation interests in the village. For example, a subset of villagers in Thmar Dan Peuv, who did not want dragon fish protection, reportedly pressured committee members to relax the conservation agreement. In other communes, committee members were threatened by professional hunters and wildlife traders, who also opposed the conservation agreements. Thus, being a committee member was potentially risky for one's safety and reputation, given the kinds of interests that stood against conservation goals at the local level. Being a committee member also meant being seen as a broker: someone who could convey villagers' informal requests to CI. This corresponds with wider observations from rural Asia, in which local leaders are brokers for the village when dealing with the outside world (Mosse 2005; Scott 1985; Tsing 1993). This brokering model appears to be the natural or de facto alternative to NGO-imposed ideas of project participation through committee making and formal meetings.

Villagers' views of "the project" (*komrong*) also revealed that CI's conservation agreements did not exist in villagers' minds as a coherent or linear set of activities. Rather, the project was locally produced and constructed through personal experiences, rumors, informal conversation, and imagination or project "imaginaries" (West 2006, 216). Through these uniquely local processes of social production (Appadurai 1990), the conservation agreements became both confused and embellished. For example, the local committees were named and renamed by villagers so many times that it seemed they had divided and multiplied. The activities of other organizations in the village, such as political parties and local NGOs, were also often wrongly attributed to CI's conservation project. In this way, the project soon existed in the local context as a set of multiple moving images, like a hologram, in which each observer perceived something different.

Local understandings of the project also depended heavily on villagers' personal interactions with CI's field staff. While villagers said that they did not know anything about what they referred to as "the organization" (*aung-kar*), they *did* know Uncle Nhet and Brother Kim, the original community engagement team. Frequently, I was told by villagers that Nhet was the man who had come to "make the community" (*twer sahakoum*) in the village, as though the community were an alien construct made by an outsider. These

The Idea in Village Life   **173**

local perspectives ultimately show how Nhet and Kim *were* the project at the local level: they were the personification of CI's intervention at the outset, which later changed with staff turnover in 2007. This shows how the "work of contextualization" (Latour 1996) was contingent on personal relationships. In other words, the project was constantly being (re)produced through various interactions between villagers and project staff, direct or implied: a process with unforeseeable outcomes (Latour 1996).

Contextualization in this case was deeply influenced by the fact that only a few villagers interacted directly and regularly with project staff. For self-proclaimed "ordinary villagers" (*neak toemeda*), and especially women, they were apparently content to observe project activities from the sidelines or to hear about it on the village grapevine. For these "ordinary villagers," project actors blended into a steady stream of outsiders visiting the village, representing government agencies, NGOs, political parties, and companies. As one villager told me: "I have heard of the conservation organization, but there are so many organizations here, I don't know what they do. . . . I've seen police and military going on patrol, but I didn't ask them about their work . . . maybe their role is to protect the forest." Thus, ordinary villagers typically avoided encounters with outsiders and were generally not inclined to ask after their activities. Many said that they "didn't dare" (*ot hien*) to ask about matters that "come from the high level," reflecting a habitual deference to hierarchy.[7]

Local views and experiences of the project, therefore, did not necessarily depend on formal NGO processes of consultation or communication. Rather, the contextualized version of the project was highly variable and arguably incoherent, especially as the community engagement team changed its composition over time, along with the ranger teams who were on rotation between field stations. CI did not recognize this as a problem, as it assumed that field staff were interchangeable and transferable.[8] This reflects their technical and policy-centered view: a view that cannot see or account for the fluid and locally contingent nature of projects in village life.

---

7. This was a frequent response in household surveys (*ot hien sua key . . . moak pee khan leu*).

8. For example, after the 2006 agreements were signed, new staff were brought in to run them, and the original field staff were transferred to other areas and tasks. Furthermore, ranger rotation was seen to be a good thing, as it deterred the formation of local relationships, which often led to corruption.

CONTEXTUALIZATION AND PROJECT IMAGINARIES

As the project became embedded in village life, unique local interpretations of the conservation agreements emerged, often leading to confusion. A key problem was that villagers had difficulty distinguishing the agreements from other project activities, especially prior community engagement activities. This meant that the agreements were not negotiated from a clean slate but were absorbed into a path-dependent local medium of villagers' earlier experiences and memories of conservation. For example, in Chumnoab, the agreement was frequently confused with the prior participatory land-use planning processes—even the commune chief had trouble distinguishing between current and past activities. Similarly, in Thmar Dan Peuv, villagers thought that the park rangers' law enforcement was a component of the conservation agreements. This shows how the agreements existed in the local realm: not as contracts, based on a common understanding between parties, but as dynamic assemblages, born out of local social processes, project history, and personal connections.

A key result of these local processes was the pervasive but erroneous perception that the conservation agreements came from the law or were the law. With the blurring of state and NGO practices, described above, it is not surprising that villagers held this misconception. Villagers regularly saw the agreements being implemented in cooperation with government actors, like the commune councils and the FA, in a political style that replicated and reinforced local state-society relations. No wonder that household surveys in 2007 revealed that over a third of all households thought they would be "arrested and fined" if they broke the conservation agreements (Milne 2009). Or, as one Indigenous elder and committee member in Tatai Leu said, "I want to cooperate with CI through the agreement, to protect my people from handcuffs." Community participation in the agreements was therefore motivated in part by local people's desire to avoid coercive law enforcement: a far cry from the neoliberal policy trope of "community choice."

Another motivation for local compliance was the perception that conservation agreements were an opportunity to secure benefits. This was especially the case in the early years (2003–2007), when villagers associated the project with well-resourced foreigners and international organizations, appearing to possess fantastical wealth and power. This was demonstrated vividly during agreement negotiations in 2007 in Thmar Dan Peuv, when CI's leadership

The Idea in Village Life

conducted a flying visit to the field with prominent stakeholders. This entailed two helicopters landing in the village, carrying an international donor, the FA director from Phnom Penh, and CI's regional director. The visit was to showcase CI's work on the conservation agreements, as part of a fundraising effort. Yet the cost of the helicopters would have been the same as the sum of the entire annual compensation package being proposed to the commune of 113 families (around US$11,000) in exchange for its delivery of conservation services, like stopping land clearing. There was bitter irony in this short helicopter visit, yet committee members and villagers smiled dutifully.

Soon, the apparent power and resources possessed by the conservation project fused with local fantasies about development, and how it might happen. As one woman in Thmar Dan Peuv said, while explaining her support for the conservation agreement: "If we do not protect dragon fish, it will become extinct. If we protect it, there will be many more foreigners coming here. This will bring development, so we can sell and buy things, and profit from being *motodop* [motorbike taxi]." Comments like this often featured alongside informal conversations about the "benefit package" (*phol proyowich*) from the agreements. When I quizzed villagers about the benefits they wanted, their responses were remarkably uniform: fix the road, get more buffalo, help the school, bring health services. It appeared as though there was a common script to prescribe "development," with benevolent outsiders being perceived as having a key role to play in this. Strikingly, Paige West (2006) observes similar patterns in her ethnography of global conservation in Papua New Guinea. In both cases, villagers saw conservation NGOs as being obliged to help. As one village chief explained to me: "Before conservation we got income from the forest and wildlife. Now CI needs to replace the lost income." Villagers therefore saw the conservation project as a development opportunity, and their cooperation with CI became one livelihood strategy among many. This view "from below" also resonates with Southeast Asia's contemporary peasant politics (see Hall et al. 2015), to which I now turn.

RIDING THE TIGER

Notions of environmentality, often wielded to critique the power of global conservation, do not do justice to the agency of local villagers. Indeed, the local interpretations and distortions of the conservation agreements that I have described point to a productive "friction" (Tsing 2005) at work here, akin to Latour's "contextualization" of projects (1996). This implies that there is more going on at the local level than just the story of global conservation and its direct impacts in the Cardamom Mountains. There is also a story of villagers' strategic responses to this, which included resistance and subversion, not just misunderstanding or reinterpretation of what CI was trying to do with its government partners.

Here, a key strategy used by villagers was "strategic representation" (Li 1996) or the telling of half-truths to advance their interests. CI's field staff knew this, and they were often skeptical of villagers' claims. One Australian advisor, for example, decided to give a numerical "truthfulness rating" for each village meeting he conducted. Similarly, one European biologist complained, "Villagers always blame outsiders for the hunting, but I don't believe them." Thus, authentic communication with villagers was often extremely difficult to achieve, especially for foreigners who had to rely on Khmer counterparts (see chapter 4). Here, I argue that the villagers' lack of authenticity in communicating with CI's field staff may be seen as a mode of "everyday resistance" against the conservation project (Scott 1985). Resistance of this kind is not directly confrontational, but it uses subtle tactics like minor acts of disobedience, spreading of rumors, and the use of "discursive strategies" such as telling metaphorical stories to contest conservation practices (Fortmann 1995). Villagers' strategies in this realm were a source of power for them, given that formal avenues for participation in the conservation project had become so constrained.

Another dynamic faced by CI's project was that village leaders often maintained various and conflicting loyalties to powerful patrons. For example, villagers engaged strategically and simultaneously with the locally influential tycoon Lim Long, party officials, local authorities, CI, and other NGOs. The interests of these parties, however, did not align when it came to natural resources. Villagers therefore tried to accommodate their various patrons' interests, either by avoiding conflicts or pitting different parties against each other (see Scott 1985). This was painfully clear in the case of two committee members who were considered by CI as "community champions." One was the committee chief in Thmar Dan Peuv, who was allegedly involved in illegal land clearing and wildlife trade alongside his efforts to protect dragon fish with CI. Another was a committee member in Roussey Chrum who apparently worked for the resource-hungry tycoon Lim Long while also helping CI to restore the local cardamom forest. Thus, village leaders often juggled their

The Idea in Village Life

loyalties between powerful outsiders, hedging their bets to secure their own and villagers' best interests. Because of this, the conservation agreements could only ever be partial commitments in the local realm: a finding that fundamentally challenges the theoretical basis for CI's policy model.

Villagers' strategic behaviors also involved a very fundamental contestation of forest conservation, for its impacts on local food security. Restrictions on shifting agriculture (*chamka*) were an inherent and deeply problematic part of the conservation project, and villagers objected bitterly. Villagers directed countless comments at the project, like: "Since CI came, we haven't been able to cut *chamka*, we are poor here"; "If we don't cut *chamka*, we have nothing to eat"; "If they don't let us cut *chamka*, and they don't give us buffalo to do lowland rice, then what do we eat?"; "I don't care [about CI] . . . if I lack rice, I go to cut *chamka* somewhere new." Thus, it was made clear that hungry villagers need to clear forest for shifting agriculture in order to survive. Here, Nhet pointed out how hunger drives people to take risks and break rules, like during the Khmer Rouge time when people risked being shot just to steal rice. The narrative of hunger is powerful in Cambodia. Villagers used it to imply that, if they were pushed too far, they would not cooperate with conservation interests.

Villagers also criticized the conservation project through jokes and insinuations, which raised major questions about the ownership of resources. For example, one commune chief expressed the terrible irony and injustice of being surrounded by natural resources that his people could not use, saying, "The chickens sit on the rice . . . but why can't they eat the rice?"[9] Similarly, in Thmar Dan Peuv, there was a local joke about the "NGO pigs"; these were the wild pigs, protected by the conservation program, that raided people's crops at night. People said, laughing, "If the NGO pig belonged to the people, then we would put it in a cage and eat it!" But this joke was not as lighthearted as it seemed. It got to the heart of what was wrong with CI's efforts to protect nature at the people's expense. Such commentary was abundant, and it directly undermined the local legitimacy of the conservation project.

Further challenges then arose as local residents complained that foreign biologists had broken their spiritual taboos against disturbing crocodiles in

---

9. The district police chief also used this expression to refer to the apparent right of local authorities and rangers to extract informal taxes from resource exploitation. The phrase is a euphemism for corruption.

the Areng River. In two famous incidents, the local guides employed to assist NGO-led crocodile research, which involved catching and tagging crocodiles, had become very sick with fevers, even leading to the death of one guide. Allegedly, this was because the guides had disturbed the crocodile spirit (*arak kropeu*), in the name of the foreigners' monitoring of this critically endangered species (*Crocodylus siamensis*). The people of Chumnoab who spoke of these events were visibly distressed. This was not just a local rumor or story but a substantive contestation, in which conservation activities were reframed as spiritually or morally wrong (see Fortmann 1995).

As CI's local legitimacy eroded, new instances of villagers' noncompliance or feigned compliance in response to the conservation agreements emerged. Villagers maintained a façade of obedience in project meetings, yet beyond CI's gaze they began to act independently, often without heed to the contractual commitments they had made to provide conservation services. A notable early example of this was the clearing of twelve hectares of forest for shifting agriculture, in Chumnoab in 2007. The area was cleared by a group of families, mainly committee members who were responsible for helping CI to implement the conservation agreements. The clearing went unreported until a helicopter overflight was made by expatriate biologists, who promptly raised the matter with local authorities, threatening legal consequences for noncompliance. In response, the local committee members feigned ignorance, claiming that they did not know the land was protected. Everyone knew otherwise, but CI could not push the matter further without jeopardizing the relationships that underpinned the conservation agreement.

Similar instances of deflecting blame occurred in Thmar Dan Peuv, where the focus of the conservation agreement was to protect the critically endangered dragon fish. Here, it was rumored that a school of dragon fish fingerlings—then valuable in the wildlife trade—had disappeared under the watch of one of the community ranger groups. Different ranger groups began to blame each other, but before the conflict escalated, a new story emerged: that a big fish had eaten the dragon fish babies. This new local story meant that no one was to blame, and the community rangers continued their work of "protection."

Such episodes, contrary to notions of environmentality, demonstrate villagers' power to produce and control knowledge about the effects of the conservation project. This leads us to one of the deepest contradictions of rule and domination: that external rulers, in this case a foreign conservation NGO in partnership with government, are only as powerful as their local brokers permit (Mackenzie 1988). Even the most reliable and amicable village representatives, who collaborated with CI's project, were also capable of deceit and strategic behavior. They were "riding the tiger" (Mackenzie 1988, 43), engaging with the conservation agreements not as the "community choice" that CI imagined but as a strategic response to a difficult situation imposed by external powers. Villagers avoided handcuffs while also maintaining some agency in a nonconfrontational way.

In this context, rigorous contractual agreements for conservation services, of the kind envisaged by CI, cannot exist. Rather, agreements in practice are subject to performative and contingent local dynamics in which facts and contract terms are always up for negotiation or subject to local interpretation. Here, CI should have learned hard lessons: that agreement transgressions cannot necessarily be systematically detected with monitoring; that conditional benefit packages cannot be enforced in a way that maintains local relationships; that an apparently powerful buyer of conservation services is in fact highly vulnerable and dependent on the goodwill of local brokers.

Conclusion: The Challenge of Project Side Effects

This chapter has explored the side effects of CI's project at the village level. Far from being a trivial matter, analysis of the side effects of conservation or development interventions can reveal their true significance. As James Ferguson explained: "Interventions . . . while 'failing' on their own terms, nonetheless, have regular effects, which include the expansion and entrenchment of bureaucratic state power, side by side with the projection of a representation of economic and social life which denies 'politics' and, to the extent that it is successful, suspends its effects" (1994, xiv–xv).

This argument, originally made in the context of the World Bank in Lesotho, holds true in this case, too, even though the context and scale of intervention were very different. As CI went about implementing its conservation agreements, a chief side effect was that it enabled the extension of government power in the protected forest. This occurred in part because CI's activities made local places and communities "legible" for government (Scott 1998)—particularly with the creation of Commune Natural Resource

Management Committees, which became new vehicles for state control over people and resources. A key problem here was that the committees, in practice, were disciplined by local authorities and subservient to the FA and commune councils: they simply could not function as representative civil society entities as originally intended.

In addition, CI's PES-like policy model and its associated field practices gave rise to a particular neoliberal subjectivity and anti-politics at the village level. That is, by insisting on negotiating the conservation agreements only through the committees and commune councils, CI closed other opportunities for village participation. This style of participation, where external facilitators invite villagers to engage in a predetermined process, is recognized as "tyrannical" (Cooke and Kothari 2001). Furthermore, by collapsing all community engagements into the conservation agreements model, CI reduced the role of the committees to one of service provision, involving the performance of tightly specified project functions like community ranger patrols. This effectively dismantled the political potential of the committees and allowed CI to avoid wider contestations over natural resources in the project area. In short, CI's framing of the communities as single actors and voluntary service providers under the conservation agreements amounted to a deft outsourcing of the local politics of conservation.

Despite these tyrannical effects, it would be wrong to assume that villagers were entirely compliant or submissive in what unfolded. The final part of this chapter showed how, as CI's project became increasingly government-aligned and top-heavy, villagers became adept at riding the tiger of global conservation. They engaged in the performance of cooperation or feigned compliance while also maintaining the possibility of outright noncompliance with CI's conservation agreements. Thus, although state power was ultimately elaborated through the committee-making processes, so too was the ability of local people to conjure or imagine new possibilities for resistance and empowerment. Given the early intentions of the committees as vehicles for community rights and representation (2002–2005), I argue that an appetite for justice was created. As CI's local legitimacy later eroded, new political dynamics then emerged: in Chumnoab, for example, some ex-committee members became key players in a politically inflammatory campaign against the proposed Areng dam (Milne 2021). CI was conspicuously absent from this radical campaign, although its early community-organizing actions probably fed into it.

Taken together, these findings offer two key lessons on the implications of project side effects and contextualization in global conservation. First is that contextualization will inevitably rework global ideas and NGO intentions, but not in a way that project actors can necessarily predict, detect, or control. In other words, project outcomes and side effects are necessarily haphazard and path-dependent, being contingent upon past events and unique conjunctures. This means that CI's conservation agreements could only ever be a "metaphor" (Mosse 2005, 11) for project action. The second lesson, however, is to recognize that NGO policy ideas and project practices *do* still matter, for these things exert influence on local material realities and village life. Here, CI's choices over project personnel and priorities gave rise to powerful and insidious side effects, for which CI did not take responsibility. This meant that CI became entangled and implicated in the unfolding of new forms of state-sanctioned control over the protected forest and its residents. A paradox therefore emerges here: that international conservation NGOs are both power*ful* and power*less* in the complex and power-laden processes of project contextualization.

To explore the ethical implications of this, I return to questions raised at the start of this chapter. If global conservation projects inevitably generate local side effects, then to what extent can project actors be held responsible for negative consequences that emerge? This is a serious question in contexts like Cambodia, where unintended project side effects can extend political violence and enable Indigenous dispossession, as seen in this case. To answer the question, I argue that project ethics lie in the domain of what NGOs *can* control, like resourcing and decision-making for which they *are* responsible. Here, CI's failure as an organization was that it did not want to see or address the complex side effects of community engagement that were unfolding through the conservation agreements. While some Khmer project staff did recognize what was going on, they were not encouraged to discuss their concerns formally with head office or expatriate staff, who might have pushed for more transparency or caution. Instead, CI's Cambodian leadership smoothed things over and got the job done, using explicit practices of anti-politics and outsourcing, enacted through the conservation agreements. CI therefore extended its relationships with powerful government interests in the Cardamom Mountains, while ignoring the processes of community marginalization and dispossession over which it presided. Unfortunately, this pattern of ethical failure would only deepen over time, as I show in the next chapter.

Chapter 6

Encountering the Violence of Corporate Conservation

Corruption is like a white-ant infestation—silent and unnoticed until part of the structure collapses; but once it is found somewhere in a building, it must be assumed to be everywhere until proved otherwise. Bosses who refuse to recognize this must, I believe, be assumed to be part of the problem. . . . They may in fact simply be naïve, but more often, I believe, they are corrupt.

—Dr. Jean Lennane, former president of Whistleblowers
Australia (Lennane 2012, 257)

This chapter provides my account of a tragic drama over corruption in CI's conservation project in Cambodia. The drama related to an illegal logging racket that was established in the Cardamom Mountains in 2009, in association with new hydropower developments. The logging, which was chiefly instigated by powerful tycoons connected to Prime Minister Hun Sen, involved selective extraction of luxury timber from the conservation area, valued at well over US$400 million, from 2009 to 2012. Apart from the movements of timber and money, this drama involved struggles over knowledge, ethics, and responsibility within CI's conservation project. Project staff were divided over how to respond to the logging, especially in relation to the apparent role of CI's government partner, the Forestry Administration. Some project staff denied the logging existed; others were complicit; and a handful disapproved but chose to do nothing. Only a few were willing to openly contest it, and for this they paid dearly, as I shall explain.

These contestations take us to the heart of debates over ethics in global conservation practice. The theme of NGO responsibility again emerges here, as it did in chapter 5, where I examined CI's role in the apparently unintended negative side effects of its project in the Cardamom Mountains. I now consider NGO conduct in institutional settings that are clearly corrupt and authoritarian. In such settings, the will to improve (Li 2007) refers to neocolonial desires to intervene for a better world, but in practice this involves navigating a vast ethical "gray zone" (Jensen 2017, 141), where control and certainty are elusive. For foreign conservation NGOs in Cambodia, this gray zone involves a complex juggling act between organizational imperatives and ethical or personal judgments, often in an atmosphere of political violence. To use a Cambodian analogy, this is a minefield of moral dilemmas and reputational risks.

My analysis of CI's conduct in this chapter shows that it navigated the minefield of conservation practice rather poorly. In particular, I show how the corporate NGO's need for organizational success and project longevity led to many, apparently small, ethical compromises over time. These compromises initially occurred in the period 2005–2007, as CI's relationships with the Cambodian government and elites in the project area became increasingly accommodating and conciliatory (see chapters 4 and 5). Just as Jean Lennane describes in relation to corrupt organizations, this was the beginning of the "white-ant infestation" (2012, 257), which later led to more overt structural failure. In other words, the conditions for failure creep in incrementally over time, often in the form of routine organizational practices, and exist well before any obvious accident or malfeasance occurs. Diane Vaughan (1996) powerfully described this phenomenon in her study of NASA's organizational culture in the 1980s, which systematically normalized risk in the lead-up to the 1986 Challenger rocket launch disaster. In this chapter, I argue that a similar process occurred within CI: ethical deviance accumulated slowly, going generally unnoticed by those on the inside of the project, until catastrophe struck in the form of a powerfully backed illegal logging operation in which CI's own staff were implicated. Making sense of the ethics of global conservation practice therefore requires a nuanced understanding of project-level organizational processes over time, as this book shows.

Another key aspect of conservation ethics emerges from the personal subjectivities and intentions of those involved. That is, deviance often tends to be a problem of organizational culture, rather than the conscious choices of individuals. To explore this, I recount my own experience of the conflicts over illegal logging in CI's project area, tracing my journey from being a CI insider in 2010 to an eventual whistleblower in 2012. I had been working part-time with CI's project in the Cardamom Mountains in 2010–2011, in a technical advisory role for the CSP's conservation agreements. Yet I soon found that my detailed knowledge of the project was too much for CI's Cambodian leadership to tolerate. This was mainly because old friends and trusted colleagues, including villagers and CI field staff, had begun to provide me with compelling data about illegal logging in the project area, which was happening under CI's watch. I felt a sense of duty to pursue the matter, following what I thought was normal professional practice. However, this provoked a top-down corporate response from CI, designed to silence me and my informants. After much struggle with my then employer, I eventually resigned. A small group of us, including Chut Wutty, then began to speak out about the logging on behalf of the voiceless forests and Indigenous people of the Cardamom Mountains.

I begin this chapter by describing the corruption that took hold within the conservation project from 2009 to 2012. Here, I show how the project was captured by powerful logging interests, which systematically exploited state authority over the protected forest. Although strongly denied by CI at the time, these logging operations have now been widely documented and publicly acknowledged (see Käkönen and Thuon 2019; Milne 2015).[1] I then describe my efforts to tackle and expose the logging, initially as a CI insider, and later as a whistleblower and outsider. Through this process, and the bitter fight over project knowledge that ensued, CI's corporate nature emerges. Here, CI's dogged instinct for self-preservation involved efforts to silence legitimate criticisms about corruption, injustice, and environmental degradation at its field site in the Cardamom Mountains.

Ultimately, by exploring how CI silenced its critics, I show how global conservation protects itself using various forms of violence. Many individuals paid dearly in the struggles that I document here: they experienced stress, illness, threats, slander, defamation, deportation, retrenchment, and forced resignation. But the man who paid the ultimate price was Chut Wutty, who was murdered by military police associated with the logging operations, near CI's ranger station in O'Som in 2012. CI's denial of any connection between Wutty's assassination and the illegal logging was an act of indirect violence, which reflects a disturbing pattern in global conservation's approach to environmental defenders more generally (Menton and Gilbert 2021). Yet CI's

---

1. Numerous media sources and primary sources are cited in peer-reviewed articles by Milne (2015) and Käkönen and Thuon (2019). Other NGOs also produced reports on the logging, which were eventually leaked.

Encountering the Violence of Corporate Conservation   **185**

strategy of denial was accompanied by more deliberate "institutional violence" too (Ahmed 2021), as seen in CI's persistent refusal to hear the voices of those who truly cared about forest destruction.

Illegal Logging in the Project Area

I returned to the Cardamom Mountains in 2010, after a three-year absence, to discover a project that had changed profoundly. Most of the community engagement team, whose work I had studied in 2007, had left CI for NGO work elsewhere. Only one of the original team members remained: Nhet, who had been transferred from Thmar Bang in the southern part of the mountains to O'Som in the north. I found that CI's community engagement, now arranged entirely through the contractual conservation agreements, had evolved in precisely the direction that I had anticipated and feared: top-down governmental engagement of local people. This was accentuated by the loss of older staff who knew the project's history of participatory mapping and advocacy for Indigenous resource rights. These problems came into focus when I arrived in Tatai Leu in 2010. Villagers I had known for years pleaded: "We are still waiting for CI to help. . . . We are worried about losing the forest." In response, I vowed to follow up with CI.

I was not naïve about the possibilities of corruption within the conservation project. My earlier research had tracked CI's transition to Khmer leadership and its consequences, not least CI's declining ability to manage its partnership with the FA, given Kiry's insistence on "smooth" (*pheaproluen*) management of government relations. However, I underestimated the serious risks of these arrangements, as did most expatriate CI staff. Early warning signs *had* been there in 2007, given regular and informal reports of corruption among rangers. Furthermore, there was a telling incident in mid-2009, when Chung, the FA manager of the protected forest, was arrested at 2:00 a.m. near the Vietnamese border in Cambodia's northeast, on charges of timber smuggling (Sokha and Shay 2009). This raised eyebrows at CI, but Chung was quickly released, and CI publicly defended him. CI's most senior expatriate in Cambodia at the time told journalists, "Past evidence has showed that he has had many years of opportunities to cut down high-value timber, but he's done the opposite" (Sokha and Shay 2009). Unfortunately, this incident was just a prelude of things to come from 2009 onward: an institutionalized form of corruption, instigated by government-backed elites in Phnom Penh, and implemented in the field under the watch of Chung and Kiry.

The systematic corruption began in 2009 in the northern part of CI's project area, at O'Som. There, construction of the Chinese-backed Stung Atay hydroelectric dam was well under way, and this made the forest vulnerable to exploitation. Key here was that dam construction involved a "reservoir clearing permit" to ensure that the area to be flooded would be cleared of forest and timber before inundation. Kiry told me that this was to prevent eutrophication caused by rotting vegetation underwater. But an underlying motivation for this permit was the extraction of high-value timber—not just from the reservoir area but from the entire expanse of the Central Cardamoms Protected Forest and the neighboring Phnom Samkos Wildlife Sanctuary. Timber extracted illegally from beyond the reservoir would simply be laundered through the site, using the extraction permit granted by the FA for reservoir clearance. Furthermore, this new and extensive logging was focused on luxury rosewood (*Dalbergia* spp.),[2] which is strictly protected under Cambodian law and prohibited for trade under the Convention on International Trade in Endangered Species (CITES). The reservoir-clearing permit therefore provided a legal fix for what became a highly lucrative and extensive illegal logging racket across the northern Cardamom Mountains.

The company that acquired the reservoir-clearing license for the Atay dam was MDS Ex-Im, owned by the then relatively unknown businessman *oknha* Try Pheap. Tellingly, he is now one of Cambodia's most prominent tycoons, whose fortune was built from the rosewood extraction described here. The title oknha is important because it signals a businessman's largesse and favor with the ruling elite. It requires a lump sum payment to the ruling party of around US$100,000, followed by ongoing public and private gifts that support Cambodia's regime at all levels (Verver and Dahles 2015). The oknha, who are addressed as "Lord" or "Excellency" in Khmer, exist in a symbiotic relationship with the ruling party. On the one hand, they enjoy privileges and licenses awarded by the state to facilitate their business activities, often including monopoly control over resources like timber. On the other hand, there is an expectation of gift giving and profit sharing through

---

2. Two species of rosewood grow in Cambodia: Thailand rosewood (*D. cochinchinensis*) and Burmese rosewood (*D. bariensis*). Locally, all species are referred in Khmer as *kronyung*.

patronage-like relationships and informal taxation that sustain government actors, whether they be park rangers or powerful officials (Milne 2015).

What happened in the Cardamom Mountains provides an exemplary case of this rather centralized and formalized system of corruption in Cambodia. MDS was awarded the timber extraction contract by the FA, which was acting in line with higher-order party demands and interests. A critical player here was the FA manager of the CCPF, Chung, who with Kiry supervised the CI-backed ranger stations in the CCPF, each housing up to ten rangers (see map 2). The rangers were a mix of FA and military police staff, funded by CI. Under this system, the logging worked as follows: park rangers ensured that MDS enjoyed protection from the law, and hence a territorial monopoly over resources in the conservation area. Meanwhile, MDS orchestrated the timber extraction, in collaboration with a handful of villagers and middlemen, and subsequent trafficking of the rosewood across Cambodia to traders in Vietnam. The rangers provided protection, forest maps, and local knowledge; MDS provided them with gifts like motorbikes, parties, and money. At the forest gate, the low-level rangers loyally recorded each truck of rosewood that left the area, taking a relatively small bribe for themselves. At the ranger checkpoint in O'Som, for example, a "bribe book" of these proceedings was kept, in which each truck and it associated bribes was documented. Remarkably, several pages of this book were photographed by one of my informants at the ranger station, who risked his safety to gather evidence on the corruption.

The meticulous recording of illicit timber flows by rangers at the O'Som checkpoint signals the well-controlled and top-down nature of the operation. The rangers were mere foot soldiers, earning US$50–100/day each, as the *real* money was amassed by MDS and more senior officials elsewhere. For example, by 2010–2011, the rosewood extraction had reached fever pitch, with between five and ten fully loaded trucks leaving O'Som every day. The value of the rosewood loaded onto these trucks was worth US$5,000–8,000 per cubic meter. Furthermore, by the time it reached the Vietnamese border— after having been trafficked across Cambodia in small pieces loaded into luxury four-wheel-drive vehicles like Land Cruisers and Range Rovers—its value was marked up by five times. This activity continued until the rosewood was exhausted in around 2013, after which villagers were left to dig up the rosewood stumps from the ground to sell by the kilo. Conservative calculations, using a range of data sources, show that over the period of intense rosewood extraction by MDS, from 2009 to 2012, a total of US$220 million was removed from O'Som—a sum that reflects the base price of rosewood and does not include profits made in subsequent trafficking.[3]

With spectacular profits at stake, the CI-sponsored rangers were effectively used by MDS to enforce its government-granted territorial monopoly over the forest. This meant that they applied the Forestry Law to prosecute "independent" cutters of rosewood, confiscating their timber and preventing them from participating in the trade. Confiscated timber was then fed into the MDS timber flows via the FA. Early on, this resulted in some spectacular conflicts, as territorial control was being established. Nhet, who observed the struggles, called it the "rosewood war": there were car chases between rivals, military helicopters sent from Phnom Penh to intervene, and dramatic timber confiscations worth millions of dollars. These events indicate early discord within the government over rosewood profits, and potentially contested patronage lines within the FA and the ruling party (Milne 2015). Certainly, there was a shake-up in 2010, when CI fired the FA manager Chung, after he was arrested a second time for timber trafficking. This prompted Chung to go and work directly for MDS, already his de facto employer, along with at least two other park rangers formerly employed by CI.[4] At this time, the director general of the FA in Phnom Penh was also deposed and sidelined—apparently for having accumulated excessive rosewood profits for himself, behind MDS's back.

This FA reshuffle also coincided with the appearance of Timber Green, a new and powerful logging group in the southern CCPF in 2010 that would eventually operate alongside MDS. The two companies took discrete logging territories—MDS in the northern CCPF and Timber Green in the south—with only occasional jostling between them in remote areas.[5] Again, the mo-

---

3. This calculation uses two data sources: (1) volumetric calculation, based on the number and size of trucks leaving O'Som during the logging period; and (2) calculation of rosewood quantities from a vegetation analysis, in a leaked NGO report about the rosewood boom. Both sums are comparable (see Milne 2015).

4. Chung is now an oknha himself after the rosewood boom. MDS also hired two former colleagues, whom I knew well, to facilitate the timber trade: both FA staff employed into CI's project.

5. MDS was awarded the contract for Pursat province, and Timber Green the contract for Koh Kong province. This divided the CCPF roughly into halves. The rosewood war was later said to be about the companies' jostling over the timber in the border area between the two provinces.

dality of logging was to launder rosewood using permits acquired from the FA for clearing hydropower reservoir areas—this time for Chinese-backed dams under construction in the Roussey Chrum and Tatai Rivers, outside of the MDS area. Timber Green's rosewood moved out through Koh Kong province, using roads upgraded by the Chinese dam builders. Yet Timber Green was a mysterious company, on paper comprised simply of three individuals with direct ties to Hun Sen's family.[6] The company's operations appeared rapidly in 2010, in top-down fashion, and enjoyed strong military support. CI's ranger teams in Koh Kong merely fell into step: the company was "untouchable," my informants told me. The rangers therefore became involved either as active facilitators of the logging or passive recipients of bribes, intimidated into silence and complicity.

Timber Green went on to extract rosewood at a similar rate to MDS, with multiple truckloads per day passing through the southern Cardamoms ranger checkpoint of Veal Pee. Villagers in Thmar Bang complained that the timber rush was affecting their families and farming. Most young men from the area had been co-opted into the logging, to the extent that farming activity dropped off in 2010. For example, villagers were paid US$2.50 for each rosewood tree that they could locate for the company, and then additional wages for participation in the logging. Given that Timber Green's target area was just as large as that of MDS, with similar forest composition, the illicit profits gained from the rosewood rush would have been roughly the same for each company. Thus, conservative estimates suggest that a total of well over US$400 million of rosewood was removed from the CCPF between 2009 and 2012 (see Milne 2015).

As the rosewood boom peaked, the logging's key players and methods were well known to local villagers, like a public secret. Everybody knew it was happening, but it was not discussed or criticized publicly. Naming and shaming was taboo, as everyone seemed to know that this would invite violent retribution from the instigators of the logging. This meant that, for park rangers and field staff involved in CI's project, it was nearly impossible *not* to be complicit. For example, Nhet, who was based in the O'Som ranger sta-

---

6. Timber Green's members included one oknha from Koh Kong province, who was able to ship timber from Sre Ambul port, and a young woman of Phnom Penh's elite, with ties to real estate in Singapore. The connection to Hun Sen was made clear when the *Phnom Penh Post* journalists reporting on Timber Green were contacted threateningly by Bayon TV, a media company owned by the prime minister's daughter.

tion, explained how he continued to refuse bribes from MDS, even though he was harassed constantly by the company's middlemen, who at some point obtained his phone number and called him incessantly. Remaining outside of the game in this way, yet being aware of its inner workings, was dangerous.

However, as I explain in the following section, CI's official line was that the logging did not exist. Only Kiry came close to acknowledging the problem, after I confronted him privately in 2011. He had said aggressively: "Sarah, you must think of the bigger picture. We can say that everyone is guilty of corruption in O'Som. Even your informant, him too!" In many ways he was right. How does one attribute individual blame or responsibility in a state-backed system that is designed for illicit extraction and underpinned by violence? What should international NGOs do when engaging with such a system? It was hard to see how global conservation could not be complicit.

Ahead loomed the ethical minefield faced by all conservation NGOs in Cambodia. As I shall now explain, CI Cambodia made errors in navigating this minefield and learned the hard way. As a Khmer colleague from another conservation NGO said to me in 2012, after Wutty's murder and significant media interest in the Cardamom Mountains, "CI stepped on the mine . . . we don't want that to happen to us." Getting through unscathed apparently requires a combination of good strategy, careful judgment, and luck. In CI's case, organizational culture played a role in its poor performance, as CI's leadership sought to deny and ignore the trouble that lay ahead.

Trying to Address the Logging from Inside CI

When I re-engaged with CI in 2010, I understood but could not participate in the ethical compromises that had become normalized in its Cambodian project. I was firm in my belief that CI, as an international organization funded by various bilateral aid and philanthropic donor agencies, had a responsibility to tackle corruption and to push for change in Cambodia. Thus, when my former colleagues and friends of many years in the field sounded the alarm about logging and corruption in the CCPF, I felt that it was my duty to raise the matter with CI's in-country management. I was convinced that CI would want to know about illegal logging in its project area and would want to take action. This belief drove me from mid-2010 until December 2011, when I eventually resigned from CI, demoralized and exhausted.

The terms of my re-engagement with CI had changed my positionality vis-à-vis the Cambodia project. As a head-office advisor based in Australia, I did not have any functional role in running the CI project in Cambodia, nor was I privy to management decisions.[7] This meant that, when I returned to Cambodia after three years' absence in 2010, I arrived as a project outsider in possession of substantial insider knowledge. Much had changed, yet it was all utterly familiar because I had intimate knowledge of the field and project history. Furthermore, I had long-standing relationships with staff and villagers in the project area. This made my arrival problematic for CI Cambodia's leadership, which consisted of two individuals who I had witnessed rise into their new roles in 2007. In some senses, I was a threat: the usual superficial performance that head office advisors received in Cambodia would not work on me, as I was capable of finding out what was happening in the field.

Rather than perceiving myself as a threat, however, I thought of myself as a skilled advisor, with important insights to share—a view that in retrospect was rather misguided. During my visits as an advisor for the CSP, I went to Thmar Bang with the field team in October 2010, and then to O'Som in February 2011. These trips meant that I saw how the field had changed since 2007: after dark and in private, villagers described the logging. Nhet also disclosed to me the workings of MDS in the northern CCPF, which he had witnessed for over a year, since he had moved to the O'Som ranger station.

It was impossible for me to ignore their quiet but desperate voices. Furthermore, it was plain to see how the corruption was undermining CI's already worn relationships with local communities and thus the long-term prospects of its investments like the conservation agreements. I therefore recommended that the CSP team in Cambodia conduct a "review" of the agreements, with my support, to provide an official way of documenting local perspectives for CI's leadership in Phnom Penh and Washington, DC. The CSP team in Cambodia was excited about the review: they saw it as an opportunity to be heard, in what had become an oppressive office environment dominated by Khmer leadership that would not tolerate questions about the conduct of CI's rangers, especially in relation to the logging.

---

7. My position was social development director for the Conservation Stewards Program. By mid-2011 I was also in discussion with CI's regional leadership about taking on the technical director position for CI Cambodia. This never eventuated, but it was a factor in my raising concerns about corruption with CI in 2011.

In 2011, I therefore worked with the CSP team to design and implement the review. The team leader in Phnom Penh, and Nhet in the field, were extremely supportive. Other team members cooperated, but I knew they were fearful: as Kiry's recent recruits, they had little knowledge of the project's history, let alone any personal values to drive a bottom-up community engagement process in the protected forest. They were also reluctant to criticize their Khmer superiors. To avoid problems, the review was designed with a technical framing. Primarily, it involved a household survey of CSP target villages, mimicking previous household surveys to measure "livelihood impacts" of the conservation agreements. The idea was to use the survey to track change, given that a baseline had been established in 2007. Although the framing was technical, the intent was to start a conversation with CI Cambodia's leadership about the state of affairs in the field.

My understanding of what was happening in the field was supplemented through collaborations with non-CI staff too. In particular, I worked with Alex, a charismatic young Khmer-speaking activist of Spanish and British descent. Fascinated with Cambodia, he had come to know Thmar Bang district in the southern CCPF very well. For the past two years, he had been in and out of the area on a bicycle, independently getting to know the villagers and their homelands. When I returned to Thmar Bang in 2010, villagers told me about Alex, and I knew that I had to meet him. Soon enough, we were regularly corresponding and discussing ways to tackle the illegal logging. We shared data and gradually developed an understanding of how Timber Green was operating in Thmar Bang, under CI's watch.

The culmination of the CSP review was scheduled for August 2011. The idea was that I would visit Phnom Penh, to work with the CSP team on analysis and report preparation. However, before I boarded the plane, there were some chilling warning signs of what would come: Kiry dismissed the four CSP field staff without discussion, informing them that an "organizational restructure" was under way. I was astounded. These were dedicated staff, financed by CI's head office on a long-term basis through grant funding beyond Kiry's control. Of course, Kiry's intent was that I would have no team to work with upon my arrival, and no informants for the upcoming CSP review. That week I also received a particularly unfriendly email from the chief administrator of CI Cambodia, who was under Kiry's command. She emailed me, copying my head office boss and CI's regional technical director, asking: "What is the purpose of this trip? Who is paying for this trip?" Unintimidated, I explained the purpose of the CSP review, along with my intention to push for the four field staff to be reinstated, in accordance with the wishes of the CSP director at the head office and in compliance with Cambodian labor law.

I had underestimated the resistance that I would encounter in Cambodia, however, and the extent of Kiry's efforts to mobilize others against me and my informants. Ominously, the same week that the four CI field staff were dismissed, Alex also lost his job. Alongside his trips to the Cardamom Mountains, Alex had been working as a translator for the Cambodian Red Cross—a national organization, under the patronage of the prime minister's wife. Apparently, Alex arrived in his employer's Phnom Penh office one morning to be told: "You are involved in nature activism, you're fired." It was never clear who tipped off Alex's employers, but Kiry certainly had the connections and knowledge of Alex's movements to do so. It seemed that a dark force field was being mobilized against those who were openly opposed to the logging in the Cardamom Mountains.

Fueled by a sense of purpose, I flew to Phnom Penh for the CSP review, still believing that good data would be enough to turn things around. I pushed to have the four field staff reinstated and was temporarily successful, due to backing from my boss in the head office. I then worked with the CSP team on the review report, which had been drafted in my absence, using recent household survey data. Tellingly, however, I found that the report's content was cautious and partial. This was because, at the last minute, the review had allegedly been "taken over" by Aung—the FA staffer who was also on the CSP team but under Kiry's command.

Aung's review report was heavily filtered. No mention was made of the rosewood logging—an omission that was especially conspicuous in the livelihoods analysis, since villagers' accounts suggested that the majority of local men had been co-opted into the logging, causing labor shortages on farms. Furthermore, with characteristic Cambodian irony, Aung's main recommendation was that the conservation agreements should be used to tackle illegal logging. Aung wanted the community rangers to "help the FA to confiscate the luxury wood" from "offenders" in the forest. This was the FA's attempt to capture the conservation agreements and integrate them into its system of corruption. As Nhet observed of Aung's actions, "He wants the luxury timber in the conservation agreement, because he wants to be involved with that." In other words, Aung wanted to secure his own authority as a legal agent in the forest, so that he too could take bribes and benefit from the timber extraction.

While the content of the review report was problematic, I thought that the key opportunity for impact would be to present our results at CI's formal all-staff meeting in Phnom Penh. So the CSP team prepared a PowerPoint presentation, with my assistance, to present the review findings and recommendations to all staff. We also drafted some key questions for the management team: not just for Kiry and Chung but also for Luke, CI's technical director, who would chair the meeting. I had high hopes for sincere and substantive engagement, but it soon became clear that Kiry and Luke had planned something else. To begin, Luke directed the meeting into bureaucratic trivialities: he explained how staff needed to complete their expense claims on time, showing them the forms that they should use for this. The diversion made me anxious and frustrated.

Finally, however, our moment came. Upon discussing the review recommendations, I first argued that the conservation agreements should not be revised to address illegal logging: "that is the responsibility of the FA, it is a law enforcement matter." But the management team ignored me. Pushing further, I said, "Actually, villagers want to know about the rosewood logging—are the rangers doing anything to stop it?" At that point Kiry snapped. He shouted back at me, pointing his finger to my face: "You can't talk like that. Otherwise, it looks like you don't know anything!" It was a confrontational moment, in part because Kiry's words were such an affront to the knowledge I had carefully gathered, based on years of research in the field. Kiry also went on to criticize Alex, whose evidence bolstered my line of questioning, saying, "Alex is like a crazy man, who knows nothing." The meeting was adjourned, without resolution.

I left feeling unsatisfied and unsettled. My next step was to seek a one-on-one meeting with Luke, the most senior CI expatriate in Cambodia. He had oversight over the entire country program, managing its relationships with the Cambodian government and CI's head office. He was also someone I had known for years, and I thought we had a good collegial relationship. We met outside of the CI office in Phnom Penh, and I put forward my concerns. I spoke in the interests of "our" organization and mission—reflecting, with utter sincerity, the professional values I thought we shared. I said, "Look, Kiry is not batting for our side, do you realize what he's covering up?" I then explained the logging operations being run by MDS and Timber Green, which were being facilitated by CI's rangers. Trusting in Luke, I was very candid and open about my sources and motivations. But my misjudgment was profound.

In retrospect, Luke's response to my allegations was indicative of a corporate, and perhaps also personal, need to deny what was happening. Luke had just received word of his promotion to a very senior role within CI, which would see him based elsewhere in the region. He was undoubtedly proud of his work and was looking for a smooth exit from Cambodia. His response to my allegations of corruption was therefore cautious and deflective: "If you really believe it, then we need evidence. . . . It's hard to get rid of these country directors once Washington has backed them. . . . It's the same with CI in the Philippines and Indonesia—they know there's some corruption there, but the country directors are just too well connected, too established . . . they're not worth challenging." I nodded respectfully, not realizing that the door was being shut in my face. He went on: "If you're going to accuse Kiry, then you need a smoking gun. We need proper evidence. And you have to follow due process too. You need to use the whistleblower function through head office. They'll take the evidence and investigate." I replied, "OK, sure. There's plenty of evidence."

Naïvely, I remained confident in CI's organizational processes and protocols—I thought that they would be a source of vindication for those who opposed the logging, and a way to push for reform in Cambodia. I was also sympathetic to Luke's need to maintain his relationship with Kiry, which was essential to the functioning of the Cambodia program. Little did I know that, in accepting Luke's recommendation to use CI's formal whistleblower function at the head office, I was walking into a trap. Cleverly, Luke had made it *my* responsibility to *prove* the alleged corruption, even though he was the senior expatriate overseeing CI's investments in Cambodia. This was the first sign of corporate denial that I would encounter: an ability to cast off personal responsibility and outsource ethical dilemmas to the larger organizational form.

The end of my visit to Phnom Penh for the CSP review was approaching—it would be my last visit to Cambodia as a CI staff member. On the morning of my departure I had arranged to see Kiry in the office, very early, when no one else was there. I had hoped that a one-on-one meeting with him would help, but he was aggressive in his pushback. I pointed out the need for accountability, saying, "You have to think of head office and the donors." But he told me to "think of the bigger picture," arguing that everyone was corrupt, and that it was impossible for rangers to police the reservoir-clearing contracts associated with the hydropower dams. He argued that his strategy was pragmatic and in CI's long-term interests, as he wanted to avoid conflict with the government. It was hard to contest, especially as he spoke forcefully and authoritatively. Only later, in 2018, would I learn of his alleged personal links to the logging: that his wife and the MDS tycoon's wife were apparently sisters.[8]

After the meeting with Kiry, I felt rattled. Something was wrong. Traveling back to my hotel room, on the back of a motorbike, I felt as though someone was following me. I looked over my shoulder nervously: so many men on motorbikes, wearing dark helmets with tinted visors. I clutched my shoulder bag, feeling vulnerable and foreign. Back in the air-conditioned expat bubble of my hotel, I began to prepare for departure. One last task remained for me: I had promised to pass on a memory stick to a trusted Khmer colleague, who had been a research assistant working with my expatriate friend in Thmar Bang over the past year. Together these researchers had collected sensitive data on CI and the corruption that was unfolding: they, too, were my informants and confidants. Furthermore, they, too, had been at the receiving end of Kiry's aggression. This had caused my now Australia-based friend to believe that her Skype and email accounts were subject to surveillance by the Cambodian government.[9] For this reason, she had physically mailed a memory stick of data to me in Australia, so that I could hand it in person to our colleague in Cambodia. But where was it? The memory stick was meant to be in my suitcase. I rummaged through everything, becoming frantic, hot with anxiety. Had someone taken it from my room?

Then I found it. I paused and observed the scene, feeling my heartbeat in my throat. The contents of my suitcase were strewn everywhere, testament to my panicked search. This was getting out of hand. Was I imagining or overreacting to Kiry's aggression? Or was this truly dangerous? Such internal dialogues of doubt and fear would become familiar to me over the coming months. Later that day, from the international departure lounge of Pochentong airport, I called Kiry. Luke had asked me to do so, to smooth things over. "I look forward to working with you," I heard myself say, "everything will be

---

8. A collaborator told me this in 2018, after his Khmer informant explained Kiry's relationship to the tycoon quite nonchalantly—as though it were so obvious and natural.

9. This concern was shared by many NGO staff and activists in Cambodia at the time. Some were convinced that their phones were tapped and that their email accounts had been hacked.

fine. I just want to do what's right for the forest and the people." My resolve was clear as I boarded the flight home.

How Corporate Processes Silence Dissent

Canberra's benign order felt reassuring upon my return from Phnom Penh. Although the CSP review had been fraught, I was at least now justified in pursuing the illegal logging issue through CI's head office channels. My strategy was to use CI's formal internal whistleblowing function to spark action, as Luke had suggested. I was still convinced that good data and good process would be enough to achieve change.

Within one week, however, my sense of conviction had evaporated. The trouble started with emails from my boss in Washington, DC, asking me to respond to a set of accusations about my behavior. The accusations came from Luke, who happened to be in DC that week, presumably arranging the details of his promotion. Breaking protocol, Luke had arranged a meeting with my boss's superior, during which he accused me of having a "conflict of interest" with field staff; of "paying bribes to Cambodian government officials" in the Ministry of Environment; and of "spreading false rumors about corruption" among CI staff in Cambodia. He also accused Nhet, one of my key allies and informants, of being "a drunk." I read and reread the allegations, which were false but familiar. I felt sick with a sense of betrayal: each accusation drew from some aspect of my personal and professional life that I had shared with Luke and his wife, in good faith, in person. It was a character assassination, perfectly implemented. I had no voice in the process. Fortunately, my boss, who was also caught by surprise, remained sympathetic to me.

The allegations of misconduct were serious, specifically targeted at having me dismissed from CI. Clearly, too, the accusers' aim was to destroy my reputation: a tactic that presumably would result in my knowledge being discredited, and my voice silenced. Initially I tried to defend myself, arguing that the accusations were motivated by my recent attempts to address corruption within CI Cambodia. But my pleas were deflected by corporate formalities at the head office. I was told by human resources that, before any dialogue could take place on the corruption issue, I should attend an appointment with their "internal auditor" via Skype. The auditor would first assess the allegations against me, seeking my response to each one, through a trial-like interview. So began my dealings with what would become a long series of corporate processes, mainly through emails and Skype calls with internal auditors, external auditors, and CI's whistleblower hotline. In retrospect, I see these processes as artifacts of CI's "audit culture," a series of corporate practices intended to achieve the appearance of public accountability (Shore 2008; Strathern 2000). Furthermore, in my personal encounters with these instruments of transparency, I found myself falling into step with the performance: I was disciplined and responsive, truly believing that the truth would eventually prevail through good bureaucratic processes.

Clinging to this belief, and needing my own sense of voice and justice, I participated in the first interview with CI's internal auditor to address the allegations against me. I knew him from his former role as a head office representative in Cambodia deployed to ensure CI's compliance with head-office systems and US laws. Ironically, one of the things he had worked on was CI Cambodia's administrative response to the US Foreign Corrupt Practices Act—a stringent new law affecting American NGOs operating overseas. Following his "success" in Cambodia, the man now interviewing me had been promoted to be CI's internal auditor. Thus, the interview was oddly loaded with Cambodian material, but I *was* given the opportunity to respond to the allegations, and I was heard. Matters seemed to be settled.

Feeling bruised but encouraged, I then sought to have my say about the corruption and set things right—I still believed that this would be possible. I therefore engaged CI's whistleblower function so that I could formally report on the illegal logging in the CCPF. Following Luke's advice, I was diligent about collecting good data from my informants and cross-checking between sources. I prepared a package of data for the external auditor, including incriminating photos of trucks loaded with rosewood, evidence of the bribes being taken by CI's rangers in O'Som, and interview data from informants about the illegal logging activity. I then handed over the data and explained everything in a single interview with CI's external auditor via Skype. I felt satisfied and excited by the possibility that my voice, and the voices of others, would finally be heard.

With anticipation, and some relief, I waited for a response from CI's management on the logging issue. While waiting, I prepared a letter to the director of human resources in the head office. My letter sought an apology, or at least some acknowledgment that the character assassination directed at me in August 2011 had been motivated by CI Cambodia's efforts to discredit my claims about corruption. I was desperate for a response. I wanted my employer to recognize what I had suffered in the name of transparency. While waiting for resolution, my stress levels remained extremely high as the weeks and months passed. I woke often in the night, haunted by the experiences of betrayal and having my voice silenced. It felt as though everything I stood for had been trampled upon, especially my values and motivation as a researcher and advocate for Indigenous people and forests in Cambodia.

Justice never came, however. Three months on, I was still waiting for a reply from CI about the corruption allegations that I had formally disclosed and substantiated. I was also still waiting for a response from human resources about how I had been treated. So, the week before Christmas I sought resolution by calling the human resources director in head office. She took the call while driving to work. I suppose she would not have taken the call if she had known that it was me. Hoping to establish a human connection, I said, "I've been waiting for months; this is really stressful, I need some kind of response." But her reply was cold: "Fair enough. I'll send you an email."

The email that I received later that day was not what I expected. There was no apology, no acknowledgment of what I had experienced. The email simply contained another set of allegations against me. It was a set of questions that I was being asked to respond to, all drawn from the original character assassination that I thought had been cleared. As I trawled through the text, I realized that this was the product of months of dialogue between Luke and the human resources director. A year later, my sympathetic boss would tell me: "I saw those two chatting at CI's annual meeting. They're tight. You never stood a chance." But at the time neither of us knew what we were up against. All I could discern from the email was that Luke had been provided with a copy of my confidential letter to human resources, and that he had been given an opportunity to respond. It seemed he did not need to prove his innocence or face questioning. Rather, he joined forces with CI's most powerful staff to sully my name and remove the annoyance of the corruption allegations that my informants and I had put forward.

At this point I realized that I was wasting energy on a fight that I could never win. CI would never acknowledge my voice or the tragedy of the logging in the Cardamom Mountains, and they would never apologize to me personally. I had been slow to see what was unfolding. It was only when sharing my experiences with a senior academic colleague—an anthropologist who had seen CI in action in Papua New Guinea—that I began to understand. He said, "You do realize that you're dealing with a corporation, don't you?" Through comments like this I found solidarity, and the fog of trauma began to clear. I also saw that I was not alone in contesting CI, and that the type of struggle I was engaged in was a quintessential one. That is, whistleblowing is a societal phenomenon, emerging from ethical disjuncture between an individual and their employer, in which dysfunctional corporate interests typically prevail (De Maria and Jan 1995). I would also later understand that the dynamics in which wronged individuals complain endlessly through bureaucratic processes, to the point of exhaustion, amount to a form of indirect violence—what Sara Ahmed has termed "institutional violence" (2021, 179)—yet another aspect of the "atmospheres of violence" faced by environmental defenders more generally (Menton, Navas, and Le Billon 2021, 51). Individuals in such struggles rarely fare well. I decided to walk away from CI, resigning through a formal and simple letter in late 2011.

Going Public, and Its Violent Spillover Effects

Freed from the contractual and indeed psychological discipline that comes with being employed by a corporate-like organization, I began to refocus on the illegal logging problem, and how it might be exposed. I was not alone: a network of forest activists had formed around the issue, and we were beginning to make contact with journalists at the *Phnom Penh Post* (then a reputable Australian-owned English-language newspaper in Cambodia). Things moved quickly. The same week that I resigned from CI, Chut Wutty entered the fray: he teamed up with journalists from the *Post* and guided them to Thmar Bang to gather data on the logging. The journalists obtained remarkable photos of trucks laden with timber and incriminating data from villagers, who went on the record. I also provided some supporting material for the write-up. The article, published December 21, 2011 (see Boyle 2011), was a sensation, sending shock waves through the NGO scene in Phnom Penh, as well as the international conservation community more broadly. For instance, the widely read *REDD-Monitor* blog, which is often critical of mainstream conservation, ran its own story based on the original article and headlined it "Conservation International Turns a Blind Eye to Illegal Logging" (Lang 2012). This, too, went viral.

It was a vindicating moment, but hardly liberating. Personally, I felt nervous about the repercussions: Would CI try to point the finger at me? Could they take legal action? Was the safety of my informants compromised? The newspaper staff were also jittery: immediately after Boyle's article was released, the *Phnom Penh Post* had received a threatening phone call from another media company in Cambodia, Bayon TV, owned by Hun Mana, one of the prime minister's daughters. The journalists were warned of potential negative repercussions from their work. This threat confirmed the alleged links between the logging racket and Cambodia's most powerful elites.

Chut Wutty was less fearful about the article's fallout, as he was now used to intimidation and death threats from the establishment. Since leaving CI a decade prior, he had started his own NGO—the Natural Resources Protection Group—which by 2011 was very active in mobilizing local communities against illegal logging. Wutty had become a public figure, known for his bold disruptions of elite-backed resource extraction, especially in the forests of Prey Lang in northern Cambodia (see Lambrick and de Smet 2015). Few members of the public knew of Wutty's old connections to CI in the Cardamom Mountains. Yet, for those involved in "managing" the CCPF, Wutty was a thorn in their side: he knew the mountains well, and he could connect the dots between the ruling party, Hun Sen's family, the Forestry Administration, the military, the logging tycoons, and CI's leadership in Cambodia.

Meanwhile, CI's official response to the *Phnom Penh Post* article was one of denial. Two days after the article was published, the international environmental blog *Mongabay* (2011) ran a post written by its managing editor titled "CI Refutes Cambodian Logging Story." Referring to the allegations in the *Post*, the blog quoted CI as saying that the article's claims were "dramatically inaccurate and patently untrue." The blog continued:

> CI said it "does not oversee enforcement and does not maintain or facilitate any checkpoints or rangers in or outside the CCPF. Rather, we provide grants to the Forestry Administration to support ongoing monitoring of the CCPF." . . . The conservation group said the large-scale logging referenced in the article was legally approved by the Cambodian government and that "CI is not involved in this work and does not engage with the company as the forest clearance for the reservoir does not take place within the CCPF". CI added that rosewood occurs in low density within the CCPF due to its geography.

The corporate sheen and arrogance of CI was now emerging. It seemed that they would not concede to any of the allegations about the logging, no matter how good the journalism or the data were. The *Mongabay* blog post drew heavily from a statement released by Luke, now one of CI's senior vice presidents. The statement was not officially circulated, but it found its way onto the *Phnom Penh Post* Facebook page in a public comment.[10] Luke's statement said: "CI Cambodia completely refutes the suggestion that it is turning a 'blind eye' to illegal logging or that it is complicit in any way with the practices alleged in the newspaper story. . . . The staff members of CI Cambodia . . . work tirelessly to support conservation of the most important natural areas in the country."

That sick feeling returned as I read those words, knowing what Luke was doing behind the scenes to silence critics and prevent CI from addressing the logging. Aside from the language of denial, and the corporate spin about CI's "success" in the Cardamom Mountains, there was also a hint of panic in Luke's use of "science" to bolster his position. For example, his arguments that the "CCPF is entirely unsuitable for rosewood to occur in significant densities" and "forest cover change maps consistently show the CCPF to be one of the least deforested areas in the entire country" were a pseudo-scientific show. Any informed reader would know that selective logging of rosewood would not appear on the forest cover change maps that he was referring to. Furthermore, Luke's claims about the vegetation of the CCPF being dominated by "pine forest and montane grasslands," unsuitable for rosewood, were incorrect.[11] He would have known this, too, but he was adept at using scientific language for CI's corporate interest. Thus, he cleverly tried to steer public debate into a discussion over scientific facts, rather than the real issue at hand. This is a now-familiar tactic of corporate power and deflection in our post-truth age (Oreskes and Conway 2010).

CI's public denial of the logging allegations initially proved to be effective. Just as climate skeptics play on uncertainty to muddy the waters of uncomfortable scientific knowledge, CI's denial strategy meant that the sta-

---

10. Obtained from the *Phnom Penh Post* Facebook page, posted December 20, 2011, accessed November 2018, in reference to the original article by Boyle (2011) https://www.facebook.com /permalink.php?story_fbid=314247368597889&id=154245617928723.

11. The *Mongabay* blog post argues that rosewood does not occur in upland montane habitat. But vegetation maps of the CCPF produced by CI show that this habitat only occurs in small portions at the very tops of the mountains.

Encountering the Violence of Corporate Conservation

tus quo in Cambodia would go unchallenged. My network of activists and informants, who were witnessing the logging firsthand, found this unacceptable. So we regrouped and restrategized: there was scope for a second *Phnom Penh Post* article, since the first had focused only on Thmar Bang. The story of MDS in O'Som, where the most blatant corruption was taking place, was still untold. At this point I collaborated more closely with the journalists. I decided to share with them the data that I had originally given to CI's whistleblower hotline, along with the story of CI's efforts to suppress internal dissent over the logging. I did not take this a decision lightly, due to potential risks to me and my informants: it would be hard for us to remain anonymous if this reached the press. Nevertheless, our sentiments reflected a strong desire for justice.

The result was a second *Post* article, published on March 26, 2012, focusing on the northern CCPF (Boyle and May 2012). Drawing from the journalists' own data from O'som, the article was damning. It detailed the logging operations, named the middlemen and traders, and explained the involvement of CI rangers. The article also firmly pointed to CI's role in suppression of the truth, with the closing words: "Community members, consultants and staff repeatedly told CI's management about the illicit timber trade that was taking place since 2009, but instead of acting on these concerns, the organization simply denied it was true. Millions of dollars in foreign donations go into CI's programs to protect the CCPF. Donors may want to know why millions of dollars in illegal timber are going back out."

With pressure mounting, CI went into damage control mode, by maintaining a firm public stance of denial. On the transnational conservation grapevine, donors, and NGO staff were apparently told that the article was "all lies," simply the product of a "disgruntled former employee."[12] Furthermore, CI's behind-the-scenes internal response, which I learned of many months later, suggested that CI was ready to play hardball in defense of its reputation. For example, all CI staff had apparently been instructed not to interact with me at all, for legal reasons. This made keeping up with my former colleagues and friends very awkward. As one of them said before a surreptitious lunch meeting, "If I'm seen talking to you, there'll be trouble." In these ways, CI staff were disciplined into silence, as part of the corporate

---

12. A sympathetic colleague working for a global conservation NGO told me this in Phnom Penh in 2012.

suppression of dissent that unfolded. I also became isolated from my former life as a CI staff member.

Alongside these NGO dynamics, frightening displays of violence were also beginning to emerge from the Cambodian elite interests behind the logging. Exactly one month after the second *Phnom Penh Post* article was published, Chut Wutty was murdered in the CCPF, about fifteen kilometers south of the O'Som ranger station maintained by CI. He was traveling with two female journalists, a Canadian and a Cambodian, intent on continuing to expose the illegal activity being conducted at the behest of MDS and Timber Green. Wutty was accosted around midday by a small group of military personnel. He was asked to hand over his camera, because he had been taking photographs of an illegal sawmill and yellow vine processing plant by the road.[13] Wutty refused stubbornly. The conflict escalated, and he was shot at close range with an AK-47. Wutty's murderer was then shot and killed by others in the military gang, in an apparently calculated move to eliminate the perpetrator and any future possibility for justice through a trial.

The assassination of Chut Wutty generated shock, grief, and fear across Cambodia, and the world. International scandal erupted, as Wutty was hailed an environmental hero and eco-warrior in the global press. His story reached the front pages of *The Guardian* and the BBC in the UK, and the *Huffington Post* in the US, and he was the subject of countless radio and television programs. In Canberra, I grieved, wrestled with anger, and connected to others who had known Wutty. Only one week before his death, I had been sitting with him at the riverfront in Phnom Penh to share data and to discuss our further collaboration in the Cardamom Mountains. I was gutted.

Amid the buzz of international press over Wutty's murder and the rosewood logging, CI's donors started to ask questions. Most major conservation donors had a stake in the Cardamom Mountains, particularly the French government's Agence Française de Développement (AFD), which was then in talks with CI about establishing a trust fund for sustainable financing of the protected forest.[14] Other funding sources, like the well-known MacAr-

---

13. The MDS tycoon was involved in illegal yellow vine extraction too. Processed yellow vine is said to be an ingredient in *yaba*, Asian amphetamine. By mid-2012 when the rosewood "rush" was waning, yellow vine became the next lucrative resource for extraction (see Otis 2014).

14. The idea was that AFD funding would match another lump sum already earmarked for the CCPF through the Moore Foundation's Global Conservation Fund, managed by CI.

Encountering the Violence of Corporate Conservation

thur Foundation and the Critical Ecosystem Partnership Fund, also had conservation investments in the Cardamom region, whose implementation depended on the presumed capacity and accountability of big international conservation NGOs, including CI.[15] The donors were understandably sensitive about the corruption allegations among their grantees: it seemed that the business model for mainstream conservation in Southeast Asia was under threat. Thus, it was rumored that one donor with active investments in the Cardamom Mountains contacted CI, saying that they would withhold funding until "things got cleaned up." This prompted CI's next move, which was to commission a formal and so-called independent review of the management of the CCPF.

Corporate Processes of Unknowing

The public performance of accountability, through apparently independent inquiries, is a classic feature of corporate responses to whistleblowing (De Maria 1999; Woodford 2012). It was therefore no surprise that CI commissioned and financed an "independent review" into the management of the CCPF in the last quarter of 2012. It is not clear how the review team was selected, but CI's choices were clearly motivated by its need to produce a credible counternarrative to allegations of CI's involvement in illegal logging that were circulating in the media. The review team consisted of five Australian forestry and remote-sensing specialists, all technocratic white men, most of whom had some knowledge of Southeast Asia.[16] For CI, a key point was that they were neutral outsiders who did not have Cambodian connections or expertise. Furthermore, with their forestry industry backgrounds and membership, they were unlikely to be bleeding-heart environmentalists or community-rights advocates, inclined to tell a critical story. They were scientific experts, skilled in producing a certain kind of selective, technical knowledge. In addition, their common links to the Tasmanian timber

---

15. These major donor organizations also employ staff who once worked for CI, making for close relationships. The joke in the conservation scene is that these people are the CI alumni, or CIA.

16. The review report states: "All authors have substantial and senior experience in forest and natural resource management, and have formal qualifications from Australian universities, and are members of the Institute of Foresters of Australia" (Flanagan, Midgley, and Turner 2012, 4).

industry—Australia's most notoriously corrupt resource sector (Beresford 2010)—implied a capacity to resist critical scrutiny.

Over three months in late 2012, the review team conducted a data collection mission in Cambodia and subsequent analysis. To their credit, they conducted forty-eight interviews with project staff and community representatives in Phnom Penh and the Cardamom Mountains, using an apparently neutral Khmer translator where required. The lead reviewers spent seven days in the field, visiting most of CI's ranger stations. This undertaking at least involved them talking to key actors in the project, even if the field trip was short and stage-managed to some degree by the managers of the CCPF. The other component of their review was a remote-sensing exercise to estimate "vegetation loss" in the CCPF and surrounds, using low-resolution satellite imagery—a technique susceptible to user manipulation and therefore not geared toward the measurement of forest degradation due to selective logging.[17]

The review team's remit was articulated in broad and general terms, as if to divert attention away from their core underlying yet unwritten objective, which was to clear CI's name. The review would document "land-use drivers" and determine the "effectiveness" of "forest cover" protection and "existing systems" supported by CI Cambodia in the CCPF (see Flanagan, Midgley, and Turner 2012, i). Carefully crafted technical language in turn sought the identification of "improvements" to the systems in place as a final outcome of the exercise. Tellingly, the final report also included the following statement under the terms of reference section about the treatment of illegal activity: "The review considered evidence of complicity or casualness of FA or CI staff in illegal trade of rosewood or other forest products (noting that such evidence may only be anecdotal and not able to be authenticated)" (Flanagan, Midgley, and Turner 2012, i).

This statement points to the review's core motivation but tempers expectations about what it will deliver. Or, as the review team leader explained to me when we met at the outset of the process, "We don't have authority to investigate corruption in the CCPF, and we don't have the qualifications. That's not the purpose of the review." He said that the FA had requested that this be a *review*, not an investigation, and that CI was following FA's wishes in this respect. In a gesture of cooperation, the review team would receive practical

---

17. Source: 2015 interview with a forest cover monitoring expert, who had previously conducted work in the Cardamom Mountains for CI and later for Global Witness in Cambodia.

assistance from the FA. Thus, the hypocrisy of the undertaking became clear: the review would not investigate corruption or follow up on the allegations that I had lodged with CI's external auditor. Rather, its fundamental purpose was to defend CI's investment and reputation.

Nevertheless, the team leader interviewed me in Phnom Penh as part of the review process. I also met with another member of the review team back in Canberra, about six months later, after the report had come out. In sharing my data and my experiences with them, I felt grateful for the opportunity to speak. Yet, in the process of speaking, I also realized that I would never actually be heard. They were not unfriendly, but they treated me as though I was a burned-out activist in need of some perspective. This was symbolized in the packet of quintessentially Australian chocolate biscuits, called Tim Tams, brought to me by the Tasmanian reviewer in Phnom Penh: he offered me the biscuits, which were melting in the heat, as a gesture from one Aussie to another, like a peace offering. We spoke candidly for more than an hour, over dinner. I at least conveyed who I was, and what I stood for. In this sense, the review met CI's stakeholder engagement requirements in the face of controversy, but the reviewers had no ability to mete out justice.

Overall, my encounters with the review team exemplify how ignorance is made in official terms, or how certain discursive practices can render uncomfortable or inconvenient things invisible (see McGoey 2012). For example, my interactions with the review team were subject to constraints and judgments that they imposed. "I know your type," said the Canberra-based reviewer, "I've seen your thesis." His words echoed those of my former colleague at CI, a sympathetic economist, who had said to me in the midst of the drama, "You're like the anthropologist who can't leave their valley." These personal experiences of being labeled by male technocrats, who so easily inhabited and deployed the discourses of economics and forestry, were gendering and marginalizing. More broadly, I learned how their power works in part by sidelining knowledge that comes from situated, ethnographic, and normative perspectives. My scholarly knowledge of Cambodia was discounted, while CI determined that a team of foreign foresters, armed with satellite imagery, could provide an authoritative answer on the scourge of corruption and violence that had taken hold in its project site.

In spite of the partial and technocratic knowledge in the review, the ultimate product was generally thorough and not entirely uncritical of CI's conduct. The report acknowledged how hard it was to do law enforcement in the CCPF, given the complexity of the terrain and the legal system, as well as what they referred to as "capacity" constraints in the FA. The reviewers also argued that CI must take some responsibility for what happened in the project area, referring to illegal activity through the euphemism of "effectiveness" as follows: "If CI continues to actively engage in and lead aspects of the CCPF program, it cannot deny its association or responsibility when issues of effectiveness are raised" (Flanagan, Midgley, and Turner 2012, 23).

This oblique statement was a far cry from the exposure of corporate wrongdoing within CI that I had hoped for. However, it did at least criticize CI's initial denial of the rosewood logging and its efforts to disassociate itself from the management of the CCPF, which had circulated in the early press statements. There would be no formal consequences for the CI Cambodia leadership. However, as one of the reviewers said to me, almost in consolation for the review's failure to tackle the corruption head on, "Look, they haven't come out of this smelling like roses." That was the closest I ever got to an acknowledgment of what happened from those aligned with CI's corporate interests.

Meanwhile, CI's selective use of the review findings provides even more insight into how big conservation organizations use knowledge production strategically, either to deny facts or generate ambiguity (see McGoey 2012). In contrast to the broad emphasis of the review's terms of reference, the executive summary that prefaced the final report of December 2012 left no doubt about its underlying corporate purpose. The opening sentence, in large font, read: "The review concludes that Conservation International is not complicit in regard to illegal activities within the Central Cardamoms Protected Forest" (Flanagan, Midgley, and Turner 2012, vii). This statement was painful to read, given the reviewers' earlier comments to me that the review was not permitted to investigate corruption. Yet CI went on to issue a press release, via its blog, to announce the findings. The headline declared "Independent Review: Central Cardamom Protected Forest has lowest deforestation rates vs. surrounding forests" (CI 2012). Never mind that the "deforestation analysis" in the review had little ability to detect selective logging of rosewood. Furthermore, the opening paragraph of CI's blog post about the review findings was deliberate in clearing CI's name: "[The review] findings identify management successes, as well as needs for management improvements that CI can address with FA. Findings also contradicted allegations made against CI in media reports from 2011 and 2012."

CI's highly selective presentation of the review, in essence a corporate whitewash, was remarkable to me at the time. Yet I now recognize how normal and commonplace it is for corporations to manipulate pseudoscientific knowledge in their interests, along with the use of lies and spin (Bakan 2012). For example, CI's blog went on to claim that the 150-page review report had "explored critical media allegations" about the CCPF, which is simply untrue. Rather, the report discussed how CI could improve its management of "stakeholder expectations," including a suggestion that CI "respond transparently and engage proactively with stakeholders, the media, and staff to address concerns" (Flanagan, Midgley, and Turner 2012, xi). This advice appears to be an indirect reference to the circumstances surrounding the review. Also telling was that the review conspicuously ignored Cambodia's corrupt political economy and the murder of Chut Wutty: vital components of the CCPF story, which by then were widely documented in international media and by anti-corruption groups (e.g., Global Witness 2010, 2012). It is likely that the Cambodian government's involvement in the "independent review" would have made these subjects taboo. But this would have suited CI, given that its main aim was to divert attention away from the illegal logging and clear its name.

By this stage, no one that I knew was prepared to unpack the details of CI's review or take its authors to task. From my perspective, feeling depleted by the murder of Chut Wutty and other injustices associated with the project, the corporate game of CI and its so-called independent review now seemed like irrelevant background noise. Yet CI's authoritative proclamation of "management success" and their dismissal of "media allegations" about corruption (see CI 2012) had taught me key lessons. I had come to see how global conservation organizations can possess a dark heart of corporate power, being impermeable, nonhuman, and infinitely capable of manufacturing apparently robust knowledge to serve their interests. It is vitally important to contest corporate power of this kind, but would-be contestants need to be prepared for what might follow.

Understanding the Violence of Corporate Nature

In this chapter I have exposed the workings of corporate conservation through an ethnographic account of CI's treatment of illegal logging within its project area in Cambodia. The corporate response, motivated by organizational self-interest, first involved ignoring the problem. Although CI denied complicity in the logging, there was ample and detailed documentation of the timber laundering that occurred under CI's watch, including numerous intimate links between CI's Khmer staff, the government, and the logging operations. Furthermore, even if CI's expatriate staff were ignorant of these goings-on, their presence and involvement in the CCPF *does* imply responsibility. As whistleblower Michael Woodford writes: "Ignorance is no defense . . . if you were there and not aware of it, then you were incompetent. If you were there, and aware of it without asking tough questions, then you were negligent" (2012, 145).

For CI's global leadership, the claim of incompetence may have offered a more humble and ethical way out. Yet this is not what happened: the production of ignorance was a key aspect of CI's corporate response to the allegations of corruption in its project area. This was achieved through the construction of highly selective corporate knowledge, which effectively erased or cast doubt on information that was inconvenient for CI. This process began with statements of denial and was followed by the suppression of individuals who tried to expose the corruption. It ended with the official removal of offending allegations, through an apparently independent, scientific review, followed by exonerating press releases from CI.

These processes tell us how knowledge management, including the filtering and silencing of inconvenient sources, is a fundamental aspect of the corporate form. Here, Rayner points to how organizations manage information that is "uncomfortable" or "out of place": they treat it like "pollution, lying on the boundaries of what is organizationally knowable and not knowable" (2012, 111). In other words, uncomfortable knowledge is existentially dangerous for organizations, especially those that rely upon external perceptions of their operations as credible and virtuous to derive financial value, as seen elsewhere in global conservation (Milne and Mahanty 2019). For this reason, organizations often have sophisticated conscious and unconscious strategies for managing difficult or dangerous information, ranging from outright denial to dismissal and diversion (Rayner 2012). This need to control knowledge, or to manage systematic gaps between talk and action in organizational life, has also been theorized as "organized hypocrisy" (Weaver 2008)—a form of institutionalized hypocrisy that arises through ongoing conflicts between internal organizational needs and the external policy environment.

The notion of organized hypocrisy, however, does not capture the potential for corporate practices to inflict institutional or symbolic violence upon their subjects (Ahmed 2021; Bourdieu 1977). Here, the production and maintenance of ignorance is inherently violent, especially when inconvenient information is ignored and critical individuals are either silenced or punished for what they know. Take, for example, CI's refusal to acknowledge the underlying motives for Chut Wutty's assassination in the Cardamom Mountains. In the press, CI attributed Wutty's murder to a "personal dispute" (*Phnom Penh Post* 2012), and his name was never mentioned in CI's independent review. Wutty's struggle with the perpetrators of illegal logging in the Cardamom Mountains was simply ignored or factored out by CI and its partners. Meanwhile, "scientific expertise" was brought to bear, apparently to settle matters, and to produce acceptable, objective knowledge for the global conservation industry. This practice of ignoring violence against people and nature, perpetrated by an NGO that was in a position of power and responsibility with regard to what was unfolding, itself amounts to an act of violence—not physical in nature, but institutional and bureaucratic (Ahmed 2021; Milne and Mahanty 2019). Here we see how corporate nature can be systematic about not hearing marginal or inconvenient voices.

For those who do speak out about wrongdoing in conservation, and are not heard, the experience of institutional violence can be very harmful. This harm relates to how corporate processes of unknowing affect individuals, emotionally and psychologically. The most obvious victims are the naysayers or whistleblowers, who come into direct contact with organizational efforts to discredit and silence them. They are dismissed, transferred, betrayed, accused of misconduct, and personally slandered. In my experience, the affective blow of being silenced and misrepresented was highly distressing, but this is a common phenomenon noted by scholars of whistleblowing and dissent (Ahmed 2021; De Maria 1999). Apart from the shock of being targeted for my ethical stance, I also grieved the loss of trust and belonging that I had once felt in my professional environment.

Occasionally I reflect upon my former colleagues in conservation, so many of whom are good people. I ask, how have they have been affected by the ethical compromises that arise in conservation practice in places like Cambodia? This question suggests yet another dimension to the violence of corporate nature: that which occurs internally or personally for NGO staff, who must constantly accommodate a form of cognitive dissonance about the virtue of their work, on the one hand, and its potential negative effects or complicity in processes of violence and corruption, on the other. The voices and subjectivities of these staff still need to be considered.

Not everyone in conservation, however, will reflect on their work in this way. As Michael Woodford explains, supporting one's company is often "like supporting a football team" (cited in Williams 2018). Implied here is an organizational culture in which failure to belong or comply is treated with disdain. Similar things have been said of the church, where failure to follow collective norms can invite accusations of heresy, as one modern-day Christian dissenter noted of his experience of ostracization in Australia: "It is almost as if you were unclean and should have a bell around your neck to warn people of your approach" (Cameron 1995, cited in De Maria 1999, 74). Thus, processes of belonging and adhering to a cause, whether that cause is saving nature or saving souls, imply processes of exclusion, or the removal of things that do not fit (Ahmed 2021). For those on the winning team, it is also necessary to cultivate disconnection from what has been removed—voices, facts, people, life itself—and the pain and injustice that this might have caused. This condition of disconnection can lead to complicity in various forms of violence, and I argue that it is an inherent feature and ethical problem in corporate nature.[18]

---

18. See Deborah Bird Rose (2011, 21–22) for a discussion of disconnection and our human capability of "turning away" from the deaths of animals and other forms of violence.

Conclusion

This book has explored how global conservation functions, through an insider's ethnography of Conservation International and its work in Cambodia. To structure my study, I followed CI's implementation of one of conservation's most powerful policy ideas: that of payments for environmental services. I traced the genesis, trajectory, and consequences of this idea in practice, examining how it was crafted into a global policy model and then implemented in the field from 2005 to 2011. Crossing scales from CI's US headquarters near Washington, DC, to the Cardamom Mountains in Cambodia, this book reveals how transnational conservation interventions are designed, enacted, and negotiated, and with what effects. My findings show how global conservation can go wrong in places like Cambodia, both practically and ethically. I argue that a key reason for this is the corporate form of big conservation NGOs, which entails organizational practices that can lead to NGO complicity in corruption, Indigenous dispossession, and environmental degradation.

While the title of this book alludes to global conservation's corporate nature, I also use this term to describe the "socio-nature" (Latour 2010) that emerges from the ideas and practices of mainstream conservation organizations. These organizations, like CI, TNC, and WWF, capture a large portion of global funding for biodiversity and channel it around the word. Critical literature tells us how these organizations use branding and marketing just like any other corporation; how their operations fail to challenge extractive and capitalist systems that threaten ecosystems and biodiversity; and how they have embraced market-based policies at the expense of social and ecological justice (Adams 2017; Brockington 2009; Büscher et al. 2014; Chapin 2004; Corson, MacDonald, and Neimark 2013). In short, this is an organizational form that has a distinctly technical, neoliberal, and territorializing gaze, driven by a global mission to govern or ameliorate people's engagements with the natural world. The contribution of this book is to have explained the inner workings and implications of this organizational form, whose chief product is corporate nature: a socio-nature that fetishizes the appearance of technical expertise and success, at the expense of diverse knowledges and ethical conduct.

The pursuit of organizational success over ethical integrity is a core aspect of corporate behavior. Joel Bakan famously declared that the corporate form is a "pathological institution" whose mandate is "to pursue, relentlessly and without exception, its own self-interest, regardless of the often harmful consequences it might cause to others" (2012, 1). This book has shown how corporate conservation functions: rather than the pursuit of profit, we see the pursuit of organizational coherence and success, which translates into funding. In the case of CI in Cambodia, I have shown how this pursuit of success involved project practices that ignored or factored out destabilizing knowledge, like insights into the social and political complexities of the field. Uncomfortable voices were silenced, inconvenient facts were removed, and struggles for justice or ethical conduct were generally avoided. For this reason, I argue that corporate nature often involves practices of symbolic and institutional violence (see Ahmed 2021; Bourdieu 1977; Menton, Navas, and Le Billon 2021). This violence is evident in the way that big conservation NGOs typically prefer to ignore rather than address injustices in the field, especially those that emerge alongside their interventions as unintended "side effects" (Ferguson 1994).

Taken together, these findings show that a paradox exists at the heart of corporate nature, in that it is both powerful and powerless. On the one hand, global conservation is politically and ideologically powerful. We see this in the persistence of potent policy ideas like PES, which seemingly defy local contexts and evidence of failure. We also see this in global conservation's capacity to ignore what is inconvenient. On the other hand, ethnographic observation reveals inherent weaknesses in global conservation practice. This perspective shows a top-heavy and clumsy form of conservation action, which is often unable to predict, control, or even detect the complex effects

Conclusion

of its interventions. Recent insights about modern endeavors of improvement corroborate this finding by suggesting that "the illusion of control" is a key goal of powerful institutions in the face of uncertainty (Scoones and Stirling 2020, 10)—especially now as the volatilities of the Anthropocene emerge.

Recognition of this paradox brings nuance to common notions of a powerful global conservation edifice, which at times can appear as a monolithic or conspiratorial neoliberal opponent, capable of appropriating natural resources around the world. Critical perspectives of this ilk are vital (see Brockington 2002; Büscher et al. 2012; Corson, MacDonald, and Neimark 2013; Fairhead, Leach, and Scoones 2012), but they can sometimes attribute too much power to global conservation by failing to recognize the cracks and contingencies of everyday practice. Scholars working in the tradition of "project ethnography" have helped to prize open global conservation in this more nuanced way (e.g., Hussain 2019; Sachedina 2010; West 2006) to reveal fragmentation, fragility, and contingency within conservation interventions. Yet, in recognizing this, we must not fail to hold global conservation to account for what it *does* control, and for what it *does* know and do. For this reason, the paradox that I describe matters: it signals complex ethical dilemmas at the heart of global conservation practice.

In this concluding chapter, I reflect on the paradoxical character of global conservation by retracing my findings from the case of CI in Cambodia. First, I return to what is powerful in global conservation, namely its policy ideas and technical hubris in the face of complexity. Second, I consider the powerlessness of global conservation, as seen in its unintended consequences and insidious side effects. Here, I point to corporate nature's tendency to reproduce and extend perversity in the places where it operates, for example by amplifying local processes of violence and dispossession, often unwittingly. Third, I examine how corporate nature deals with uncertainty and contingency in the field through a performative emphasis on organizational success. Here I point to systemic processes that I observed of avoiding and not acknowledging problematic dynamics in project implementation, such as abuses of government power and Indigenous dispossession. I also explain how these practices of strategic ignorance can become normalized over time within conservation organizations (see McGoey 2012; Vaughan 1996), to the extent that various forms of violence and unethical conduct can emerge. Ultimately, these characteristics and effects of corporate nature imply that mainstream global conservation cannot produce desirable, life-inspiring, and diverse socio-natures for the future. I therefore conclude the book by exploring how my findings can inform a new ethics of practice for nature conservation.

Policy Ideas and the Power of Corporate Nature

This book has shown how policy ideas underpin the production of corporate nature. This is because they lend purpose, function, and structure to global conservation action. Scholars of development have observed similar patterns: policy ideas provide a script or metaphor for interventions (Mosse 2005); they are the ghost in the machine of bureaucracy (Shore and Wright 1997). By tracing CI's adoption and deployment of PES, I have shown how policy ideas can become organizational devices in conservation too, as they are carefully crafted into silver bullets that offer neat solutions or technical fixes to intractable problems. Here is the appeal: policy fixes can be marketed to donors, publics, governments, and other stakeholders. PES has been a particularly attractive policy idea in this sense, given its market-inspired apparent simplicity. When my research began in the early 2000s, PES was an economists' thought experiment. Now, it is considered a mainstream conservation strategy, alongside other tools like the creation of protected areas (Burivalova et al. 2019).

This policy success, however, has little to do with empirical measures of effectiveness. Rather, it emerges from the way that global conservation produces knowledge and sees the world. Having examined how CI designed and implemented its PES-like conservation agreements, I note three key aspects to the politics of knowledge in this case, which apply to global conservation practice more broadly.

First is the discursive power of conservation policy, which refers to its ideological contours and assumptions about the world. Here, policy ideas or models can function like "political technologies" (Foucault 1977) in their ability to format knowledge and shape the subjectivities of those involved. The idea of PES was particularly powerful in this sense, with its neoliberal notions of rational choice, apolitical service provision, and the ability of market forces to transcend the complications of local context. I observed, across scales and over time, how CI's PES model led to a neoliberal and apolitical formatting of the field, which simplified local social, political, and environmental problems. In particular, local communities were treated as willing service providers, which had the effect of narrowing their potential role in conservation practice and in political life more generally.

The second aspect of knowledge politics that I observed is what gets filtered out or unseen by global conservation NGOs. This process involves practitioners selectively "seeing" in order to render the world "legible" for their interventions (Scott 1998; Vetterlein 2012). Global conservation does this by factoring out extraneous noise and information because these things may expose weaknesses or undermine its policy-based interventions. Maintaining a façade of effectiveness and control is essential for organizational survival and policy success (Milne and Mahanty 2019; Scoones and Stirling 2020). In global development organizations, too, this is a "behavioral characteristic," whereby dissonance between the external environment and internal bureaucratic needs must be constantly managed, resulting in "organized hypocrisy" (Weaver 2008, 34). I observed this phenomenon within CI, as project actors constantly juggled the demands of the PES policy model with the contingencies of the field in Cambodia. Clever brokers actively filtered field knowledge to fit the project, but foreign technical advisors typically did not recognize this, meaning that they failed to see the full scale of dissonance between CI's policy ideas and local realities.

The third aspect of conservation's knowledge politics observed in this book relates to epistemology. In short, global conservation possesses a technical-reductionist epistemology, which simplifies the field and erases the specificities of place and context (Brosius and Hitchner 2010; Li 2007). This is an epistemology of disconnection, which prevents the field from being "situated" (see Peluso 2012). Within this framing of the world, it becomes possible for generic policy ideas or global tools to be translated from one site to the next, as I witnessed in CI's global PES program. Here, the underlying assumption is that policy models function in the same way everywhere. This leads technical experts to ask about whether a policy model "works," as through it were a treatment for a sick patient. Correspondingly, we see the rise of quasi-experimental methods, which try to test or prove the effectiveness of a given conservation tool (McKinnon et al. 2015). These logics of expertise and oversight, which ignore context, are fundamental to corporate nature.

Overall, the discursive and epistemological aspects of mainstream conservation that I identify here can help to explain the remarkable persistence of ideas like PES. As John Quiggin argues, despite disastrous failures and fundamental critique, the ideas of "market liberalism" keep coming back like zombies or "dead ideas" that still walk among us (2012, 3). Similarly, Jamie Peck writes that "zombie neoliberalism" is a "mutable, mongrel model of governance" in which the foundational and utopian ideals of market rule remain in the background, as "dead but dominant" (2010, 106–108). To sustain itself, neoliberal governance is "inescapably, and profoundly, marked by compromise, calculation and contradiction" (Peck 2010, 106). This is where organized hypocrisy plays a role: it tells us that powerful policy ideas can function like a living dead, sustained by a combination of ideological belief and selective forms of knowledge production. No matter what challenges arise, faith in the idea will sustain purpose and progress.

CI's embrace of PES in Cambodia demonstrates this ability to keep on believing in spite of near-impossible field realities. After the scandals related to illegal logging from 2009 to 2012, CI largely rebooted in Cambodia—a process aided by the generally short and accommodating institutional memories of NGOs and donors. Subsequent reforms to Cambodia's protected areas also modified local institutional arrangements (see Souter et al. 2016). In this new terrain, CI has repositioned itself as a loyal government advisor, especially on PES. For example, in 2016, CI sponsored a Cambodian government delegation to Costa Rica for officials to see how PES leads to "green growth" (Simpson and Souter 2017). There, the Cambodians were hosted by one of CI's vice presidents, former environment minister of Costa Rica, Carlos Manuel Rodriguez—a man who is evangelical about how PES can transform national economies. Rodriguez published a blog about the visit, writing, "To protect nature and boost economy, Cambodia must follow Costa Rica's lead" (2016). This enthusiasm appears to have caught on, with Prime Minister Hun Sen's recent backing of a national PES policy for Cambodia (UNDP 2019). Memory is therefore selective, as past problems are subsumed into a narrative of "lessons learned" in the longue durée of policy ideas that serve power.

In sum, compelling policy ideas like PES are fundamental to the workings of global conservation. They shape its intervention logics; they are crucial for branding and fundraising; and they support organizational coherence across scales. Global conservation is therefore in large part an industry whose chief product is the policy fix or generic solution. Its modus operandi is to generate winning ideas, which are then rolled out or scaled up around the world. Yet, in order for these ideas to work, global conservation must systematically

Conclusion

factor out evidence of local complexity or dissonance within its field projects. Corporate nature is therefore constituted through a self-referencing system of knowledge that is strictly technical, apolitical, and not situated.

Unintended Consequences and Side Effects

While policy ideas signal much of what is powerful in corporate nature, its clumsiness or lack of control in practice tells us that this power can be hollow or paradoxical. Having traced the fate of policy ideas and good intentions across scales, in the case of CI in Cambodia, this book finds that global conservation can often struggle to "translate" and "contextualize" (Latour 1996) its ideas in the field. For instance, I showed how CI's global policy idea of conservation agreements was transformed almost beyond recognition during its implementation in Cambodia. Key conceptual elements of the PES-like policy were lost in translation, including CI's notions of performance-based payments, conditionality, and community choice. My findings show how these policy transformations were caused by an array of cross-cultural misunderstandings between foreigners and Khmers, and strategic or political manipulations on the Cambodian side. Here, project brokers juggled across tricky project "interfaces" (Long 2001) between Khmer and foreign worlds, as well as government and NGO systems. The policy transformations that occurred show how global conservation's technical fixes often do not unfold in predictable or controllable ways, especially in places like Cambodia.

More problematically, I found that CI's mistranslated policy model also generated a series of side effects in local governance and politics. Ferguson (1994) first explained how development interventions are significant not necessarily for their intended outcomes but for their side effects, such as the elaboration of bureaucratic state power. This book shows how a similar phenomenon unfolded around CI's project in Cambodia. That is, by introducing new processes and ideas for governing people and nature, alongside the financing and empowerment of Cambodian government officials, CI contributed to the elaboration of state power in the Cardamom Mountains. Key here was that CI's activities made the field legible (Scott 1998) for government through processes of land-use mapping and committee making. Although these processes were meant to empower local communities and strengthen their resource claims, the effect was the opposite: government manipulation and co-option of CI's project structures only extended and reinforced state "territorialization" (Vandergeest and Peluso 1995) of the forests and natural resources in the project area. A narrowing of political space also occurred as new "environmental subjectivities" (Agrawal 2005) emerged in the project area through CI's facilitation of local committees for natural resource management.

Unfortunately, given Cambodia's political context, the state power that CI helped to elaborate was both predatory and authoritarian. Timing played a role here, as CI's engagement in Cambodia occurred alongside a consolidation of power by the Cambodian People's Party throughout the country from 2005 onward (Morgenbesser 2019; Norén-Nilsson 2016). In this governance setting, many NGOs were left with little option other than to fall into step with the incumbent regime (e.g., Frewer 2013). But CI's role here was different from other NGOs and problematic because of its partnership with the Forestry Administration, through which CI became complicit in state-making processes that amplified government control over people and resources in the field. Although CI could do little in the face of strong government influence, it did make key strategic choices about who to empower and who to hear in the context of its government relations. In this sense, CI's project succumbed to a "normalization of deviance" (Vaughan 1996), through almost constant deference to government and party interests, the implications of which I explore in the next section.

For now, with the focus on unintended consequences and side effects, I argue that global conservation cannot control everything that happens in the field. Furthermore, by fixating on global policy and technical solutions, mainstream conservation organizations can become ill equipped to direct or even to detect the effects of their interventions. Corporate nature's tendency to blinker itself from local context and format knowledge around its policy logics therefore leads to unpredictable project side effects, which can reproduce or even accentuate illiberal governance conditions at sites of intervention.

Organizational Deviance in the Face of Perversity

When global conservation fails to recognize how its ideas are transformed in practice, and with what side effects, a range of ethical problems arise. In other words, when conservation NGOs systematically fail to see problems,

Conclusion

or fail to respond to problems they see, then various forms of organizational deviance and hypocrisy can emerge (Vaughan 1996; Weaver 2008). In the case of CI in Cambodia, it was the gradual creep of government influence within NGO realms of the project that undermined the integrity and capacity of the operation. CI effectively allowed its Cambodian project to become a pseudo-state entity, or a black box over which the NGO's head office had little directive or ethical control.

This situation eventuated because Cambodian actors in the project, under constant political pressure, became adept at subverting NGO structures and intentions. In particular, with CI's appointment of a Khmer country director in 2007, most government relations and project dealings with CI's partner the Forestry Administration were rendered opaque to foreigners' eyes. While CI's head office claimed to be building local partnerships and capacity, in practice CI Cambodia was facilitating government interests in the protected forest. Over time, this hindered the project's ability to contest elite-backed, illicit resource extraction. In the field, powerful tycoons and companies grabbed land and resources without consequence, while some CI-facilitated community committees were co-opted by party officials. In tandem, CI was not responsive to villagers' pleas for help with these problems. Patterns were therefore set for the final blow in 2009, when CI's Cambodia team was unable and unwilling to address the risks of government-backed hydropower dam construction in the heart of the Cardamom Mountains. This story shows how global conservation can operate hand in hand with predatory political regimes, becoming complicit in the servicing of elite interests and the silencing of others.

Some pragmatic observers would argue that CI had little choice in the circumstances outlined above. How else can an international NGO do biodiversity conservation in Cambodia? This question applies across global conservation, where projects are implemented in weak or authoritarian governance contexts. For many practitioners, it is apparently strategic not to rock the boat with incumbent political regimes, for the sake of biodiversity. While this is not necessarily ethically wrong, decisions to engage with corrupt or authoritarian governments do lead conservation NGOs into an ethical gray zone, as this book has shown. What becomes important then, ethically speaking, is the way that international NGOs and their staff choose to navigate the multitude of delicate decisions and compromises that constitute the gray zone.

This book has illustrated critical ethical dimensions in NGO decision-making and values, in fraught political environments. For example, CI's choices about staff roles and capabilities fundamentally shaped the organization's practices of engagement in Cambodia. With most technical staff being resource economists and conservation biologists, little emphasis was placed upon their acquisition of cultural knowledge or Khmer language skills. This meant that CI relied heavily on key Khmer brokers to implement its project. These brokers, however, enjoyed a lot of discretion over how the project unfolded in practice, including what information was fed to foreign advisors and head office staff. Unfortunately, there were few checks and balances in place to monitor what was really happening. CI even seemed to be happy with these arrangements: technical oversight was apparently in place, and the minutiae of conservation management could be left to a Cambodian black box.

CI's management approach, of outsourcing the politics of conservation to local brokers and partners, had major ethical implications—especially as corruption associated with illegal logging set in around the project. It is unclear whether CI anticipated the risks of its approach. Regardless, its organizational practices were to blame for what unfolded, because they generated various forms of institutional blindness and associated risks. First, there was the familiar problem of epistemological blind spots. Biologists, for instance, are not trained to notice or analyze social and political complexity. Second, there was a form of willful blindness at work too. That is, even as CI's foreign staff were informed of problems in the field, the organization preferred to look the other way, or to factor out what was complicated. CI's organizational practices therefore exhibited a strong preference for reductionist and technical forms of knowledge, which privileged the voices of staff who were willing to simplify complexity.

Overall, these insights convey how the corporate form in global conservation navigates perversity. Here, global ideas and expertise are performed, while experiences of weakness or incompetence are hidden. At an institutional level, this implies the presence of ongoing dissonance between stated NGO goals and external realities, the denial of which can become habit. Institutionalized dissonance is therefore a key marker of corporate nature, and it chiefly emerges from organizational practices that absorb or ignore perversity in the field.

Ethical Pitfalls and Violence in Corporate Nature

My account of CI's behavior in Cambodia shows that global conservation does not just fail to address complexity and injustice in the field, but it is also capable of actively ignoring problems or covering them up. For this reason, I argue that corporate nature has a special relationship with ignorance, which in turn contributes to global conservation's capacity to inflict indirect violence against Indigenous people and environmental defenders, among others. CI's refusal to acknowledge the links between Chut Wutty's murder and his anti-logging stance in the Cardamom Mountains, for example, is indicative of this kind of violence. So too was CI's subsequent "independent review" of the CCPF project, which was effectively used to clear CI's name in the face of media allegations about park rangers' complicity in the illegal logging.

While these events were dramatic, they do not represent an isolated case in global conservation. Rather, they illustrate wider dynamics of big international NGO complicity in violence and environmental degradation in diverse field settings (Menton and Gilbert 2021; Milne and Mahanty 2019; Survival International 2021). My contribution is to have shown how this indirect violence emerges in part from the production of ignorance about the negative side effects and ethical failings of global conservation. As conservation scholars have suggested, there is often stony silence when things go wrong in the field—or worse, critical observers who try to expose the injustices of conservation can find themselves being silenced or sidelined by big NGOs (Brosius and Hitchner 2010; Igoe and Sullivan 2009; Survival International 2021). These patterns reveal how global conservation organizations strive to achieve conformity and apparent coherence in their project operations, above all else. Chiefly, this entails the removal of people and voices that do not fit into corporate visions of purpose and action, in order to secure "success." Studying how organizations deflect complaints and contestation, or how they discount certain forms of knowledge, becomes pertinent here (Ahmed 2021). Importantly, we must ask after the shadow of corporate knowledge, to study its "anti-epistemology" (Galison 2004)—and a key way to do this is to explore instances of whistleblowing.

My account of whistleblowing in this book shows that it takes organizational effort to maintain ignorance, and that this effort is a key defense mechanism in corporate conservation. In general, the corporate form requires that its staff are compliant, or willing to enact their employer's ideas and imperatives. Problems then arise when certain individuals are more rigorously or personally engaged with the ethics of what they do. As De Maria explains, "dissenters and whistleblowers are ethical overreachers, forever going beyond what the prevailing orthodoxy says are the central values" (1999, 76). Internal dissent is therefore an inevitable feature of the corporate form, and it requires ongoing management or disciplinary action by corporate leadership. My findings show that these insights hold true in global conservation: critics are often treated as a nuisance because they threaten the illusions upon which the whole enterprise depends.

Tellingly, whistleblowers rarely plan to dissent or seek conflict. Time and again, we see how ethical conflicts within organizations emerge in increments, eventually to become long and unforeseeable processes of attrition, from which the dissenting individual rarely emerges unscathed (De Maria 1999). As I shared in this book, these experiences of not being heard, being deflected, or being discredited by a large organization, usually one's employer, are violent in nature. In Sara Ahmed's research on how complaints are handled in universities (2021), I see many parallels with the ways global conservation treats dissenters. Indeed, there are some common institutional parameters here: big conservation NGOs and universities are ostensibly not-for-profit organizations that aim to deliver public goods. In this context, complaints or dissonance can threaten organizational survival. For this reason, dissent provokes a corporate response, as Ahmed illustrates in her essay on institutional damage limitation: "Say, a ship is sinking: watch out! Damage control is used to stop the ship from going down by locking off the damaged area from other ship's compartments. The containment of damage becomes necessary to stop the whole thing from sinking. The complainers are perhaps located here: in that damaged room, keeping the whole thing afloat by what they are expected to take in and take on" (2019, 1).

These notions of "taking in" or "taking on" reflect the personal, ethical, and affective impacts of institutional violence. For those who get shut out of the ship, or locked in the damage control room, their loss of agency and alienation can be debilitating. There is also the whistleblower's mystification over how "they" can continue with business as usual: they must sleep, eat, live, and work, having been complicit or actively involved in ethical misconduct or institutional violence. Organizational staff's ability to persist

Conclusion

highlights what it takes to be an insider: a level of disconnection from the wider effects of the organization in which one is embedded. Hannah Arendt famously characterized this kind of human behavior in bureaucracies as "non-thinking" ([1964] 1976). However, the "will to improve" (Li 2007) that drives so much NGO work also plays a role here: it can act like a pair of rose-colored glasses, which permit the denial of certain uncomfortable truths or enable complicity with unjust forms of power and exploitation.

Conservationists' collective and subjective experiences of this will to improve—seen in their drive to save ecosystems and biodiversity—therefore require some scrutiny. I say this not to distract from the urgency of our planetary crisis but to call for greater ethical sensitivity and awareness in the course of conservation action. Here, I recall my own experience: conservation work is so compelling that it often leaves little room for self-doubt or critical reflection. Unerring commitment to the cause of saving nature can become a vocation or even an identity, but this condition can also bring pitfalls. More ethnographic research into the personal perspectives of conservation workers is therefore necessary (see Kiik 2018). In particular, by understanding more about how individuals interact with the ethical dimensions of their work and the actions of their employers, new avenues for conservation ethics may emerge. Here, Judith Butler's reflections on Hannah Arendt point to the importance of individuals *thinking about their intentions* in the course of any collective endeavor. To have "intentions," argues Butler, "is to think reflectively about one's own action as a political being, whose own life and thinking is bound up with the life and thinking of others" (2011). And so, by recognizing conservation's entanglements and connections, along with our own personal ones, a new ethics of practice may begin to emerge. This offers a pathway out of mainstream conservation's strong tendencies to remove inconvenient knowledge and silence critical voices for the sake of its own perpetuation.

Reimagining Conservation Practice

This book has largely focused on how things can go wrong in global conservation. Specifically, I have identified core problems with knowledge making and organizational culture that produce what I have called corporate nature. I have shown how problems arise because of global conservation's technical hubris; its systematic disconnection from context and place; and its willful ignorance of complexity and perversity, even when social injustice and ecological destruction emerge at its field sites. From this analysis of key failings, I now argue that we can identify three points of departure for undoing what is wrong. First, if we take the problem of technical hubris and imagine its opposite, then we find practices of humility and a fresh recognition of diverse knowledges and ontologies. Second, regarding the problem of disconnection, in its opposite we find an imperative to establish meaningful relationships with people and place, or nature-society relations that are grounded in principles of connection and reciprocity. Third, from the problem of willful ignorance, in its opposite we find new practices of listening and seeing. These might entail special efforts to hear marginal voices—Indigenous, activist, subaltern, nonhuman, more-than-human—and to bear witness to social and ecological injustices on the ground.

It is as though, by turning global conservation inside out, we discover what we have always intuitively known about our entangled socio-natural condition. Radical and critical voices have already begun to convey this message. Some argue, for example, that the logics and reasoning that led us into the ecological crisis cannot lead us out of it (Eisenstein 2018). Others show how we must disentangle ourselves from the dominant institutions of capitalism and modernity in order to move forward (Büscher and Fletcher 2020). Similarly, Donna Haraway (2016) argues that individualism and human exceptionalism cannot help us to imagine what will be required to live on our damaged planet. Only a radically relational and interconnected way of being with nature can enable us to "stay with the trouble" (Haraway 2016; see also Tsing et al. 2019). These insights signal that there is no easy fix for mainstream conservation: change will not simply come with new management principles or policy ideas to retrofit onto the existing machinery. The task at hand is far more radical: a "conservation revolution" is required (Büscher and Fletcher 2020).

Yet this revolution is not about starting from scratch. There is growing recognition that we already have or will find what we need by decolonizing our approach to nature, including decolonizing our minds and institutions from the tentacles of colonial power and capital (Adams and Mulligan 2003; Collard, Dempsey, and Sundberg 2015; Kashwan et al. 2021). Correspondingly, Indigenous scholars around the world have begun to articulate their philosophies and practices for the whole of humanity, pointing to how Indigenous ontologies and ways of relating to nature offer foundational insights for sustainability and conservation practice (e.g., Arabena 2015; Kimmerer 2013; Yunkaporta 2019). From their messages, we hear of interbeing between people and nature; we hear of the nonhuman as kin; and we hear of the need for reciprocity between humans and nonhumans. For Deborah Bird Rose and her Indigenous collaborators in northern Australia, this set of relationships is nothing less than "world-making," and it implies an ethical disposition in which we must always ask: "Are self and others flourishing? Are the possibilities for life enhanced?" (Rose 2011, 12). These are practical questions, too, for everyone, to guide new approaches in caring for nature and all of Earth's inhabitants.

In considering how these radical, Indigenous, and decolonial threads might tie together, I suggest that an "ethic of care" can offer foundational guidance for conservation practice. In this vein, Büscher and Fletcher have proposed "convivial conservation" (2020)—a movement to house radical and decolonial ideas for saving nature, inspired by Ivan Illich's (1973) notion of conviviality. Here, Illich observed that to solve our environmental crisis, we need to establish a shared insight that people are happier if they can work together and care for each other. Importantly, Rose (2011) extended these principles of connection and care to multispecies communities, drawing from Indigenous ontologies in Australia. For her, "connectivity ethics" are not rule-bound but are "open, uncertain, attentive, participatory, contingent"; they are grounded in practices of love that "keep faith with life" (Rose 2011, 141–143). Similarly, Indigenous botanist Robin Wall Kimmerer (2013) shows how experiences of care co-emerge with intimate, material connections with the more-than-human. Reflecting on her own and others' practices of field biology, she suggests that these practices of care and connection can become a practical ethics for all of humanity: "Doing science with awe and humility is a powerful act of reciprocity with the more-than-human world . . . [It] can be a way of forming intimacy and respect with other species that is rivalled only by the observations of traditional knowledge holders. It can be a path to kinship" (Kimmerer 2013, 252).

I raise these ethical propositions of multispecies care and connection because they have major implications for global conservation. It is not just the mainstream conservation edifice that is at stake here but nature-society itself (Latour 2010). This book has illustrated an undesirable form of nature-society that emerges from mainstream conservation practice today: corporate nature is the product of organizational practices that lack humility, open-endedness, and open-heartedness in their engagements with people and places. A new ethics for nature conservation must therefore dissolve the imperatives of technical thinking and the corporate form, through radically relational, decolonial, and situated practices. Only then will it be possible to care for self, each other, and all species on this planet in life-inspiring ways.

References

Adams, William. 2017. "Sleeping with the Enemy? Biodiversity Conservation, Corporations and The Green Economy." *Journal of Political Ecology* 24: 243–257.

Adams, William, and David Hulme. 2001. "Conservation and Community: Changing Narratives, Policies and Practices in African Conservation." In *African Wildlife and Livelihoods: The Promise and Performance of Community Conservation*, edited by D. Hulme and M. Murphree, 9–23. Oxford: James Currey.

Adams, William, and Jon Hutton. 2007. "People, Parks and Poverty: Political Ecology and Biodiversity Conservation." *Conservation and Society* 5, no. 2: 147–83.

Adams, William, and Martin Mulligan, eds. 2003. *Decolonising Nature: Strategies for Conservation in a Post-Colonial Era*. London: Earthscan.

Adams, William, and Chris Sandbrook. 2013. "Conservation, Evidence and Policy." *Oryx* 47, no. 3: 329–35.

Agrawal, Arun. 2005. "Environmentality: Community, Intimate Government, and the Making of Environmental Subjects in Kumaon, India." *Current Anthropology* 46, no. 2: 161–90.

Agrawal, Arun, and Clark Gibson. 1999. "Enchantment and Disenchantment: The role of Community in Natural Resource Management." *World Development* 27, no. 4: 629–49.

Ahmed, Sara. 2019. "Damage Limitation." *Feminist Killjoys*, February 15, 2019. https://feministkilljoys.com/2019/02/15/damage-limitation/.

Ahmed, Sara. 2021. *Complaint!* Durham, NC: Duke University Press.

Amnesty International. 2022. *"Our Traditions Are Being Destroyed': Illegal Logging, Repression, and Indigenous Peoples' Rights Violations in Cambodia's Protected Forests."* ASA 23/5183/2022. London: Amnesty International. https://www.amnesty.org/en/documents/asa23/5183/2022/en/.

Anderson, Ben, and Colin McFarlane. 2011. "Assemblage and Geography." *Area* 43, no. 2: 124–27.

Anderson, David, and Eeva Berglund. 2003. *Ethnographies of Conservation: Environmentalism and the Distribution of Privilege*. New York: Berghahn Books.

Appadurai, Arjun. 1990. "Disjuncture and Difference in the Global Cultural Economy." *Theory, Culture & Society* 7: 295–310.

Appadurai, Arjun. 1996. *Modernity at Large: Cultural Dimensions of Globalization*. Minneapolis: University of Minnesota Press.

Appleton, Michael, Ros Bansok, and Jenny Daltry. 2000. *Biological Survey of the Cardamom Mountains Region, Southwest Cambodia*. Cambridge and Phnom Penh: Flora and Fauna International and the Government of Cambodia, Ministry of Environment and Wildlife Protection Office.

Arabena, Kerry. 2015. *Becoming Indigenous to the University: Reflections on Living Systems, Indigeneity and Citizenship*. Melbourne: Australian Scholarly Publishing.

Arendt, Hannah. (1964) 1976. *Eichmann in Jerusalem: A Report on the Banality of Evil*. New York: Penguin Classics.

Baird, Ian. 2010. "The Construction of Indigenous Peoples in Cambodia." In *Alterities in Asia: Reflections on Identity and Regionalism*, edited by Leong Yew, 155–76. London: Routledge.

Bakan, Joel. 2012. *The Corporation: The Pathological Pursuit of Profit and Power*. London: Constable & Robinson Ltd.

Balboa, Cristina. 2014. "How Successful Transnational Non-governmental Organizations Set Themselves up for Failure on the Ground." *World Development* 54: 273–87.

Balmford, Andrew, Aaron Bruner, Philip Cooper, Robert Costanza, Stephen Farber, et al. 2002. "Economic Reasons for Conserving Wild Nature." *Science* 297: 950–53.

Balmford, Andrew, and Tony Whitten. 2003. "Who Should Pay for Tropical Conservation, and How Could the Costs Be Met?" *Oryx* 37, no. 2: 238–50.

Barron, Porter. 2003. "Striking Oil: An Illicit Industry Thrives in the Cardamom Mountains." *Cambodia Daily*, December 13–14, 2003.

Bashi, Solomon. 2007. "Starvation under the Democratic Kampuchea Regime." Unpublished manuscript, Documentation Centre of Cambodia, Phnom Penh.

Beavan, Nancy, Sian Halcrow, Bruce McFadgen, Derek Hamilton, Brendan Buckley, Tep Sokha, Louise Shewan, Ouk Sokha, Stewart Fallon, John Miksic, et al. 2012. "Radiocarbon Dates from Jar and Coffin Burials of the Cardamom Mountains Reveal a Previously Unrecorded Mortuary Ritual in Cambodia's Late- to Post-Angkor Period (15th to 17th Centuries AD)." *Radiocarbon* 54, no. 1: 1–22.

Beban, Alice. 2021. *Unwritten Rule: State-making Through Land Reform in Cambodia*. Ithaca, NY: Cornell University Press.

Beresford, Quentin. 2010. "Corporations, Government and Development: The Case of Institutional Corruption in Tasmania." *Australian Journal of Political Science* 45, no. 2: 209–25.

References **231**

Biddulph, Robin. 2014. *Cambodia's Land Mapping and Administration Program.* WIDER Working Paper No. 2014/086. Helsinki: United Nations University World Institute for Development Economics Research (UNU-WIDER). https://www.econstor.eu/handle/10419/103010.

Billo, Emily, and Allison Mountz. 2016. "For Institutional Ethnography: Geographical Approaches to Institutions and the Everyday." *Progress in Human Geography* 40, no. 2: 199–220.

Bit, Seanglim. 1991. *The Warrior Heritage: A Psychological Perspective of Cambodian Trauma.* California: Seanglim Bit.

Bizot, François. 2003. *The Gate.* London: The Harvill Press.

Blaikie, Piers. 1995. "Changing Environments or Changing Views? A Political Ecology for Developing Countries." *Geography* 80, no. 3: 203–14.

Blaikie, Piers. 2006. "Is Small Really Beautiful? Community-Based Natural Resource Management in Malawi and Botswana." *World Development* 34, no. 11: 1942–57.

Blunt, Peter, and Mark Turner 2005. "Decentralisation, Democracy and Development in a Post-Conflict Society: Commune Councils in Cambodia." *Public Administration and Development* 25: 75–87.

Bourdieu, Pierre. 1977. *Outline of a Theory of Practice.* Cambridge: Cambridge University Press.

Boyce, James. 2003. *Aid, Conditionality and War Economies.* University of Massachusetts Political Economy Research Institute Working Paper Series No. 70. Amherst: University of Massachusetts.

Boyle, David. 2011. "Logging in the Wild West." *Phnom Penh Post,* December 21, 2011. https://www.phnompenhpost.com/national/logging-wild-west.

Boyle, David, and May Titthara. 2012. "Blind Eye to Forest's Plight." *Phnom Penh Post,* March 26, 2012. https://www.phnompenhpost.com/national/blind-eye-forest %E2%80%99s-plight.

Brandon, Katrina, and Michael Wells. 1992. "Planning for People and Parks: Design Dilemmas." *World Development* 20, no. 4: 557–70.

Brockington, Dan. 2002. *Fortress Conservation: The Preservation of the Mkomazi Game Reserve, Tanzania.* Oxford: James Currey.

Brockington, Dan. 2009. *Celebrity and the Environment: Fame, Wealth and Power in Conservation.* New York: Zed Books.

Brockington, Dan, Rosaleen Duffy, and James Igoe. 2008. *Nature Unbound: Conservation, Capitalism and the Future of Protected Areas.* London: Routledge.

Brohman, John. 1995. "Economism and Critical Silences in Development Studies: A Theoretical Critique of Neoliberalism." *Third World Quarterly* 1, no. 2: 297–318.

Brosius, J. Peter. 1999a. "Analyses and Interventions: Anthropological Engagements with Environmentalism." *Current Anthropology* 40, no. 3: 277–309.

Brosius, J. Peter. 1999b. "Green Dots, Pink Hearts: Displacing Politics from the Malaysian Rain Forest." *American Anthropologist* 101, no. 1: 36–57.

Brosius, J. Peter, and Sarah Hitchner. 2010. "Cultural Diversity and Conservation." *International Social Science Journal* 61, no. 199: 141–68.

Brosius, J. Peter, and Diane Russell. 2003. "Conservation from Above: An Anthropological Perspective on Transboundary Protected Areas and Ecoregional Planning." *Journal of Sustainable Forestry* 17, no. 1: 39–66.

Brosius, J. Peter, Anna Lowenhaupt Tsing, and Charles Zerner. eds. 2005. *Communities and Conservation: Histories and Politics of Community-Based Natural Resource Management*. Walnut Creek, CA: AltaMira Press.

Bryant, Raymond. 2002. "Non-governmental Organizations and Governmentality: 'Consuming' Biodiversity and Indigenous People in the Philippines." *Political Studies* 50, no. 2: 268–92.

Bryant, Raymond, and Sinead Bailey. 1997. *Third World Political Ecology*. London: Routledge.

Burivalova, Zuzana, Thomas F. Allnutt, Dan Rademacher, Annika Schlemm, David S. Wilcove, and Rhett Butler. 2019. "What Works in Tropical Forest Conservation and What Does Not: Effectiveness of Four Strategies in Terms of Environmental, Social and Economic Outcomes." *Conservation Science and Practice* 1, no. 6: e28. https://doi.org/10.1111/csp2.28.

Büscher, Bram. 2008. "Conservation, Neoliberalism, and Social Science: A Critical Reflection on the SCB 2007 Annual Meeting in South Africa." *Conservation Biology* 22, no. 2: 229–31.

Büscher, Bram. 2013. *Transforming the Frontier: Peace Parks and the Politics of Neoliberal Conservation in South Africa*. Durham, NC: Duke University Press.

Büscher, Bram, Wolfram Dressler, and Robert Fletcher, eds. 2014. *Nature Inc.: Environmental Conservation in the Neoliberal Age*. Tucson: University of Arizona Press.

Büscher, Bram, and Robert Fletcher. 2020. *The Conservation Revolution: Radical Ideas for Saving Nature Beyond the Anthropocene*. London: Verso Books.

Büscher, Bram, Sian Sullivan, Katja Neves, Jim Igoe, and Dan Brockington. 2012. "Towards a Synthesized Critique of Neoliberal Biodiversity Conservation." *Capitalism Nature Socialism* 23, no. 2: 4–30.

Butler, Judith. 2011. "Hannah Arendt's Challenge to Adolf Eichmann." *The Guardian*, August 29, 2011. https://www.theguardian.com/commentisfree/2011/aug/29/hannah-arendt-adolf-eichmann-banality-of-evil.

Callon, Michel. 1986. "The Sociology of an Actor-Network: The Case of the Electric Vehicle." In *Mapping the Dynamics of Science and Technology*, edited by M. Callon, J. Law, and A. Rip, 19–34. London: Palgrave Macmillan.

Campbell, Lisa. 2012. "Seeing Red: Inside the Politics of IUCN's Red List." *Conservation and Society* 10, no. 4: 367–80.

Campbell, Lisa, Catherine Corson, Noella J. Gray, Kenneth I. MacDonald, and J. Peter Brosius. 2014. "Studying Global Environmental Meetings to Understand Global Environmental Governance: Collaborative Event Ethnography at the Tenth Conference of the Parties to the Conventions on Biological Diversity." *Global Environmental Politics* 14, no. 3: 1–20.

Carrier, James, and Paige West, eds. 2009. *Virtualism, Governance and Practice: Vision and Execution in Environmental Conservation*. New York: Berghahn Books.

References

Castree, Noel. 2008. "Neoliberalising Nature: The Logics of Deregulation and Reregulation." *Environment and Planning A: Economy and Space* 40, no. 1: 131–52.

Castree, Noel, and George Henderson. 2014. "The Capitalist Mode of Conservation, Neoliberalism and the Ecology of Value." *New Proposals: Journal of Marxism and Interdisciplinary Inquiry* 7, no. 1: 16–37.

Cepek, Michael. 2011. "Foucault in the Forest: Questioning Environmentality in Amazonia." *American Ethnologist* 38, no. 3: 501–15.

Chandler, David. 1991. *The Tragedy of Cambodian History: Politics, War and Revolution Since 1945*. Chiang Mai: Silkworm Books.

Chapin, Mac. 2004. "A Challenge to Conservationists." *World Watch Magazine* (November/December): 17–31.

Chomitz, Kenneth, and Kanta Kumari. 1998. "The Domestic Benefits of Tropical Forests: A Critical Review." *World Bank Research Observer* 13, no. 1: 13–35.

Christoff, Peter. 1996. "Ecological Modernisation, Ecological Modernities." *Environmental Politics* 5, no. 3: 476–500.

Cleaver, Francis. 1999. "Paradoxes of Participation: Questions of Participatory Approaches to Development." *Journal of International Development* 11: 597–612.

Cleaver, Francis. 2002. "Moral Ecological Rationality, Institutions and the Management of Common Property Resources." *Development and Change* 31, no. 2: 361–83.

Cock, Andrew. 2016. *Governing Cambodia's Forests*. Copenhagen: NIAS Press.

Collard, Rosemary-Claire, Jessica Dempsey, and Juanita Sundberg. 2015. "A Manifesto for Abundant Futures." *Annals of the Association of America Geographers* 105, no. 2: 322–30.

Conrad, Joseph. (1899) 2007. *Heart of Darkness*. London: Penguin Classics.

CI (Conservation International). 2012. "Independent Review: Central Cardamom Protected Forest Has Lowest Deforestation Rates vs. Surrounding Forests." Press release, December 20, 2012. Accessed November 2018. https://www.conservation.org/NewsRoom/pressreleases/Pages/Independent-Review-Central-Cardamom-Protected-Forest--Has-Lowest-Deforestation-Rates-vs--Surrounding-Forests--1219-484.aspx.

CI (Conservation International). 2015a. "Science and Innovation at CI." Accessed September 2015. http://www.conservation.org/how/pages/science-and-innovation.aspx.

CI (Conservation International). 2015b. "Gary Edson Steps Down as President of Conservation International." Press release, October 9, 2015. Accessed May 2019. https://www.conservation.org/NewsRoom/pressreleases/Pages/Gary-Edson-Steps-Down-as-President-of-Conservation-International.aspx.

CI (Conservation International). 2018. "Annual Report for 2018." Accessed September 2019. https://www.annualreports.com/HostedData/AnnualReportArchive/C/Conservation-International_2018.pdf.

CI (Conservation International). 2019. "Board of Directors." Accessed May 2019. https://www.conservation.org/about/Pages/board-of-directors.aspx.

CI (Conservation International). 2020. "Conservation Stewards Program." Accessed May 2020. http://www.conservation.org/projects/Pages/conservation-stewards -program.aspx.

Cooke, Bill, and Uma Kothari, eds. 2001. *Participation: The New Tyranny?* London: Zed Books.

Corson, Catherine. 2016. *Corridors of Power: The Politics of Environmental Aid to Madagascar.* New Haven, CT: Yale University Press.

Corson, Catherine, Lisa M. Campbell, Peter Wilshusen, and Noella J. Gray. 2019. "Assembling Global Conservation Governance." *Geoforum* 103 (July 2019): 56–65.

Corson, Catherine, Kenneth I. MacDonald, and Benjamin Neimark. 2013. "Grabbing 'Green': Markets, Environmental Governance and the Materialization of Natural Capital." *Human Geography* 6, no. 1: 1–15.

Croissant, Aurel. 2019. "Cambodia in 2018: Requiem for Multiparty Politics." *Asian Survey* 59, no. 1: 170–76.

Crush, Jonathan, ed. 1995. *Power of Development.* London: Routledge.

Curley, Melissa. 2004. "The Role of the Non-Profit Sector in Transitional Asian Economies: Cambodia Ten Years After UNTAC." Paper for the 15th Biennial Conference of the Asian Studies Association of Australia, June 29–July 2, 2004, Canberra.

Curley, Melissa. 2018. "Governing Civil Society in Cambodia: Implications of the NGO Law for the 'Rule of Law'." *Asian Studies Review* 42, no. 2: 247–67.

Dauvergne, Peter, and Genevieve LeBaron. 2014. *Protest Inc.: The Corporatization of Activism.* Cambridge: John Wiley & Sons.

De Maria, William. 1999. *Deadly Disclosures: Whistleblowing and the Ethical Meltdown of Australia.* Adelaide: Wakefield Press.

De Maria, William, and Cyrelle Jan. 1995. "Behold the Shut-eyed Sentry!" *Crime, Law and Social Change* 24, no. 2: 151–66.

Devas, Nick. 1996. "Reshaping Government at the Local Level in Cambodia: With an Example of Urban Water Supply in Battambong." *Public Administration and Development* 16: 31–41.

Diepart, Jean-Christophe, and Laura Schoenberger. 2016. "Concessions in Cambodia: Governing Profits, Extending State Power and Enclosing Resources from the Colonial Era to the Present." In *The Handbook of Contemporary Cambodia*, edited by Katherine Brickell and Simon Springer, 177–88. London: Routledge.

Diepart, Jean-Christophe, and Sem Thol. 2018. *Cambodian Peasantry and Formalization of Land Rights: Historical Perspectives and Current Issues.* Paris: French Technical Committee on Land Tenure and Development (CTFD).

Dryzek, John. 1997. *The Politics of the Earth: Environmental Discourses.* Oxford: Oxford University Press.

Easterly, William. 2006. *The White Man's Burden: Why the West's Efforts to Aid the Rest Have Done So Much Ill and So Little Good.* London: Penguin Press.

Edwards, Michael. 2008. *Just Another Emperor? The Myths and Realities of Philanthrocapitalism.* London: Demos/The Young Foundation.

References

Eisenstein, Charles. 2018. *Climate: A New Story*. Berkeley, CA: North Atlantic Books.

Ellis, Carolyn, Tony Adams, and Arthur Bochner. 2011. "Autoethnography: An Overview." *Forum: Historical Social Research* 36, no. 4: 273–90.

Ellison, Katherine. 2003. "Renting Biodiversity: The Conservation Concessions Approach." *Conservation in Practice* 4, no. 4: 20–29.

Escobar, Arturo. 1999. "After Nature: Steps to an Antiessentialist Political Ecology." *Current Anthropology* 40, no. 1: 1–30.

Fairhead, James, and Melissa Leach. 1995. "False Forest History, Complicit Social Analysis: Rethinking Some West African Environmental Narratives." *World Development* 23, no. 6: 1023–35.

Fairhead, James, and Melissa Leach. 2003. *Science, Society and Power: Environmental Knowledge and Policy in West Africa and the Caribbean*. Cambridge: Cambridge University Press.

Fairhead, James, Melissa Leach, and Ian Scoones. 2012. "Green Grabbing: A New Appropriation of Nature?" *The Journal of Peasant Studies* 39, no. 2: 237–61.

Ferguson, James. 1994. *The Anti-Politics Machine: 'Development', Depoliticization, and Bureaucratic Power in Lesotho*. Minneapolis: University of Minnesota Press.

Ferraro, Paul, and Agness Kiss. 2002. "Direct Payments to Conserve Biodiversity." *Science* 298: 1718–19.

Ferraro, Paul, and Subhrendu Pattanayak. 2006. "Money for Nothing? A Call for Empirical Evaluation of Biodiversity Conservation Investments." *PLoS Biology* 4, no. 4: 0482–88.

Flanagan, Aidan, Stephen Midgley, and Russell Turner. 2012. *Review of Conservation International's Activities in the Central Cardamoms Protected Forest*. Arlington, VA: Conservation International Foundation.

Forestry Administration (FA). 2008. "Country Paper on Forestry Outlook 2020." Accessed October 2021 from Open Development Mekong Database. Phnom Penh: Forestry Administration of Cambodia.

Fortmann, Louise. 1995. "Talking Claims: Discursive Strategies in Contesting Property." *World Development* 23, no. 6: 1053–63.

Foucault, Michel. 1977. *Discipline and Punish: The Birth of the Prison*. Translated by A. Sheridan. New York: Vintage.

Foucault, Michel. 1980. *Power/Knowledge: Selected Interviews and Other Writings 1972–77*. New York: Pantheon.

Frewer, Tim. 2013. "Doing NGO Work: The Politics of Being 'Civil Society' and Promoting 'Good Governance' in Cambodia." *Australian Geographer* 44, no. 1: 97–114. https://doi.org/10.1080/00049182.2013.765350.

Galison, Peter. 2004. "Removing Knowledge." *Critical Inquiry* 31, no. 1: 229–43.

Galtung, Johan. 1969. "Violence, Peace and Peace Research." *Journal of Peace Research* 6, no. 3: 167–91.

Geertz, Clifford. 2008. "Thick Description: Toward an Interpretive Theory of Culture." In *The Cultural Geography Reader*, edited by Timothy Oakes and Patricia L. Price, 28–39. London: Routledge.

Global Witness. 2010. "Sacking of Cambodia's Forest Chief Unconvincing as Move Against Illegal Logging." April 9, 2010. https://www.globalwitness.org/en/archive /sacking-cambodias-forest-chief-unconvincing-move-against-illegal-logging/.

Global Witness. 2012. "Death of a Comrade." April 26, 2012. https://www.global witness.org/en/campaigns/environmental-activists/death-comrade/.

Global Witness. 2016. "On Dangerous Ground." June 20, 2016. https://www.global witness.org/en/campaigns/environmental-activists/dangerous-ground/.

Goldman, Michael. 2005. *Imperial Nature: The World Bank and the Making of Green Neoliberalism*. New Haven, CT: Yale University Press.

Gottesman, Evan. 2004. *Cambodia After the Khmer Rouge: Inside the Politics of Nation Building*. Chiang Mai: Silkworm Books.

Gusterson, Hugh. 1997. "Studying Up Revisited." *PoLAR*, 20: 114–19.

Hajer, Maarten. 1995. *The Politics of Environmental Discourse*. Oxford: Clarendon Press.

Hall, Ruth, Marc Edelman, Saturnino M. Borras Jr., Ian Scoones, Ben White, and Wendy Wolford. 2015. "Resistance, Acquiescence or Incorporation? An Introduction to Land Grabbing and Political Reactions 'From Below'." *Journal of Peasant Studies* 42, nos. 3–4: 467–88.

Hansen, Matthew, Peter Potapov, Rebecca Moore, Matthew Hancher, Svetlana Turubanova, Alexandra Tyukavina, et al. 2013. "High-Resolution Global Maps of 21st-Century Forest Cover Change." *Science* 342, no. 6160: 850–53.

Haraway, Donna. 1997. *Modest_Witness@Second_Millenium.FemaleMan©_Meets_ On coMouse™*. New York: Routledge.

Haraway, Donna. 2016. *Staying with the Trouble: Making Kin in the Chthulucene*. Durham, NC: Duke University Press.

Hardner, Jared, and Richard Rice. 2002. "Rethinking Green Consumerism." *Scientific American* 286, no. 5: 70–77.

Harrison, Elizabeth. 2003. "The Monolithic Development Machine?" In *A Moral Critique of Development: In Search of Global Responsibilities*, edited by Philip Q. van Ufford and Anta K. Giri, 101–17. London: Routledge.

Harvey, Paul, Rachel Slater, and John Farrington. 2005. "Cash Transfers: Mere 'Gadaffi Syndrome', or Serious Potential for Rural Rehabilitation and Development?" *Overseas Development Institute Series: Natural Resource Perspectives* 97 (March): 1–4.

Hickey, Sam, and Giles Mohan. 2004. *Participation: From Tyranny to Transformation?* New York: Zed Books.

Hilhorst, Dorothea. 2003. *The Real World of NGOs: Discourse, Diversity and Development*. London: Zed Books.

Hobart, Mark, ed. 1993. *An Anthropological Critique of Development: The Growth of Ignorance*. London: Routledge.

Hockley, Neal. 2003. "Park and Free Ride." *The Economist*. Letters Section, September 20, 2003.

Holmes, George. 2011. "Conservation's Friends in High Places: Neoliberalism, Networks, and the Transnational Conservation Elite." *Global Environmental Politics* 11, no. 4: 1–21.

References

Holmes, George. 2012. "Biodiversity for Billionaires: Capitalism, Conservation and the Role of Philanthropy in Saving/Selling Nature." *Development and Change* 43, no. 1: 185–203.

Hughes, Caroline. 2003. *The Political Economy of Cambodia's Transition 1991–2001.* London: Routledge.

Hughes, Caroline. 2006. "Cambodia." *Institute of Development Studies Bulletin* 37, no. 2 (March).

Hughes, Caroline, and Tim Conway. 2003. *Understanding Pro-Poor Political Change: The Policy Process—Cambodia.* 2nd draft, August 2003. London: Overseas Development Institute.

Hummel, Christiaan, Dimitris Poursanidis, Daniel Orenstein, Michael Elliott, Mihai Cristian Adamescu, Constantin Cazacu, Guy Ziv, Nektarios Chrysoulakis, Jaap van der Meer, and Herman Hummel. 2019. "Protected Area Management: Fusion and Confusion with the Ecosystem Services Approach." *Science of the Total Environment* 651, no. 2: 2432–43.

Hussain, Shafqat. 2019. *The Snow Leopard and the Goat: Politics of Conservation in the Western Himalayas.* Seattle: University of Washington Press.

Hutton, Jon, William M. Adams, and James Murombedzi. 2005. "Back to the Barriers? Changing Narratives in Biodiversity Conservation." *Forum for Development Studies* 32, no. 2: 341–70.

Igoe, James. 2010. "The Spectacle of Nature in the Global Economy of Appearances: Anthropological Engagements with the Spectacular Mediations of Transnational Conservation." *Critique of Anthropology* 34, no. 2: 375–97.

Igoe, James. 2017. *The Nature of Spectacle: On Images, Money, and Conserving Capitalism.* Tucson: University of Arizona Press.

Igoe, James, and Dan Brockington. 2007. "Neoliberal Conservation: A Brief Introduction." *Conservation and Society* 5, no. 4: 432–49.

Igoe, James, and Sian Sullivan. 2009. *Problematizing Neoliberal Biodiversity Conservation: Displaced and Disobedient Knowledges.* London: International Institute for Environment and Development (IIED).

Illich, Ivan. 1973. *Tools for Conviviality.* New York: Harper and Row.

IPBES (Intergovernmental Science-Policy Platform on Biodiversity and Ecosystem Services). 2019. "Nature's Dangerous Decline 'Unprecedented' Species Extinction Rates 'Accelerating.'" Intergovernmental Science-Policy Platform on Biodiversity and Ecosystem Services. Media release. Accessed July 2020. https://www.ipbes.net/news/Media-Release-Global-Assessment.

Jacobsen, Trude, and Martin Stuart-Fox. 2013. *Power and Political Culture in Cambodia.* Singapore: Asia Research Institute, National University of Singapore.

Jasanoff, Sheila. 2004. "Ordering Knowledge, Ordering Society." In *States of Knowledge: The Co-Production of Science and Social Order,* edited by S. Jasanoff, 13–45. Oxon: Routledge.

Jeanrenaud, Sally. 2002. *People-oriented Approaches in Global Conservation: Is the Leopard Changing Its Spots?* London and Brighton: International Institute for Environment and Development and Institute of Development Studies.

Jensen, Casper B. 2017. "Integrating Human to Quality: Capacity Building Across Cambodian Worlds." *The Cambridge Journal of Anthropology* 35, no. 1: 131–45.

Jepson, Paul. 2005. "Governance and Accountability of Environmental NGOs." *Environmental Science & Policy* 8: 515–24.

Käkönen, Mira, and Try Thuon. 2019. "Overlapping Zones of Exclusion: Carbon Markets, Corporate Hydropower Enclaves and Timber Extraction in Cambodia." *The Journal of Peasant Studies* 46, no. 6: 1192–1218.

Kashwan, Prakash, Rosaleen V. Duffy, Francis Massé, Adeniyi P. Asiyanbi, and Esther Marijnen. 2021. "From Racialized Neocolonial Global Conservation to an Inclusive and Regenerative Conservation." *Environment: Science and Policy for Sustainable Development* 63, no. 4: 4–19. https://doi.org/10.1080/00139157.2021.1924574.

Keeley, James, and Ian Scoones. 2014. *Understanding Environmental Policy Processes: Cases from Africa.* London: Routledge.

Kelly, Alice. 2013. "Conservation Practice as Primitive Accumulation." In *New Frontiers of Land Control,* edited by N. Peluso and C. Lund, 23–42. London: Routledge.

Kerr, Ron. 2008. "International Development and the New Public Management: Projects and Logframes as Discursive Technologies of Governance." In *The New Development Management,* edited by S. Dar and W. Cooke, 91–110. New York: Zed Books.

Kiernan, Ben. 1996. *The Pol Pot Regime: Race, Power and Genocide in Cambodia under the Khmer Rouge, 1975–79.* New Haven, CT: Yale University Press.

Kiik, Laur. 2019. "Conservationland: Toward the Anthropology of Professionals in Global Nature Conservation." *Critique of Anthropology* 39, no. 4: 391–419.

Killeen, Tim. 2012. *The Cardamom Conundrum: Reconciling Development and Conservation in the Kingdom of Cambodia.* Singapore: NUS Press.

Kimmerer, Robin W. 2013. *Braiding Sweetgrass: Indigenous Wisdom, Scientific Knowledge and the Teachings of Plants.* New York: Penguin Books.

Kingdon, John. 1984. *Agendas, Alternatives and Public Choices.* Boston: Little, Brown and Company.

Kirsch, Harald. 2005. "The Use of Geo-Information Tools and Products in Participatory Land Use Planning (PLUP) in Rural Cambodia." *Pacific News* 23 (January/February): 4.

Kirsch, Stuart. 2018. *Engaged Anthropology: Politics Beyond the Text.* Oakland: University of California Press.

Kiss, Agnes. 2004. "Making Biodiversity Conservation a Land Use Priority." In *Getting Biodiversity Projects to Work: Towards More Effective Conservation and Development,* edited by T. McShane and M. Wells, 98–123. New York: Columbia University Press.

Knowles-Morrison, Jenny. 2010. "From Global Paradigms to Grounded Policies: Local Socio-Cognitive Constructions of International Development Policies and Implications for Development Management." *Public Administration and Develop-*

References

ment: The International Journal of Management Research and Practice 30, no. 2: 159–74.

Kremen, Claire, John Niles, M. Dalton, G. C. Daily, P. Ehrlich, J. Fay, D. Grewal, and R. Guillery. 2000. "Economic Incentives for Rain Forest Conservation Across Scales." *Science* 288: 1828–32.

Lamb, Vanessa, Laura Schoenberger, Carl Middleton, and Borin Un. 2017. "Gendered Eviction, Protest and Recovery: A Feminist Political Ecology Engagement with Land Grabbing in Rural Cambodia." *The Journal of Peasant Studies* 44, no. 6: 1215–34.

Lambrick, Fran, and Vanessa de Smet. 2020. *I Am Chut Wutty.* Journeyman Pictures. 57 minutes. https://www.youtube.com/watch?v=ndnC_6wY8OI.

Lang, Chris. 2012. "Conservation International Turns a Blind Eye to Illegal Logging in the Cardamom Mountains, Cambodia." *REDD-Monitor,* January 19, 2012. https://redd-monitor.org/2012/01/19/conservation-international-turns-a-blind-eye-to-illegal-logging-in-the-cardamom-mountains-cambodia/.

Lang, Chris. 2018. "ExxonMobil Strikes US\$200 Billion Offshore Oil Reserves in Guyana, Gives US\$10 million to Conservation International." *REDD-Monitor,* August 7, 2018. https://redd-monitor.org/2018/08/07/exxonmobil-strikes-us 200-billion-offshore-oil-reserves-in-guyana-gives-us10-million-to-conservation -international/.

Larsen, Peter B., and Dan Brockington. 2018. *The Anthropology of Conservation NGOs: Rethinking the Boundaries.* London: Palgrave Macmillan.

Lashaw, Amanda. 2013. "How Progressive Culture Resists Critique: The Impasse of NGO Studies." *Ethnography* 14, no. 4: 501–22.

Lather, Patti. 1986. "Research as Praxis." *Harvard Educational Review* 56, no. 3: 257–78.

Latour, Bruno. 1996. *Aramis, or the Love of Technology.* Cambridge, MA: Harvard University Press.

Latour, Bruno. 2010. "An Attempt at a 'Compositionist Manifesto.'" *New Literary Theory* 41, no. 3: 471–90.

Lea, Tess. 2008. *Bureaucrats and Bleeding Hearts: Indigenous Health in Northern Australia.* Sydney: UNSW Press.

Leach, Melissa, and Robin Mearns, eds. 1996. *The Lie of the Land: Challenging Received Wisdom on the African Environment.* Oxford: James Currey.

Le Billon, Philippe. 2000. "The Political Ecology of Transition in Cambodia 1989–1999: War, Peace and Forest Exploitation." *Development and Change* 31: 785–805.

Le Billon, Philippe. 2002. "Logging in Muddy Waters: The Politics of Forest Exploitation in Cambodia." *Critical Asian Studies* 34, no. 4: 563–86.

Ledgerwood, Judy, and John Vijghen. 2002. "Decision-making in Rural Khmer Villages." In *Cambodia Emerges from the Past: Eight Essays,* edited by Judy Ledgerwood, 90–150. DeKalb: Northern Illinois University Center for Southeast Asian Studies.

Lennane, Jean. 2012. "What Happens to Whistleblowers, and Why." *Social Medicine* 6, no. 4: 249–58.

Lewis, David, Anthony Bebbington, Simon Batterbury, Alpha Shah, Elizabeth Olson, M. Shameem Siddiqi, and Sandra Duvall. 2003. "Practice, Power and Meaning: Frameworks for Studying Organizational Culture in Multi-Agency Rural Development Projects." *Journal of International Development* 15: 541–57.

Lewis, David, and David Mosse, eds. 2006. *Development Brokers and Translators: The Ethnography of Aid and Agencies.* Bloomfield, CT: Kumarian Press.

Li, Tania. 1996. "Images of Community: Discourse and Strategy in Property Relations." *Development and Change* 27: 509–27.

Li, Tania. 2002. "Engaging Simplifications: Community-Based Resource Management, Market Processes and State Agendas in Upland Southeast Asia." *World Development* 30, no. 2: 265–83.

Li, Tania. 2007. *The Will to Improve: Governmentality, Development and the Practice of Politics.* Durham, NC: Duke University Press.

Long, Norman. 2001. *Development Sociology: Actor Perspectives.* London: Routledge,

Long, Norman, and Ann Long, eds. 1992. *Battlefields of Knowledge: The Interlocking of Theory and Practice in Social Research and Development.* London: Routledge.

Lorimer, Jamie. 2015. *Wildlife in the Anthropocene: Conservation After Nature.* Minneapolis: University of Minnesota Press.

Loughlin, Neil, and Sarah Milne. 2021. "After the Grab? Land Control and Regime Survival in Cambodia Since 2012." *Journal of Contemporary Asia* 51, no. 3: 375–97.

Luco, Fabienne. 2002. *Between a Tiger and a Crocodile: Management of Local Conflicts in Cambodia, An Anthropological Approach to Traditional and New Practices.* Phnom Penh: UNESCO Culture of Peace Programme.

MacDonald, Christine. 2008. *Green, Inc.: An Environmental Insider Reveals How a Good Cause Has Gone Bad.* Guilford, CT: The Lyons Press.

MacDonald, Kenneth. 2010. "The Devil Is in the (Bio)diversity: Private Sector 'Engagement' and the Restructuring of Biodiversity Conservation." *Antipode* 42: 513–50. https://doi.org/10.1111/j.1467-8330.2010.00762.x.

MacDonald, Kenneth, and Catherine Corson. 2012. "'TEEB Begins Now': A Virtual Moment in the Production of Natural Capital." *Development and Change* 43, no. 1: 159–84.

MacKenzie, John. 1988. *The Empire of Nature: Hunting, Conservation and British Imperialism.* Manchester: Manchester University Press.

Mahanty, Sango. 2022. *Unsettled Frontiers: Market Formation in the Cambodia-Vietnam Borderlands.* Ithaca, NY: Cornell University Press.

Marchese, Christian. 2015. "Biodiversity Hotspots: A Shortcut for a More Complicated Concept." *Global Ecology and Conservation* 3 (January): 297–309.

Marcus, George, ed. 1983. *Elites: Ethnographic Issues.* Albuquerque: University of New Mexico Press.

Marcus, George. 1995. "Ethnography in/of the World System: The Emergence of Multi-Sited Ethnography." *Annual Review of Anthropology* 24: 95–117.

References

Markowitz, Lisa. 2001. "Finding the Field: Notes on the Ethnography of NGOs." *Human Organization* 60, no. 1: 40–46.

Marschke, Melissa. 2012. *Life, Fish, and Mangroves: Resource Governance in Coastal Cambodia.* Ottawa: University of Ottawa Press.

Marston, John, and Huoer Chhoeun. 2015. "A 'People's' Irrigation Reservoir on the Tonle Sap Floodplain." In *Conservation and Development in Cambodia: Exploring Frontiers of Change in Nature, State and Society,* edited by Sarah Milne and Sango Mahanty, 238–57. Oxon: Routledge.

Martin, Marie. 1997. *Les Khmers Daeum, 'Khmers de l'origine': Société Montagnarde et Exploitation de la Forêt, de l'écologie à l'histoire.* Paris: Presses de l'Ecole Française d'Extrême-Orient.

McAfee, Kathleen. 1999. "Selling Nature to Save It? Biodiversity and the Rise of Green Developmentalism." *Environment and Planning D: Society and Space* 17, no. 2: 133–54.

McCarthy, Donal, Paul Donald, Jörn Scharlemann, Graeme Buchanan, Andrew Balmford, Jonathan Green, et al. 2012. "Financial Costs of Meeting Global Biodiversity Conservation Targets: Current Spending and Unmet Needs." *Science* 338, no. 6109: 946–49.

McCarthy, James. 2006. "Neoliberalism and the Politics of Alternatives: Community Forestry in British Columbia and the United States." *Annals of the Association of American Geographers* 96, no. 1: 84–104.

McElwee, Pamela. 2016. *Forests Are Gold: Trees, People, and Environmental Rule in Vietnam.* Seattle: University of Washington Press.

McGoey, Linsey. 2012. "Strategic Unknowns: Towards a Sociology of Ignorance." *Economy and Society* 41, no. 1: 1–16.

McGoey, Linsey. 2015. *No Such Thing as a Free Gift: The Gates Foundation and the Price of Philanthropy.* London: Verso Books.

McKinnon, Madeleine, Michael Mascia, Wu Yang, Will Turner, and Curan Bonham. 2015. "Impact Evaluation to Communicate and Improve Conservation Non-Governmental Organization Performance: The Case of Conservation International." *Philosophical Transactions of the Royal Society B* 370: 2014028220140282. http://doi.org/10.1098/rstb.2014.0282.

Menton, Mary, and Paul R. Gilbert. 2021. "BINGOs and Environmental Defenders: NGO Complicity in Atmospheres of Violence and the Possibilities for Decolonial Solidarity with Defenders." In *Environmental Defenders: Deadly Struggles for Life and Territory,* edited by Mary Menton and Philippe Le Billon, 228–44. Oxon: Routledge.

Menton, Mary, Grettel Navas, and Philippe Le Billon. 2021. "Atmospheres of Violence: On Defenders' Intersecting Experiences of Violence." In *Environmental Defenders: Deadly Struggles for Life and Territory,* edited by Mary Menton and Philippe Le Billon, 51-63. Oxon: Routledge.

Merry, Sally E. 2011. "Measuring the World: Indicators, Human Rights, and Global Governance." *Current Anthropology* 52 (S3): S83–95.

Migdal, Joel. 2001. *State in Society: Studying How States and Societies Transform and Constitute One Another*. Cambridge: Cambridge University Press.

Millennium Ecosystem Assessment (MEA). 2005. *Ecosystems and Human Wellbeing: Synthesis*. Washington, DC: Island Press.

Milne, Sarah. 2002. *Report on Livelihoods in Tatai Leu and Roussey Chrum Communes*. Phnom Penh: Conservation International.

Milne, Sarah. 2009. "Global Ideas, Local Realities: The Political Ecology of Payments for Biodiversity Conservation Services in Cambodia." PhD diss., University of Cambridge.

Milne, Sarah. 2012. "Grounding Forest Carbon: Property Relations and Avoided Deforestation in Cambodia." *Human Ecology* 40, no. 5: 693–706.

Milne, Sarah. 2015. "Cambodia's Unofficial Regime of Extraction: Illicit Logging in the Shadow of Transnational Governance and Investment." *Critical Asian Studies* 47, no. 2: 200–28.

Milne, Sarah. 2017. "On the Perils of Resistance: Local Politics and Environmental Struggle in Cambodia." *International Institute of Asian Studies—The Newsletter* 78 (Autumn): 32–33.

Milne, Sarah. 2021. "Resist or Comply? Experiences of Violence Around Hydropower Dams in Cambodia." In *Environmental Defenders: Deadly Struggles for Life and Territory*, edited by Mary Menton and Philippe Le Billon, 167–79. Oxon: Routledge.

Milne, Sarah, and William Adams. 2012. "Market Masquerades: Uncovering the Politics of Community-Level Payments for Environmental Services in Cambodia." *Development and Change* 43, no. 1: 133–58.

Milne, Sarah, and Sango Mahanty, eds. 2015. *Conservation and Development in Cambodia: Exploring Frontiers of Change in Nature, State and Society*. London: Routledge.

Milne, Sarah, and Sango Mahanty. 2019. "Value and Bureaucratic Violence in the Green Economy." *Geoforum* 98: 133–43.

Milne, Sarah, Sango Mahanty, Phuc To, Wolfram Dressler, Peter Kanowski, and Maylee Thavat. 2019. "Learning from 'Actually Existing' REDD+: A Synthesis of Ethnographic Findings." *Conservation & Society* 17, no. 1: 84–95.

Milne, Sarah, and Eduard Niesten. 2009. "Direct Payments for Biodiversity Conservation in Developing Countries: Practical Insights for Design and Implementation." *Oryx* 43, no. 4: 530–41.

Milne, Sarah, Kimchoeun Pak, and Michael Sullivan. 2015. "Shackled to Nature? The Post-Conflict State and Its Symbiotic Relationship with Natural Resources." In *Conservation and Development in Cambodia: Exploring Frontiers of Change in Nature, State and Society*, edited by Sarah Milne and Sango Mahanty, 28–50. Oxon: Routledge.

Mittermeier, Russell, Patricio Robles Gil, Michael Hoffman, John Pilgrim, Thomas Brooks, Cristina Goettsch Mittermeier, John Lamoreux, and Gustavo da Fonseca. 2004. *Hotspots Revisited: Earth's Biologically Richest and Most Endangered Terrestrial Ecoregions*. Washington, DC: CEMEX.

Mongabay. 2011. "CI Refutes Cambodian Logging Story." December 23, 2011. https://news.mongabay.com/2011/12/ci-refutes-cambodian-logging-story/.

Morgenbesser, Lee. 2019. "Cambodia's Transition to Hegemonic Authoritarianism." *Journal of Democracy* 30, no. 1: 158–71.

Mosse, David. 2001. "Social Research in Rural Development Projects." In *Inside Organisations: Anthropologists at Work*, edited by David Gellner and Eric Hirsch, 159–82. Oxford: Berg.

Mosse, David. 2004. "Is Good Policy Unimplementable? Reflections on the Ethnography of Aid Policy and Practice." *Development and Change* 35, no. 4: 639–71.

Mosse, David. 2005. *Cultivating Development: An Ethnography of Aid Policy and Practice*. London: Pluto Press.

Mosse, David. 2015. "Misunderstood, Misrepresented, Contested? Anthropological Knowledge Production in Question." *Focaal* 72: 128–37.

Muradian, Roldan, Murat Arsel, Lorenzo Pellegrini, Fikret Adaman, Bernardo Aguilar, Bina Agarwal, Esteve Corbera, Driss Ezzine De Blas, Joshua Farley, Géraldine Froger, et al. 2013. "Payments for Ecosystem Services and the Fatal Attraction of Win-Win Solutions." *Conservation Letters* 6, no. 4: 274–79.

Myers, Norman, Russell Mittermeier, Cristina Mittermeier, Gustavo da Fonseca, and Jennifer Kent. 2000. "Biodiversity Hotspots for Conservation Priorities." *Nature* 403: 853–58.

Nader, Laura. 1969. "Up the Anthropologist: Perspectives Gained by Studying Up." In *Reinventing Anthropology*, edited by Dell Hymes, 284–311. New York: Pantheon Books.

Neef, Andreas, and Siphat Touch. 2012. "Land Grabbing in Cambodia: Narratives, Mechanisms, Resistance." Paper presented at the international conference on Global Land Grabbing II, Cornell University, Ithaca, New York, October 17–19, 2012.

Neef, Andreas, Siphat Touch, and Jamaree Chiengthong. 2013. "The Politics and Ethics of Land Concessions in Rural Cambodia." *Journal of Agricultural and Environmental Ethics* 26, no. 6: 1085–1103.

Nevins, Joseph, and Nancy Lee Peluso. 2008. "Introduction: Commoditization in Southeast Asia." In *Taking Southeast Asia to Market: Commodities, Nature, and People in the Neoliberal Age*, edited by Joseph Nevins and Nancy Lee Peluso, 1–24. Ithaca, NY: Cornell University Press.

Niesten, Eduard, and Richard Rice. 2004. "Sustainable Forest Management and Conservation Incentive Agreements." *International Forestry Review* 6, no. 1: 56–66.

Norén-Nilsson, Astrid. 2016. *Cambodia's Second Kingdom: Nation, Imagination, and Democracy*. Ithaca, NY: Cornell University Press.

Öjendal, Joakim, and Kim Sedara. 2006. "*Korob, Kaud, Klach*: In Search of Agency in Rural Cambodia." *Journal of Southeast Asian Studies* 37, no. 3: 507–26.

O'Leary, Moire, and Nee Meas. 2001. *Learning for Transformation: A Study of the Relationship Between Culture, Values, Experiences and Development Practice in Cambodia*. Battambang, Cambodia: Krom Akphiwat Phum.

Oreskes, Naomi, and Erik Conway. 2010. "Defeating the Merchants of Doubt." *Nature* 465, no. 7299: 686–87.

Otis, Daniel. 2014. "The Secret Garden: Yellow Vine." *Southeast Asia Globe*, May 9, 2014. https://southeastasiaglobe.com/the-secret-garden-yellow-vine-cambodia-southeast-asia-globe/.

Ouk, Kimsan, and Chetha Chay. 2013. "Central Cardamom Conservation Program." In *Evidence-based Conservation: Lessons from the Lower Mekong*, edited by Terry Sunderland, Jeffrey Sayer, and Minh-Ha Hoang, 187–201. New York: Routledge.

Ovesen, Jan, Ing-Britt Trankell, and Joachim Ojendal. 1996. *When Every Household Is an Island: Social Organisation and Power Structures in Rural Cambodia*. Uppsala Research Reports in Cultural Anthropology, No. 15. Stockholm, Sweden: Department of Cultural Anthropology, Uppsala University and Sida.

Oxfam. 2008. *Smart Development: Oxfam's Briefing Paper on Making Aid Work*. Washington, DC: Oxfam America.

Paley, Richard. 2015. "Managing Protected Areas in Cambodia: The Challenge for Conservation Bureaucracies in a Hostile Governance Environment." In *Conservation and Development in Cambodia: Exploring Frontiers of Change in Nature, State and Society*, edited by S. Milne and S. Mahanty, 159–77. Oxon: Routledge.

Pasgaard, Maya, and Tania F. Nielsen. 2016. "A Story of 'Communities': Boundaries, Geographical Composition and Social Coherence in a Forest Conservation Project, Northern Cambodia." *Geografisk Tidsskrift-Danish Journal of Geography* 116, no. 2: 134–46.

Peck, Jamie. 2010. "Zombie Neoliberalism and the Ambidextrous State." *Theoretical Criminology* 14, no. 1: 104–10.

Peet, Richard, and Michael Watts, eds. 2004. *Liberation Ecologies: Environment, Development, Social Movements*. London: Routledge.

Peluso, Nancy. 2012. "What's Nature Got to Do with It? A Situated Historical Perspective on Socio-Natural Commodities." *Development and Change* 43, no. 1: 79–104.

Phalan, Ben, Malvika Onial, Andrew Balmford, and Rhys Green. 2011. "Reconciling Food Production and Biodiversity Conservation: Land Sharing and Land Sparing Compared." *Science* 333, no. 6047: 1289–91.

Phnom Penh Post. 2012. "Cardamom Solution Remains an Option." June 5, 2012. https://www.phnompenhpost.com/post-plus/cardamom-solution-remains-option.

Prum, Virak. 2005. "Reforming Cambodian Local Administration: Is Institutional History Unreceptive for Decentralization?" *Forum of International Development Studies* 30: 97–121.

Quiggin, John. 2012. *Zombie Economics: How Dead Ideas Still Walk Among Us*. Melbourne: Black Inc. Books.

Ramutsindela, Maano, Marja Spierenburg, and Harry Wels. 2011. *Sponsoring Nature: Environmental Philanthropy for Conservation*. London: Earthscan.

Rayner, Steve. 2012. "Uncomfortable Knowledge: The Social Construction of Ignorance in Science and Environmental Policy Discourses." *Economy and Society* 41, no. 1: 107–25.

Redford, Kent, and Steven Sanderson. 2000. "Extracting Humans from Nature." *Conservation Biology* 14, no. 5: 1362–64.

Roberts, Andrew. 2015. "Lost in Transition: Landscape, Ecological Gradients and Legibility on the Tonle Sap Floodplain." In *Conservation and Development in Cambodia: Exploring Frontiers of Change in Nature, State and Society*, edited by Sarah Milne and Sango Mahanty, 71–92. Oxon: Routledge.

Rock, Florain. 2001. *Participatory Land Use Planning (PLUP) in Rural Cambodia: Manual for Government Staff and Development Workers.* Phnom Penh: Ministry of Land Management, Urban Planning and Construction, Government of Cambodia.

Rodriguez, Carlos-Manuel. 2016. "To Protect Nature and Boost Economy, Cambodia Must Follow Costa Rica's Lead." *Conservation International.* Accessed November 2018. https://www.conservation.org/blog/to-protect-nature-and-boost-economy-cambodia-must-follow-costa-rica-s-lead.

Rodríguez, Jon-Paul, Andrew Taber, Peter Daszak, Raman Sukumar, C. Valladares-Padua, S. Padua, L. F. Aguirre, R. A. Medellín, M. Acosta, A. A. Aguirre et al. 2007. "Globalization of Conservation: A View from the South." *Science* 317, no. 5839: 755–56.

Roe, Emery. 1991. "Development Narratives, or Making the Best of Blueprint Development." *World Development* 19, no. 4: 287–300.

Rose, Deborah B. 2011. *Wild Dog Dreaming: Love and Extinction.* Charlottesville: University of Virginia Press.

Rose, Nikolas. 1999. *Powers of Freedom: Reframing Political Thought.* Cambridge: Cambridge University Press.

Rottenburg, Richard. 2009. *Far-fetched Facts: A Parable of Development Aid.* Translated by A. Brown and T. Lampert. Cambridge, MA: MIT Press.

Royal Government of Cambodia (RGC). 2017. *National Protected Area Strategic Management Plan 2017–2031.* Phnom Penh: Royal Government of Cambodia.

Sachedina, Hassan. 2010 "Disconnected Nature: The Scaling Up of African Wildlife Foundation and Its Impacts on Biodiversity Conservation and Local Livelihoods." *Antipode* 42, no. 3: 603–23.

Sachs, Jeffrey. 2005. *The End of Poverty: Economic Possibilities for Our Time.* New York: Penguin Books.

Sam, Rith. 2003. "Jolie Money Sets Up Conservation Zone in Wild West." *The Phnom Penh Post.* August 15, 2003. Accessed February 2022. https://www.phnompenhpost.com/national/jolie-money-sets-conservation-zone-wild-west.

Samuelson, Paul. 1948. "Consumption Theory in Terms of Revealed Preference." *Economica* 15, no. 60: 243–53.

Save Cambodia's Wildlife (SCW). 2006. *Atlas of Cambodia: National Poverty and Environment Maps.* Phnom Penh: Save Cambodia's Wildlife.

Scheper-Hughes, Nancy. 1995. "The Primacy of the Ethical: Propositions for a Militant Anthropology." *Current Anthropology* 36, no. 3: 409–40.

Scoones, Ian, and Andy Stirling. 2020. *The Politics of Uncertainty: Challenges of Transformation*. London: Routledge.

Scopis, Sheila. 2011. "Cambodia's String Economy." PhD diss., Melbourne School of Land and Environment, University of Melbourne.

Scott, James. 1976. *The Moral Economy of the Peasant: Rebellion and Subsistence in Southeast Asia*. New Haven, CT: Yale University Press.

Scott, James. 1985. *Weapons of the Weak: Everyday Forms of Peasant Resistance*. New Haven, CT: Yale University Press.

Scott, James. 1990. *Domination and the Arts of Resistance: Hidden Transcripts*. New Haven, CT: Yale University Press.

Scott, James. 1998. *Seeing Like a State: How Certain Schemes to Improve the Human Condition Have Failed*. New Haven, CT: Yale University Press.

Seymour, Francis, and Navroz Dubash. 2000. *The Right Conditions: The World Bank, Structural Adjustment, and Forest Policy Reform*. Washington, DC: World Resources Institute.

SFI (Sustainable Forestry Initiative). 2002. "Forest Conservation News Today: Cambodia Protects Forested Mountains, Cracks Down on Illegal Logging." Accessed May 15, 2008. Forest Conservation Portal: http://forests.org/archived_site/today/recent/2002/caadlawp.htm.

Shore, Cris. 2008. "Audit Culture and Illiberal Governance: Universities and the Politics of Accountability." *Anthropological Theory* 8, no. 3: 278–98.

Shore, Cris, and Susan Wright, eds. 1997. *Anthropology of Policy: Critical Perspectives on Governance and Power*. London: Routledge.

Simpson, Virginia, and Nicholas J. Souter. 2017. "The Future of Payments for Ecosystem Services in Cambodia." *Cambodian Journal of Natural History* 2017: 1–3.

Slocomb, Margaret. 2004. "Commune Elections in Cambodia: 1981 Foundations and 2002 Reformulations." *Modern Asian Studies* 38, no. 2: 447–67.

Smith, Dorothy. 1987. *The Everyday World as Problematic: A Feminist Sociology*. Toronto: University of Toronto Press.

Soenthrith, Saing, and John Maloy. 2007. "Military Police Kill Woman; Circumstance Disputed." *The Cambodia Daily*, March 6, 2007.

Sokha, Cheang, and Christopher Shay. 2009. "Forest Agent Caught with Rare Timber." *Phnom Penh Post*, July 30, 2009. https://mail.phnompenhpost.com/national/forest-agent-caught-rare-timber.

Souter, Nicholas, Virginia Simpson, Alistair Mould, Jonathan Eames, Thomas Grey, Ross Sinclair, Tracy Farrell, Joel Jurgens, and Andrew Billingsley. 2016. "Will the Recent Changes in Protected Area Management and the Creation of Five New Protected Areas Improve Biodiversity Conservation in Cambodia?" *Cambodian Journal of Natural History* 1: 1–5.

Starling Resources. 2008. *Cardamom Mountain Protected Area Network Conservation Trust Fund Business Plan*. Prepared on behalf of Conservation International and Flora and Fauna International, October 2008. Bali: Starling Resources. http://

www.admcf.org/wp-content/uploads/2016/12/1-Resource-Cardamom-Mountain -Conservation-Trust-Fund-Business-Plan-October-2008.pdf.

Strathern, Marilyn. 2000. "The Tyranny of Transparency." *British Educational Research Journal* 26, no. 3: 309–21.

Sullivan, Michael. 2016. *Cambodia Votes: Democracy, Authority and International Support for Elections 1993–2013*. Copenhagen: NIAS Press.

Survival International. 2021. "WWF Accused of Deceit, Cover-Ups and Dishonesty in US Congressional Committee Hearing." October 27, 2021. https://survivalinter national.org/news/12683.

Sutherland, William, Andrew Pullin, Paul Dolman, and Teri Knight. 2004. "The Need for Evidence-Based Conservation." *Trends in Ecology and Evolution* 19, no. 6: 305–8.

Svadlenak-Gomez, Karin, Tom Clements, Charles Foley, Nikolai Kazakov, Dale Lewis, Dale Miquelle, and Renae Stenhouse. 2007. "Paying for Results: WCS Experiences with Direct Incentives for Conservation." In *Protected Areas and Human Livelihoods*, edited by Kent Redford and Eva Fearn, 117–30. WCS Working Paper No. 32, December 2007. Bronx, NY: Wildlife Conservation Society.

Tacconi, Luca. 2015. *Regional Synthesis of Payments for Environmental Services (PES) in the Greater Mekong Region*. Working Paper 175. Bogor: CIFOR.

Terborgh, John. 1999. *Requiem for Nature*. Washington, DC: Island Press.

Thaler, Gregory. 2021. "Ethnography of Environmental Governance: Towards an Organizational Approach." *Geoforum* 120: 122–32.

Trembath, Jodie-Lee. 2018. "Expats, Tourists and 'Matter Out of Place.'" *The Familiar Strange*, May 10, 2018. https://thefamiliarstrange.com/2018/05/10/expats-tourists -matter-out-of-place/.

Tsing, Anna. 1993. *In the Realm of the Diamond Queen: Marginality in an Out-of-the-Way Place*. Princeton, NJ: Princeton University Press.

Tsing, Anna. 2005. *Friction: An Ethnography of Global Connection*. Princeton, NJ: Princeton University Press.

Tsing, Anna, Heather Anne Swanson, Elaine Gan, and Nils Bubandt, eds. 2019. *Arts of Living on a Damaged Planet*. Minneapolis: University of Minnesota Press.

Un, Kheang. 2019. *Cambodia: Return to Authoritarianism*. Cambridge: Cambridge University Press.

Un, Kheang, and Sokbunthoeun So. 2009. "Politics of Natural Resource Use in Cambodia." *Asian Affairs: An American Review* 36, no. 3: 123–38.

UNDP (United Nations Development Programme). 2007. *Developing an Integrated Protected Area System for the Cardamom Mountains*. Accessed June 21, 2009. http://www.undp.org/gef/portfolio/writeups/bd/cambodia.html

UNDP (United Nations Development Programme). 2019. *National Human Development Report 2019: Cambodia*. Phnom Penh: UNDP. Accessed May 2020. http://hdr.undp.org/en/content/national-human-development-report-2019 -cambodia.

van Ufford, Philip Q., and Anta Giri, eds. 2003. *A Moral Critique of Development: In Search of Global Responsibilities*. London: Routledge.

Vandergeest, Peter, and Nancy Peluso. 1995. "Territorialization and State Power in Thailand." *Theory and Society* 24, no. 3: 385–426.

Vaughan, Diane. 1996. *The Challenger Launch Decision: Risky Technology, Culture, and Deviance at NASA*. Chicago: University of Chicago Press.

Verver, Michiel, and Heidi Dahles. 2015. "The Institutionalisation of *Oknha*: Cambodian Entrepreneurship at the Interface of Business and Politics." *Journal of Contemporary Asia* 45, no. 1: 48–70.

Vetterlein, Antje. 2012. "Seeing Like the World Bank on Poverty." *New Political Economy* 17, no. 1: 35–58.

Waldron, Anthony, Arne O. Mooers, Daniel C. Miller, Nate Nibbelink, David Redding, Tyler S. Kuhn, J. Timmons Roberts, and John L. Gittleman. 2013. "Targeting Global Conservation Funding to Limit Immediate Biodiversity Declines." *Proceedings of the National Academy of Sciences* 110: 12144–48.

Weaver, Catherine. 2008. *Hypocrisy Trap: The World Bank and the Poverty of Reform*. Princeton, NJ: Princeton University Press.

Wells-Dang, Andrew. 2010. "Political Space in Vietnam: A View from the 'Rice-Roots'." *The Pacific Review* 23, no. 1: 93–112.

West, Paige. 2006. *Conservation Is Our Government Now: The Politics of Ecology in Papua New Guinea*. Durham, NC: Duke University Press.

West, Paige, James Igoe, and Dan Brockington. 2006. "Parks and Peoples: The Social Impact of Protected Areas." *Annual Review of Anthropology* 35: 251–77.

Williams, Ruth. 2018. "'Like Supporting a Football Team': Why Whistleblowers Are Shunned at Work." *The Sydney Morning Herald*, October 22, 2018. https://www.smh.com.au/business/workplace/like-supporting-a-football-team-why-whistle blowers-are-shunned-at-work-20181008-p508hl.html.

Work, Courtney. 2019. "Chthonic Sovereigns? '*Neak Ta*' in a Cambodian Village." *The Asia Pacific Journal of Anthropology* 20, no. 1: 74–95.

Woodford, Michael. 2012. *Exposure: From President to Whistleblower at Olympus*. London: Penguin.

Wunder, Sven. 2005. *Payment for Environmental Services: Some Nuts and Bolts*. Occasional Paper No. 42, Centre for International Forestry Research. Bogor: CIFOR.

WWF (World Wildlife Fund). 2001. *The Forests of the Lower Mekong Eco-Region Complex*. Phnom Penh: World Wildlife Fund.

Yunkaporta, Tyson. 2019. *Sand Talk: How Indigenous Thinking Can Save the World*. Melbourne: Text Publishing.

Zeller, Tom. 2011. "Conservation International Duped by Militant Greenwash Pitch." *Huffington Post*, May 17, 2011. https://www.huffingtonpost.com.au/2011/05/17/conservation-international-lockheed-martin-video_n_863205.html

Index

Agence Française de Développement (AFD), 204

Angkor civilization, 90, 102, 117

animism, 102; in the Cardamom Mountains, 103, 177, 178

anthropology: of development, 9, 16; environmental, 49; of policy, 17, 71, 77, 216; of projects, 9, 24, 33–35, 49, 121, 215

Arendt, Hannah, 225

Areng Valley, 102–4, 139, 144, 157, 160, 161, 178; proposed dam, 114, 160, 161, 180

avoided deforestation, 82, 115, 142

big international nongovernment organizations (BINGOs), 10–12, 14–15, 22, 24, 121

BINGOs (big international nongovernment organizations), 10–12, 14–15, 22, 24, 121

biodiversity: caretakers of, 85; destroyed by logging, 7; global assessments, 10; surveys in the field, 88–89, 106, 109, 112, 118; hotspots, 5, 11, 36, 38; loss, 12, 63; protecting, 57–58, 84, 97; as public good, 60–61; threats to, 106, 110, 112, 118, 213; value of, 16, 62, 89, 117

biodiversity conservation: in Cambodia, 97–100, 221; Cardamom Mountains as

site for, 5, 106–11; and development, 18, 57–60, 63–65; dollars spent on, 11, 38; ethics of, 121, 150, 161, 181–83, 216, 221; as intervention, 16–18; transnational aspects of, 24, 26–28, 34, 41–42, 98, 118, 120–23, 134, 147–48. *See also* transnational conservation projects

Buddhism, 102

Bush, Wes, 39

Cambodia: Forestry Law, 97, 105, 113, 142, 170, 188; forests, 95–97, 142; geography, 89–90, 98; global conservation, 100, 106–7, 117–18, 213, 219, 223; government, 7, 20, 27, 63, 99, 123–131; history, 90–91; Khmer Rouge regime, 47, 88, 90–91, 104, 112, 115; NGOs, 93, 97, 98, 99, 113, 121, 148; participatory land-use planning, 113, 152–53; political culture, 47, 91, 93, 150, 159; politics, 92–95, 220; society and environment, 89–91, 94–96

Cambodian National Rescue Party (CNRP), 93

Cambodian People's Party (CPP), 92, 94, 109, 156, 159

cardamom, 100, 101, 146

Cardamom Mountains: 1950s French maps, 103; geography, 94–95, 100–101; history, 103–5; Indigenous people, 101–3, 184; livelihoods, 101–2, 105, 112, 150, 164, 171, 175, 193; logging, 6–8, 52, 99, 182, 186, 193; protected areas (map), 2–3

Cargill, 40

CCPF (Central Cardamoms Protected Forest). *See* Central Cardamoms Protected Forest (CCPF)

Central Cardamoms Protected Forest (CCPF): conservation agreements in, 115–17; creation of, 97, 109, 113; early community engagement in, 46–47, 51, 70, 109, 111–17; illegal logging, 111, 130, 188–90, 198; independent review of, 205, 206, 208; role of park rangers, 7–8, 108–11, 113, 117, 124, 127–36, 173, 177, 185–89, 191, 195, 198, 203

Chumnoab, 161, 167, 171, 174, 178, 180

CI (Conservation International). *See* Conservation International (CI)

CI's project in Cambodia: author's account, 31–33; case study of, 9, 25–28; key characters in, 43; design of, 109–12; local conflicts with, 27, 105, 113–15, 175–79; origins of, 107–09; villagers' views of, 171–74. *See also* Central Cardamoms Protected Forest (CCPF); conservation agreements; corruption

CI field staff: and commune leaders, 143; dismissals, 193; as informants, 184; monitoring agreement compliance, 144, 145; relationships with government, 158–66, 183, 187, 194; relationships with villagers, 114–15, 135–37, 144–45, 154, 166, 172–73, 176. *See also* community engagement

CI staff: economists and their ideas, 36, 39–40, 57–59, 61–65, 82, 207, 222; ethical failure, 220–22; expatriate, 109, 132–34, 135–36, 185; leadership transition in Cambodia, 126; and Milne's research, 49–50, 56; and change in mission state-

ment, 37; technical approach, 36–38, 75, 109; tension with government counterparts, 124–28, 130, 133–36; translation of policy in the field, 143–45. *See also* CI field staff

CNRP (Cambodian National Rescue Party), 93

collaborative event ethnography, 34

committees: in the Cardamom Mountains, 151–53, 157–60, 161, 162–63, 164, 169–70; committee-making, 137, 171–72, 180; and commune councils, 162–64, 168, 180; and conservation agreements, 143, 162–66, 169; as environmental subjects, 166–71; government control over, 160–61, 169–71, 220–21; historical precedents in Cambodia, 95; and PLUP, 112–14, 152–53, 162; as political disturbance, 156–58; political interference in, 156–58; purpose of, 155; as service providers, 28, 86, 170, 180, 217

Commune Natural Resource Management Committees (CNRMCs), 114, 152, 153, 162. *See also* committees

communities: in Cambodian development, 137–38, 143, 147, 161, 169, 172; choice in entering conservation agreements, 28, 64, 72, 85, 143–44, 156, 174; participation in CI's conservation project, 52, 66, 114, 151–54, 159, 162–68, 176, 180; strategic responses to conservation, 174–79. *See also* community engagement

community-based natural resource management (CBNRM), 18, 21, 65, 68, 71

community engagement: CI's approach, 47, 65–66, 151–55, 162; CI's team in Cambodia, 114, 117, 160, 162–63, 166, 168, 185; complexities of, 149, 155; silencing villagers' voices, 166, 221; threats of violence against CI team, 126, 157

conservation agreements: businesslike, 40, 167; in Cambodia, 42, 70, 115–18; CI's adoption of, 56, 65–71, 84–86; CI's

Index

251

operationalization of, 56, 71–77, 85; core idea, 64; CSP model, 77–78, 183; costs and benefits of, 117, 158, 165; design of, 64–65, 76, 138; financing, 61, 65, 66, 131, 144; guiding premise, 62; illegal logging, 193–94; livelihood impacts, 43, 51, 75, 192; local compliance with, 139, 144–45, 163, 164–65, 174, 178, 180; local experiences of, 149, 151, 174–75; matrix for, 80–81; negotiations, 155, 166, 180; PES-like, 27, 41, 72, 109, 141, 145, 216; procedures manual, 154; rapid solution, 60; validation of, 67. *See also* community engagement; implementation of conservation agreements

conservation agreements model, 58, 68, 71, 137, 180

conservation and development: conflicts between, 59–60; ethnographic studies of, 9, 34, 120, 215; harmonizing between, 57–59; local narratives of, 145, 149–50, 172, 175; policy narratives, 57–60; win-win solutions, 8, 14, 63, 73. *See also* ICDPs

Conservation International (CI): board of, 39; in Cardamom Mountains, 107, 111, 112, 122, 161; and Chut Wutty, 6, 8, 201, 204, 211; criticism of, 40–41, 184; CSP model, 76–77; direct payments, 60, 63, 67, 70, 71; discourses, 38; economists, 58, 61, 62, 66, 72, 75; enabling government power in Cambodia, 21, 127–32, 141, 179, 219–21; funding, 12, 38, 205; global leadership, 112, 210; and illegal logging, 202–3; independent review of, 205–9, 223; Milne's observations, 9, 15, 22, 26, 31, 33; Milne's relationship with, 43, 46, 48, 51–53; mission statement, 12, 37; neoliberal conservation, 39, 65, 85; organizational culture, 190; relationship with the Cambodian government, 123–24, 130–31, 135, 158–59, 183; response to corruption allegations, 197–200.

See also Central Cardamoms Protected Forest (CCPF); CI field staff; CI staff; CI's project in Cambodia; committees; community engagement; conservation agreements; hotspots

conservation policies: adjusting incentives, 62; crafting, 25; discursive nature, 29, 55, 56, 77, 154, 216; economists, 80, 141; ideas, 18, 22, 48, 213, 216

conservation practice: capitalism's synergy with, 39; contesting, 176; ethics, 161, 182, 211; gaps between global ideas and local realities, 15; insights, 227; intentions, 50; power relations, 16, 217. *See also* organised hypocrisy; side-effects; transnational conservation projects; transnational intervention

Conservation Stewards Program (CSP): arrival in Cambodia, 155; director, 69–70, 72, 115, 193; donor, 67, 75; manual, 154; policy model, 72, 76–79, 84; program, 26, 51, 68, 71, 74, 117; review in Cambodia, 191–94, 195, 197. *See also* conservation agreements

contextualization (of projects), 171, 181, 145–46, 171–75, 176, 181

convivial conservation, 9, 227

corporate nature: definition, 6, 24–26, 29, 214; ethics of practice, 148, 225; making of, 16, 28, 54, 120; and management of dissonance, 29, 215, 222; paradox at heart of, 214–15; and policy ideas, 216–19, 220; power of, 55, 216–19; practices of disconnection, 120, 148; and project knowledge, 54, 120, 184; relationship to ignorance, 24, 28–29, 223; silencing of dissent, 15, 197–200, 223; socio-nature, 213–14, 215–16; violence of, 28, 209–12, 214, 215, 223–25

corruption: allegations, 136, 195, 199, 205, 207, 209–10; in Cambodia, 126–27, 187, 190; in the CCPF, 203, 206; CI's response, 52, 182, 184, 185–86, 196,

corruption (*continued*)
 207; Hun Sen's government, 6, 97, 130,
 182, 193; and logging, 52, 96, 190; Milne
 addressing, 197–99; review's failure to
 tackle in the CCPF, 208; undermining
 relationships in CI, 190–95
CPP (Cambodian People's Party), 92, 94,
 109, 156, 159
Critical Ecosystem Partnership Fund, 205
crocodile (Siamese), 103, 107, 112, 116, 117,
 139, 144, 177–78

deforestation, 6, 26, 60, 99, 156, 208
deviance, normalization of, 124, 147, 183,
 215, 220–21
direct payments, 26, 57–58, 59, 62–64,
 68–71, 115
discourses: in conservation, 17, 18, 84;
 economistic, 83–84, 207; of intervention,
 38, 109–10; neoliberal, 65; of oversight,
 83–84; policy as discourse, 17–18, 156;
 technical, 38, 88, 106
dispossession: CI presiding over, 165, 181; of
 peasant farmers in Cambodia, 95, 96, 99;
 Indigenous, 181, 213, 215; role of conservation, 13, 181, 213, 215
dissonance: accommodation of, 16; cognitive, 211; in the field, 23, 24, 144, 219;
 institutionalized, 222; management of
 by NGOs, 8–9, 22, 23, 28–29, 217, 222;
 moments of, 8, 125, 139; between policy
 ideas and local reality, 217; production
 of, 23. *See also* ignorance; organized
 hypocrisy
dragon fish, 111, 116, 117, 144, 157, 172, 175,
 176, 178,

economic theories, 13, 58–59, 61–62, 69, 84;
 and conservation agreements, 71–73
epistemology: anti-epistemology, 223; blind
 spots, 222; positivist, 22; dominant in
 global conservation, 49, 53, 217; reductionist, 148, 217; of disconnection, 217

ethics: of care, 227; of conservation practice,
 148, 183, 211, 215, 220, 223–25; corporate nature, 148, 225; ethical conduct,
 214, 215, 225; ethical failure in conservation, 28, 181, 223; insider ethnography, 9,
 29, 32, 48; of institutional ethnography,
 32–33, 35; multispecies, 227; of research,
 48; of transnational projects, 121, 124,
 181
ethnography: auto-ethnography, 35, 53;
 characters that feature in, 43; of conservation, 34, 175; of CI's policy ideas,
 27–29, 34, 48; as engaged research, 34;
 ethnographic exit, 33; generating ethical
 practice, 29; insider, 26, 32, 52–54, 213;
 institutional, 32–35; multi-positioned,
 26, 32, 35, 49–50, 191; of projects, 9, 18–
 22, 24, 33, 35, 43, 49, 121
expatriates: advisors, 76, 83, 133, 139; being
 foreign, 30–31, 119–20; in Cambodia,
 113, 124–26; CI directors, 125, 135; in the
 field, 66, 88, 133; life of, 31–32; in NGOs,
 98, 109, 111–12, 123, 128, 132–35
ExxonMobil, 40

FA (Forestry Administration), 97, 124, 126–
 31, 141–42, 187–89, 206–7
Ferguson, James, 17, 21, 150, 161, 179, 219
field (the field): expatriates in, 66, 88, 133;
 field stories, 43; fieldwork, 83, 88, 119,
 121, 132, 151; information from, 139, 146;
 knowledge about, 19; legibility of, 15, 78,
 80, 161, 179; Milne in, 48–49, 191–92,
 194; multisited phenomenon, 34; offices
 and, 42–43, 76–77, 136, 139, 148; participant observation in, 121; policy ideas
 in, 70, 147; problems in, 222–23; realm
 of intervention, 78, 88, 118; situating the
 field, 88–89, 118, 217; social construction
 of, 83; violence in, 15, 53, 214
Ford, Harrison, 36, 39
Forestry Administration (FA), 97, 124, 126–
 31, 141–42, 187–89, 206–7

Index   **253**

forests: Forest Estate, 96–97, 99, 105, 108, 138, 141–42; Forestry Law, 97, 105, 113, 142, 170, 188; indigenous words and concepts, 138; and state-making, 92, 94–97; logging concessions, 96–97, 105, 137; protection, 6, 46, 97–98; sacred, 103; territorialization of, 106, 141, 220

GEF (Global Environment Facility), 107
global conservation: accountability in, 11–12; business models, 14, 22; in Cambodia, 100, 106–7, 117–18, 213, 219, 223; and capitalism, 14; corporate form of, 154, 209, 213, 222; discourses, 16–17; ethnographies of, 53–54; evidence-based, 22; funding, 10, 12, 98; the industry, 9–11, 36, 211, 218; interventions, 16, 23, 28, 89, 217; investors, 86; neoliberal, 13, 14, 39, 80; neoliberal ideas in, 24, 65, 80; non-thinking staff, 225; protectionism, 58; NGO practices, 14–15, 28, 150; paradigms, 37; paradoxical character of, 215; and predatory political regimes, 221; strategies, 14, 58–59, 216; transnational dimensions, 19–20; treatment of dissenters, 224
Global Environment Facility (GEF), 107
Gordon and Betty Moore Foundation, 12, 38, 107

Haraway, Donna, 6, 9, 226
HCI (Healthy Communities Initiative), 66
Healthy Communities Initiative (HCI), 66
hotspots, 5, 11, 36, 38, 60
Huffington Post, 204
hydropower dams, 99, 100, 110, 131, 160, 196

ignorance: in conservation projects, 15, 23, 47, 223; of expatriates, 120, 139; non-knowledge, 15, 140, 148; production of, 15, 28, 210–11; sociology of, 226; strategic, 23, 24, 207, 215, 223
illegal logging: and Cambodian government, 7, 28, 99; CI denial, 8, 43, 184,

202–3, 210; in CI's project area, 52, 148, 182, 183–84, 185–90, 209, 222; ethnographic rendering, 53; exposing, 200; Hun Sen, 182; independent review by CI, 205, 209, 211, 223; rangers' complicity in, 221, 223; reports in *Phnom Penh Post*, 8, 200–204; of rosewood, 187–89, 208; tackling, 192, 193; whistleblowers, 28, 52, 197, 198; Wutty's struggle, 211
Illich, Ivan, 227
IMF (International Monetary Fund), 96
implementation of conservation agreements: enabling conditions, 78–79; from 2006 onward, 115–17; four key brokers, 43–45, 122; as a global policy idea, 25, 132–33, 149–50, 153, 219; government power in, 52, 118, 127–32, 179, 220; preferred translators, 136; project system, 41–43, 122; success of, 83, 131, 132, 138–40, 144, 147. *See also* community engagement; conservation agreements
Indigenous: dispossession, 181, 213, 215; ontology, 226–27; people, 20, 21, 27, 36, 89, 95; perspectives, 82; rights, 65, 114, 147, 150, 185; scholars, 226. *See also* Khmer Daeum
institutional ethnography, 33, 35
institutional violence, 24, 185, 200, 211, 214, 224
integrated conservation and development projects (ICDPs), 18, 57, 66, 114, 146; vs. conservation agreements, 57–64
International Monetary Fund (IMF), 96

Jolie, Angelina, 98

Khmer Daeum, 102, 103, 105
Khmer language, 31, 46, 222. *See also* translation
Khmer Rouge, 47, 88, 90–91, 104, 112, 115
Khmer staff, 125–26, 129, 133–35

knowledge: about the field, 76; economistic, 222; filtering/selective, 89, 138, 140, 205; global, 148, 150; inconvenient, 225; knowledge-making, 14–15, 17, 24, 137, 139–40, 148; local, 47, 187; management, 210; non-knowledge, 15, 140, 148; politics of, 16, 216–17; production of, 33, 43, 49, 52, 54, 138–39, 147; scholarly, 46, 207; technical, 205, 222; translation of, 122. *See also* epistemology

Koh Kong, 108, 189

land-grabbing, 90, 94, 99–100

Latour, Bruno, 19, 23, 33, 41, 68, 121, 133, 145, 146, 149, 171

legibility: of the field, 15, 78, 80, 219; for government, 17, 161, 179; for interventions, 217

Long, Lim, 144, 156, 157, 158, 176

MacArthur Foundation, 12, 204–5

MAFF (Ministry of Agriculture, Forestry, and Fisheries), 97–98, 107, 108, 128

Martin, Marie, 101, 102

Massachusetts Institute of Technology, 75

MDS Ex-Im, 186–90, 191, 194, 196, 203–4

Mead, David, 108

Ministry of Agriculture, Forestry, and Fisheries (MAFF), 97–98, 107, 108, 128

Ministry of Environment (MoE), 97–98, 107

MoE (Ministry of Environment), 97–98, 107

Mongabay, 201–2

Monsanto, 40

Moore Foundation, 12, 38, 107

Mosse, David, 121–22, 123, 134, 140, 145, 147, 181

Mouhot, Henri, 90

The Nature Conservancy (TNC), 10, 36, 213

neoliberal conservation, 13, 14, 25, 39, 80

neoliberal thinking, 27, 55, 65, 72, 169

NGOs (nongovernmental organizations). *See* nongovernmental organizations (NGOs)

nongovernmental organizations (NGOs): in Cambodia, 93, 97–99, 113, 121; choice between advocacy and government alignment, 6, 129, 165; Chut Wutty's murder, 5, 7–9; compromise, 128; conduct, 182; corporate-friendly, 13; corporate culture, 15, 24, 37; funding, 12, 14, 97, 114, 156; government involvement, 161, 179; influence, 121; intentions, 22, 147, 181, 221; managing dissonance, 23; need for success, 15, 23, 24, 28, 38, 140, 144, 147, 183, 214, 216–17; NGO–government relations, 98, 123, 125, 135, 137, 169; practices, 14–15, 147, 169, 174; professionalism, 8, 88, 129, 184, 194; projects, 20, 89, 98, 120, 181, 183; promotional imagery, 15, 39; resistance to NGO activities, 126, 176; silencing of dissent, 15, 197–200, 223; solutions, 14, 18, 22, 24, 43, 56, 60, 63, 74, 80, 86; staff, 19, 111, 125, 126, 128, 168, 203; work, 28, 32, 185; workers, 31, 46, 47, 171. *See also* BINGOs; conservation practice; conservation projects; dissonance; knowledge; transnational

O'Som, 184–86, 187–88, 189–91, 198, 203–4

organized hypocrisy, 210, 211, 217–18, 221. *See also* dissonance

Paris Peace Accords, 91

participatory land-use planning (PLUP), 112, 113–14, 115, 128, 139, 152–53

payments for environmental services (PES): adoption and deployment, 55, 216; conditionality, 58–59, 144–45, 219; idea of, 84, 216, 218; implementation of, 20, 25, 27, 29; narratives, 58; and neoliberal thinking, 27, 28, 60, 216; paying for behavior change, 58, 85; policy model in practice, 180, 216–17; transforming national economies, 218. *See also* conservation agreements; direct payments

Index

255

PES (payments for environmental services). *See* payments for environmental services (PES)

Pheap, Try, 186

Phnom Penh Post, 8, 200–201, 202, 203, 204

policies (CI): documents, 61, 73; ideas, 67, 131–32, 141, 147, 149–50; intentions, 171; misinterpretations of, 146; model, 141, 145, 154; statements, 62; transformation in practice, 21, 28, 140, 141–46, 147, 219–20

policy: corporate nature, 216–19, 220; global conservation, 29, 121, 216, 218, 219; knowledge, 15, 17, 24–25, 55, 220; logics, 27, 55, 56, 75, 220; narratives, 17–18, 29, 56–65, 145; operationalization, 71; transformation in practice, 141–46, 219–20; translation, 27, 121, 147, 219. *See also* global conservation; conservation policies; discourse

policy environment, 56

policy transformations, 141–46, 219–20. *See also* contextualization; uncertainty

political ecology, 18; situated (political ecology) of conservation, 88, 89

Prey Lang, 201

projects: brokers, 43, 121, 122–23, 132–35, 137, 139; contextualization, 171, 181, 219; project ethnography, 9, 24, 33, 35, 49, 215; translation, 41–42, 121, 122–23, 147; transnational, 32, 120, 121, 122, 148

quasi-experimental approaches, 22, 74, 75–76, 217

REDD-Monitor blog, 200

REDD+ (reducing emissions from deforestation and forest degradation), 25, 60, 142

Redford, Robert, 40

resin trees, 101, 105

resistance: Areng dam, 114, 160, 180; to conservation agreements, 145, 163–65, 174, 178, 180; to logging, 28, 201, 223;

to NGOs, 126; protest, 113, 157–58; riding the tiger, 175–79, 180; strategic responses, 151, 176–79

Rio Tinto, 40

Roberts, Julia, 40

rosewood, 7; logging, 186–89, 193–94, 204, 206, 208; density in CCPF, 201–2

Roussey Chrum, 157–58, 163–64, 176, 189

scaling up, 10, 27, 43, 74

Seligman, Peter, 36, 37, 40, 66, 70

Sen, Hun, 6–7, 90, 91, 92, 94, 97, 99, 100, 109, 110, 128, 182, 189, 201, 218; Cambodian People's Party (CPP), 92, 97, 109; deforestation, 6–7; Economic Land Concessions, 99; environmental reforms, 100; and the FA, 128; family, 189, 201; hydropower dams, 110; illegal logging, 182; PES policy, 218; regime, 90; top-down government, 94; Vietnamese installation of Cambodia's leadership, 91

shifting agriculture, 82–83, 101, 103, 112–14, 138, 170, 177, 178

side-effects: of conservation, 106, 161; of development interventions, 16; ethical implications for CI, 179–81, 214, 219–20; significance of, 21, 150. *See also* James Ferguson

Sihanouk, Norodom, 90–91

socio-nature: corporate nature, 24, 148, 214, 215–16; multi-natural, 6; produced by conservation NGOs, 24, 213, 215–16

Starbucks, 40

studying up, 32–33

Tatai Leu, 164, 165

territorialization: consequences, 99; of forests, 106, 141, 220; by government, 118, 141, 219–20; by NGOs, 106

The Economist, 60

The Guardian, 204

Thmar Bang: cardamom forest, 146; communes of, 115, 153, 157; dispossession

Thmar Bang (*continued*)
and exploitation, 165; expatriate friend in, 196; landscapes of, 104; elite interests, 144, 156, 164–65, 177; protests at the ranger station, 113; soldiers relocated, 108; trouble with illegal activity, 130; Wutty guiding journalists, 200. *See also* Cardamom Mountains

Thmar Dan Peuv, 157, 167, 172, 174–75, 176, 177–78

Timber Green, 188–89, 192, 194, 204

Tonle Sap Lake, 89–90

translation (Khmer-English), 133, 138

translation (process), 20, 27, 41–42, 121–23, 138, 147

transnational conservation projects: alignment with local power structures, 158, 162; brokering 132–37, 139–41, 146–48, 172, 217; community participation, 114, 159, 169–71; corruption within, 111, 184, 185; government control within, 52, 118, 127–32, 156; information filtering, 15, 76, 136, 138, 140, 146–47, 193, 210, 217; social life of, 18–20; structural inequalities in, 119–20. *See also* CI's project in Cambodia; conservation practice; transnational intervention

transnational intervention: anthropology of 16–21, 33–34, 38; dissonance and incoherence in, 22–24, 121, 215; technical framing of, 67, 73, 76–78; realm of intervention, 79, 88, 89, 100, 106, 118; crafting of 109–11; policy processes in, 32, 120–22; side-effects of, 179–80, 214–15. *See also* ignorance; uncertainty

uncertainty (in NGO projects), 18, 29, 202, 215

United Nations Convention on Biological Diversity, 97

United Nations Transitional Authority in Cambodia (UNTAC), 91

USAID, 12, 34, 70, 71

unintended consequences (of NGO action), 21–22, 150, 215, 219–20. *See also* side-effects

Vietnam, 106, 112, 187

Vietnamese border, 185, 187

Vietnamese forces, 91, 104

Vietnamese regime in Cambodia, 95, 159

Vietnam War, 91, 108

violence: complicity of NGOs, 211–12, 214, 215, 223; displays of, 204; in the field, 15, 53, 214; indirect, 9, 184, 200, 223; institutional, 24, 185, 200, 211, 214, 224; political, 181, 183; threats of, 126

Walton, Rob, 12, 39

whistleblowers, 52, 183–84, 195, 198, 203, 224; organizational responses to, 212

Woodford, Michael, 210, 212

World Bank, 21, 23, 56–58, 60–61, 179

World Parks Congress, 61

World Wildlife Fund (WWF), 10, 11, 54, 59, 71, 107, 213

Wutty, Chut, 5–8, 28, 47, 93, 110, 184; gathering data on the illegal logging, 200; informant, 110; mobilizing local communities, 201; murder of, 5–8, 184, 204, 209, 211, 223; speaking out about the illegal logging, 184; work with Milne, 47

About the Author

Sarah Milne is a senior lecturer at the Australian National University, in the field of political ecology. Sarah gained her doctorate in geography from the University of Cambridge (2010). She is the author of *Conservation and Development in Cambodia: Exploring Frontiers of Change in Nature, State, and Society* (edited with Sango Mahanty, 2015). Sarah has combined research and practice for over twenty years in the fields of community development and international conservation, mainly in Cambodia.